WOMEN, WORK AND SOCIAL RIGHTS

Canada in Historical and Comparative Perspective

Cecilia M. Benoit

University of Victoria

Prentice Hall Allyn and Bacon Canada
Scarborough, Ontario

Canadian Cataloguing in Publication Data

Benoit, Cecilia, 1954-
  Women, work and social rights

Includes bibliographical references and index.
ISBN 0-13-022049-3

1. Women — Employment — Canada — History. 2. Women employees —
Government policy — Canada — History. 3. Women employees — Canada — Social conditions.
4. Sexual division of labor — Canada — History.
I. Title.

HD6099.B46 2000   331.4'0971   C99-930971-4

© 2000 Prentice-Hall Canada Inc., Scarborough, Ontario
Pearson Education

Prentice-Hall, Inc., Upper Saddle River, New Jersey
Prentice-Hall International (UK) Limited, London
Prentice-Hall of Australia, Pty. Limited, Sydney
Prentice-Hall Hispanoamericana, S.A., Mexico City
Prentice-Hall of India Private Limited, New Delhi
Prentice-Hall of Japan, Inc., Tokyo
Simon & Schuster Southeast Asia Private Limited, Singapore
Editora Prentice-Hall do Brasil, Ltda., Rio de Janeiro

ISBN 0-13-022049-3

Vice President, Editorial Director: Laura Pearson
Acquisitions Editor: Nicole Lukach
Marketing Manager: Christine Cozens
Developmental Editor: Carina Blåfield
Production Editor: Cathy Zerbst
Copy Editor: Jennifer A. Lambert
Production Coordinator: Wendy Moran
Art Director: Mary Opper
Cover Design: David Cheung
Cover Image: Photodisc
Page Layout: Christine Velakis

1 2 3 4 5 04 03 02 01 00

Printed and bound in Canada.

Visit the Prentice Hall Canada Web site! Send us your comments, browse our catalogues, and more
at **www.phcanada.com**. Or reach us through e-mail at **phabinfo_pubcanada@prenhall.com**.

Contents

Chapter 3: Capitalism and Women's Work

Chapter 4: Welfare States and Women's Social Rights

Chapter 5: Midwives' Work and Social Rights

Chapter 6: Women's Work and Social Rights: Looking to the Twenty-first Century   148

List of Tables and Figures

Preface

The meaning of work in human societies has been transformed by recent feminist criticism of traditional "male-stream" interpretations. *Women, Work, and Social Rights* refines this criticism by analyzing historical and cross-national differences and similarities. First, our understanding of work is extended by illustrating important differences and similarities between and among women workers in different time periods. Second, this book goes beyond the monolithic view of the modern capitalist state to show that more "women-friendly" states design social policies that actually enhance the economic and social status of the majority of women.

Women, Work, and Social Rights highlights the variation in women's work situations and access to social rights across time and place. This historical perspective gives voice to the diversity of women in Canada during times predating capitalism, as well as during subsequent stages of capitalism up to the present day. While Canada serves as the main setting, both the United States and Sweden provide windows of cross-national similarity and contrast. The book aims to show that women's inequality at work, although frequent across time, has not been universal. To the contrary, the historical record reveals societal arrangements where women enjoyed rough equality with men within the economy and family, revealing also that these societies have tended to be relatively egalitarian along class and racial lines.

Women, Work, and Social Rights shows that some capitalist societies with comprehensive welfare states maintain a shared model of paid work and family life. A case in point is the welfare state in Sweden, which remains intact even during the recent period marked by seemingly intensifying capitalism. Even the "country cousins" of Canada and the United States have important differences, with the Canadian welfare state more caring of women workers than that of its neighbour to the south.

Students, policy-makers, and those interested in understanding the main issues confronting women workers in the next millennium will find much food for thought in this historical and cross-national investigation of the gendered nature of work in human societies and the role of societal institutions in reducing inequality between women and men.

Acknowledgments

Growing up in a family where both males and females worked long and hard, it strikes me that an important difference between my male and female kin was that the men had the luxury of ending their day before the women, who were still required to perform the countless work activities that kept bodies fed, clean, healthy, and emotionally stable. I thank my sisters, Joan, Theresa, and Christina, for their hard work and companionship over the years, and our dear mother, who knew how to work hard while maintaining a sense of humour when facing hardships that I find hard to imagine.

This book has been a long time in the making and would not have been possible without the intellectual stimulation and practical assistance of many colleagues and friends. Lesley Biggs, Robbie Davis-Floyd, Ivy Lynn Bourgeault, Alena Heitlinger, Pat Kaufert, and Dena Carroll enlightened me through their intellectual curiosity about women's work and their views about the gains made and yet to be made in regard to women's social rights. I am very grateful that Darby Carswell gave her thoughtful editorial comments on early drafts. Special thanks to Bonnie Johnstone, Karen Burch, and Jan MacLeod, who shared old photos and memories of the work lives of their own female kin. I warmly thank Bill McCarthy, Alan Hedley, Zheng Wu, and Larry Picco, who, in their own special ways, have showed strong support for my research by offering critical commentary and going out of their way to educate me. The Åbo Akademi University in Finland and the University of Victoria provided the generous financial support that made this book possible. Many colleagues in the Departments of Sociology at both of these institutions gave both encouragement and insightful guidance. Special thanks to Sirpa Wrede for sharing her thorough historical knowledge and astute understanding of the nature of women-friendly welfare states. To the midwives who have taken time out of their busy schedules to answer my interview questions and allowed me to observe them at work, thank you for enriching my knowledge of women providers who care for other women, and showing me the complexity that this relationship involves. I also appreciate the assistance provided by David Stover, Nicole Lukach, Carina Blåfield, and Cathy Zerbst at Prentice Hall Canada, who guided the book along its various stages of production. Special thanks to Jennifer Lambert for her fine editorial work on the final drafts.

Statistics Canada information is used with the permission of the Ministry of Industry. Information on the availability of the wide range of data from Statistics Canada can be obtained from Statistics Canada's Regional Offices, its World Wide Web site at http://www.statcan.ca, and its toll-free number: 1-800-263-1136. Earlier versions of certain parts of this book have appeared, in different forms, in *Canadian Journal of Sociology, Social Science & Medicine*, and "Rediscovering Appropriate Care: Maternity Traditions and Contemporary Issues in Canada," in *Health and Canadian Society*, edited by David Coburn, Carl D'Arcy, and George Torrance (Toronto: University of Toronto Press, 1998), and "Professionalizing Canadian Midwifery: Sociological Perspectives," in *The New Midwifery: Reflections on Renaissance and Regulation*, edited by Farah Shroff (Toronto: The Women's Press, 1997).

This book is dedicated to Annika and Mikael. Thank you for your patience, help, love, and humour. You both ease the daily stress associated with my kind of hard work.

INTRODUCTION

"We shall never be able to understand the social processes going on around us so long as we tacitly or overtly deny the part played by the givers and receivers of "care" and "service," the victims of socialisation processes, the unpaid labourers in the processes of production and reproduction." (Stacey, 1981: 189)

No society can function without the work of its members. Even today we spend most of our waking hours getting ready for work, working, or enjoying the fruits of other people's labour. Our leisure time at a restaurant involves the *paid* work of many, which might include farmers, fishers, butchers, vendors, dishwashers, chefs, bartenders, servers, and food managers. At the same time, our dinner out is likely to have involved the *unpaid* work of many others associated with these paid workers—the person who did the family's grocery shopping, the person who prepared the evening meal in between doing the week's laundry, or the parent who chauffeured the children to and from school, and later helped them with their homework before dropping them at the hockey game. Work—whether paid or unpaid—is so fundamental to understanding human societies that it is the "inescapable starting point for all of social inquiry" (Heilbroner, 1985: 9).

The truth of the matter is that unpaid work seldom receives the kind of societal recognition typically awarded to paid work; this bias runs as well through much of the sociological research on work. While we have at hand a sizeable sociological literature that focuses on the interplay between employment, industry, and society—and is concerned particularly with the effect of changing market conditions and technology on the situation of paid workers—unpaid work is rarely given a central place in the analysis. In the introduction to their book on work in Canadian society (1998: xvi), Harvey Krahn and Graham Lowe acknowledge that human work, broadly defined, includes "both paid and unpaid work, activities ranging from the legal to the illegal, and from the highest esteemed to the undesirable and despised," yet nevertheless dedicate the rest of the book almost exclusively to examining paid work activities—i.e., "jobs." Likewise do Randy Hudson and Teresa Sullivan (1995: 3) define the purpose of work as the production of "material goods and services, which may be consumed by the worker or sold to someone else. Work includes not only paid labor but also self-employed and unpaid labor, including that of housewives and 'househusbands'."

Yet these authors also proceed, after a brief historical interlude, to focus without exception on the organization of paid work under capitalist systems of relations, ignoring the fact that capitalism itself is dependent on the invisible unpaid labour of the many people not included in the labour statistics that form the basis of these sociological analyses.

This bias towards paid work is shared by Statistics Canada analysts, who provide daily updates and year-end reports on employment and unemployment levels and the productivity of various industries and employment growth areas. Alarm bells ring when the country's unemployment rate hits a certain mark, but seldom is it pointed out that to be "out of work" does not necessarily mean that a person is not working. In fact, it may be the case that an individual's unpaid domestic or childcare activities are so demanding or complex that she or he is unable to be "available for work," as is required for one to be considered an "active worker."[1] According to Chris Tilly and Charles Tilly (1997: 89), this bias towards paid/market work is endemic: "only a prejudice bred by Western capitalism and its industrial labour markets fixes on strenuous effort expended for money payment outside the home as real work, relegating other efforts to amusement, crime, and mere housework."

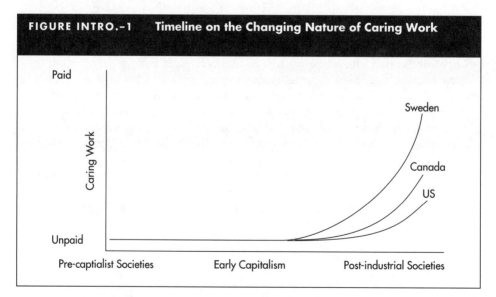

FIGURE INTRO.-1   Timeline on the Changing Nature of Caring Work

As outlined in Figure 1, this book takes a broader view of women's work as encompassing both paid and unpaid labour (including domestic work, childcare, and voluntary activities). Evaluations of paid and unpaid work have varied according to time and place. Historically, both women's and men's labour had use-value only. Even with the onset of capitalism in the sixteenth century, the vast majority of women spent their days performing essential but nevertheless unpaid work. This continued to be the norm for women long after most men gained access to paid work beginning in the nineteenth century and—especially in Canada and Sweden—into the early part of the twentieth century. The major shift from non-paid to paid work for women in Canada, Sweden, and the United States occurred in the twentieth century.

The most recent data shows that Sweden, due chiefly to its large public sector, where much of women's paid work is located, reports the highest participation of women in paid work, followed by Canada, with the US close behind. Alongside rights common to other industrial capitalist societies, such as freedom of association, universal suffrage, and equality before the law, what might be called the "right to care" has been institutionalized as a social principle in Sweden. This has resulted in strong public support for health and social services for those in need of care (the sick, children, elders, disabled, etc.), and at the same time society's recognition of the work of caring. This book examines how even Canada and the US, country cousins in so many respects, differ in regard to their citizens' right to care, as well as their acknowledgment of the work done by those who care for others. In many key dimensions Canada emerges as more "caring" than its neighbour to the south.

Of course, like many things in life, work is not the same thing for women and men. Interlacing the book's central theme of the broad nature of human work is the fundamental fact that all human work is *gendered*; both paid and unpaid work is structured by a system of gender relations, which is in turn embedded in all other social institutions. This gendered system of social relations need not necessarily be oppressive for one or the other sex. In some small-scale societies women and men enjoyed relative equality, even if their work roles may have been complementary rather than interchangeable. In capitalist societies, where market forces have a major influence over all aspects of human life, gender-based social relations tend to favour men over women, to be structured on *gender inequality*. But even in this respect there are no universals. As noted above and elaborated in later chapters, in some capitalist countries where the right to care has been institutionalized—including present-day social democracies such as Sweden—relations between men and women are relatively egalitarian compared to those countries where caring work remains invisible and undervalued.

As with inequalities based on access to wealth and/or power, "male advantage" is not in our genes, but rather in our social institutions. Gender inequality is the outcome of unequal social relations that are found only at some times and in some places. This perspective goes against a "grand narrative of patriarchy" that runs through much of the feminist scholarship on women's work and the state, including research on the gendered underpinnings of the professions (Walby, 1990; Witz, 1990). The central problem concerns confusion regarding patriarchy as a descriptive tool for understanding unequal social relations between women and men in particular historical instances, and patriarchy as an explanatory tool for theorizing the basic structure of human societies in general. Patriarchy used in the latter sense results in a circular argument: the gendered organization of work is described as inevitably patriarchal, and the explanation for its existence is patriarchy.

Heidi Hartmann (1979: 11) defines patriarchy "as a set of social relations between men, which have a material base, and which, though hierarchal, establish and create interdependence and solidarity among men that enable them to dominate women." Sylvia Walby (1986: 46) makes the same tautological argument when she states that "patriarchy is distinctive in being a system of interrelated structures through which men exploit women. The distinctiveness of the patriarchal system is marked by the social relations which enable men to exploit women." Jeff Hearn (1982: 195–96) draws a similar conclusion about the pan-historic patriarchy underlying the "full" and "semi" professions, when he states that "full professionalization comes when the activity is fully dominated by men—in both management and the ranks. It is the fate that awaits the semi-professions."

Patriarchy, then, is a zero-sum power relationship, with men always in the dominant position and women in the subordinate one. As such we are left with no way to conceptualize variation in power relations between men and women in their work activities in particular times and places. Wither historical change and cross-national variation in gender-work relations? In fact, why even pose this question if the answer is already established?

It can be argued that *not* to pose this (admittedly difficult) question is to fail to do justice to human agency, the material existence or "lived experiences" of people in their social context (Acker, 1989). It makes little sociological sense, for example, to conclude that daily life in Canada's historical small-scale agricultural societies, organized on the basis of matrilineal descent, were patriarchal, even if men in these societies appear to have had advantages over women in certain respects. On the other hand, it is appropriate to describe many of the patrilineal fishing societies found on Canada's northwest coast prior to European contact as patriarchal, and the same can be said in regard to the pre-capitalist agricultural societies of Upper and Lower Canada (see Chapter 3 for a detailed discussion).

Nor is it meaningful to conclude that the relations between contemporary Swedish women and men are based on a zero-sum power game. As discussed in Chapter 6, over the past two decades Swedish women have increased their presence in national government such that they are approaching near parity with male counterparts. Though this is less so in North America, there has been an incremental increase in women's political representation in both Canada and the US. At the same time, significant national variation remains between the two North American countries in regard to women's access to political power, with Canadian women scoring higher than their US colleagues (Inter-Parliamentary Union, 1998).

In brief, I employ the term patriarchy very cautiously, reserving its use to refer to specific types of historical societies and adopting the more neutral "gender relations," which may involve male domination or advantage, but also leaves open for analysis the relative equality between the sexes in work and family life in particular times and places. This approach is in line with one taken by other feminist scholars writing on women's (and men's) work (Bradley, 1989), and is also endorsed by Anna Pollert (1996: 655), who argues that "concept of 'gender relations' is far more productive: it cannot be as easily reified into structure and problematises, rather than assumes, its nature. This not only allows for the detailed exploration of the persistence of male power domination, but also leaves room for the more subtle play of gendering men and women."

I take this argument one step further, and attempt to show that just as the concept of patriarchy fails to grasp the complex ways in which the lives of women and men are gendered, so too does the "grand narrative of capitalism" need to be challenged at the onset. It is indeed the case that no capitalist society has been found to exist without social class inequality.

However, typically overlooked by those who believe that a pervasive capitalism homogenizes all social relations among individuals, within households, and across economies and polities, reducing them to an outgrowth of profit accumulation, is the significant variation that exists across capitalist societies in regard to social class inequality, as well as the non-capitalist economic, social, and political practices found in specific societies that go some way in levelling economic differences. This book challenges the recent "globalization narrative" that is based on the notion of the supremacy of multinational corporations to "fuse and obliterate the boundaries of production and consumption through the pervasive domination of all levels of consumer culture and everyday life" (Deshpande and Kurtz, 1994: 35).

Capitalism's globalization narrative depicts a world ruled by an all-powerful market with the capacity to invade and ultimately transform all that it confronts, including national governments should they stand in its path (Miyoshi, 1993). However, what may in fact be occurring is a more discriminate movement of capital interests linking particular countries together in "commodity chains," while leaving some countries out entirely, either because they are deemed unprofitable or because of national resistance to capital's encroachment (Kiely, 1998).

A subplot of the globalization narrative is post-Fordism, which is based on the prediction that the globalization of capitalism has caused the "end of work" as we have known it in post-World War II capitalist societies, and what has emerged is the substitution of sophisticated information technologies for human labour, changes in industry from mass to lean and flexible production, the shrinking of the global workforce, and the dawn of a new historical phase—the near jobless society of the twenty-first century. According to Jeremy Rifkin (1995: 3), "for the first time, human labor is being systematically eliminated from the production process. Within less than a century, "mass" work in the market sector is likely to be phased out in virtually all of the industrialized nations of the world."

Thus, goes the post-Fordist argument, regardless of national differences in culture and politics, the end result will be the same—like the predictions underlying the globalization script—a homogeneous world where capital rules, machines are dominant, and work (i.e., paid work) is the preserve of a small elite of knowledge-workers controlling the new technologies. Not only do these predictions ignore the enormous sum of human work that has never been a part of "jobs"—and is unlikely to disappear in the emerging "world without workers"—but also left out of the analysis are the significant differences between countries in regard to their citizens' access to secure employment with fringe benefits, and the degree and severity of long-term unemployment.

Even when they challenge the grand patriarchy script, feminists, too, sometimes fall into the same trap as globalization and post-Fordist writers when considering the forces of capitalism, overlooking the significant variation among different types of capitalist societies in regard to the societal value of women's paid and unpaid work (Pollert, 1996). Recent feminist scholarship examining welfare states in capitalist societies in regard to their support for women's economic independence is a step forward (Orloff, 1993; O'Connor, 1996; Gornick, 1997). This work allows for close examination of the ways in which different types of welfare states partly buffer the impact of capitalism on women's lives, and promote a different agenda that involves recognition for women's caring work in the formal economy and within the family. The empirical data reveals significant cross-national variation, even within the capitalist world, regarding the degree to which their welfare states can be shown to be "women-friendly." In brief, even within capitalist societies, welfare state social policies figure highly in daily life, and can make the difference between a solo mother living in poor or moderate circumstances; between caring work made visible and valued or its opposite; and between relative equality between the sexes and pronounced inequality (Ruggie, 1984; Polakow, 1993; Lewis, 1993). As Diane Sainsbury (1996: 221) notes, even in the recent decade and a half of welfare-state restructuring across industrial capitalist societies, national variation in social policies remains strong, and there is no evidence of a trend towards either "convergence" of welfare state policies or their "residualization"[2] (see Chapter 2).

The aim of this book is to address the deficiencies in research mentioned above by studying women's work across time and place. The focus is mainly on Canada, with windows[3] on the US and Sweden that place the Canadian context in a comparative view. Canada has rich Aboriginal gender systems, a legacy of two colonial heritages later combined with a cultural mosaic of immigrants, and a relative absence in the comparative scholarship on women's work and social rights. Many scholars write of "North America" when they are referring specifically to the United States, overlooking the unique features of Canadian history and society that have moulded its economy and welfare state in ways that differ from its neighbour to the south. On the other hand, much of the Canadian literature on this topic stops short of drawing comparisons between Canada and other industrial capitalist countries; those that do so tend to confine their comparisons to English-speaking parts of Anglo-America in the modern era. This book addresses these concerns by centring the analysis on Canada and drawing points of similarity and contrast by discussing aspects of the evolution and present-day organization of the US minimal welfare state and the Swedish comprehensive welfare state.

THE STRUCTURE OF THE BOOK

The first chapter, "Conceptualizing Women's Work and Social Rights," provides the reader with an overview of the research literature in sociology on human work, and exposes its bias towards paid work while overlooking women's caring activities. It contains a critical discussion of the theoretical debates about the nature of late capitalism that revolve around the concepts of globalization and post-Fordism, as well as the mainstream and feminist perspectives on welfare states.

Chapter 2, "Women's Work and Social Rights in the Pre-capitalist Era," seeks to rectify the fault in much of the literature about the nature of women's work situations predating capitalism. Based on the alternative premise that there is no immutable gender contract across human societies under which women's work activities are forever and always rendered secondary to those of men, this chapter begins the historical examination of gendered work with a focus on early Canada. As in subsequent chapters, windows are opened on the United States and Sweden in order to place women's situation in early Canada in perspective.

In Chapter 3, "Capitalism and Women's Work," I examine the changes in women's paid and unpaid work in four phases of capitalist development. Capitalism extensively changed the social organization of work and family life, but the consequences were not the same for women and men. The chapter shows, among other things, that as capitalism advanced, it impaired the important productive roles women performed in the pre-capitalist era, both undermining and impeding their economic involvement in the free market and narrowing their role to societal spaces that were deemed female and private, with a change in ideology of women's proper place emerging as well in order to justify this new gender system.

"The Welfare State and Women's Social Rights," Chapter 4, discusses the evolution of the particular mix of employment and general social policies found in present-day Canada, the United States, and Sweden. This section is intended to illustrate the significant variation among the three countries regarding women's economic independence and recognition for their unpaid caring work. This cross-national investigation shows as well that while some social policies have been eliminated in the last decade and a half, and the benefit levels of others reduced, new social programs and welfare state funding have at the same time emerged in all three countries, indicating the complicated nature of welfare state reform as the century draws to a close.

Chapter 5, "Midwives' Work and Social Rights," draws on my own primary and secondary comparative research on midwives' work and social rights in Canada, the US, and Sweden. This chapter offers the reader a specific case study of the book's main theme: the significant historical and present-day variation in gender equality regarding work and social rights in the three countries. Sweden has long valued midwives as central to its public health care system, has granted them relatively high occupational status, and has simultaneously provided important employment and general social rights in order for Swedish midwives to balance their paid and non-paid work. Conversely, until recently, midwives have been marginalized in Canada, and even today in those provinces where they have legal status and public funding, the model of professional work implemented pays little attention to the midwives' other caring roles in families. In the US, the situation of midwives is in many respects even more precarious than that of their Canadian counterparts, due not least to the corporate takeover of health care work by large US-based insurance companies.

The final chapter, "Women's Work and Social Rights: Looking to the Twenty-first Century," summarizes the arguments of preceding chapters and relates the book's general findings to the interconnected bodies of literature presented in Chapter 1. With regard to the historical picture of pre-capitalist societies and the present-day social organization of the three countries examined, there is no evidence of inevitable "patriarchy" across time and in place; even within capitalist societies, class, gender, and other inequalities are much more pronounced in some countries than in others. The chapter illustrates that the concepts of globalization and post-Fordism, although useful in generating hypotheses, are not fully adequate in understanding the complicated and somewhat contradictory employment picture in these three countries. The book concludes with a plea for a wide analysis of women's work across time and in place. Such an analysis must necessarily pay close attention to who performs the caring work fundamental to every society, and the rewards they receive for this consequential work.

ENDNOTES

[1] According to the Canadian Labour Force Survey (LFS), "unemployed persons are those who were without work during the reference week and were available for work and a) were on temporary layoff during reference week with an expectation of recall, or b) had actively looked for work in the past four weeks, or c) had a new job to start within four weeks from reference week" (Statistics Canada, 1998b: 31).

[2] Residualization involves expansion of the market in welfare state benefits and services, and reduction of social provision to a skeleton safety net that is utilized by the individuals only when in dire straits and all other resources fail.

[3] The window technique is adapted from Valerie Polakow (1993).

CONCEPTUALIZING WOMEN'S WORK AND SOCIAL RIGHTS

"Analysts should not rest with an adumbration of social rights for 'typical' worker-citizens—such ungendered citizens do not exist. Men make claims as worker-citizens to compensate for failures in the labor market; women make claims as workers, but also as members of families." (Orloff, 1993: 308)

INTRODUCTION

There is no single area of sociological theorizing from which to draw concepts that help us understand the organization of women's work and their access to social rights. The conceptual literature on this general topic can be found in four overlapping areas of inquiry: 1) scholarship on the gendered nature of caring work; 2) sociological theorizing on the professions; 3) analyses of welfare states; and 4) writings on post-Fordism. The central concepts in all four domains of sociological inquiry are discussed in turn below, concluding with the conceptual perspective that frames subsequent chapters.

WOMEN'S CARING WORK AND ITS ORIGINS

Work is a basic human activity embedded in the very fabric of all human societies. It is connected in some way to all other human activity, including the reproduction and maintenance of workers. Thus a list of activities included under the umbrella of "work" must be as exhaustive as possible. As Herbert Applebaum (1992: 571) puts it: "modern work and the modern work ethic is based on industrial society in which most people work for wages …. [Yet] wage work does not exhaust all the work performed in society, particularly household work and voluntary work without which modern society could not function."

Understood in its broadest sense, work involves creating and serving for one's own and perhaps dependents' direct consumption, or in exchange for pay or material support. Paid work includes goods produced and services performed for an income, while activities discharged voluntarily for personal or others' consumption (e.g., household work, childcare, caring for disabled or elderly persons, and community service) is unpaid work, and may be (but is not always) accompanied by non-monetary rewards such as companionship or opportunities for creative growth. Most of the activities that fall under the rubric of unpaid work are in some way connected with caring for others, which frequently is considered as analogous to "women's work." But caring work can also be performed for pay, as in the case of the so-called "caring professions," such as teaching, nursing, social work, and midwifery.

But why is caring work (unpaid and paid) typically assigned to women? Is caring work intrinsic to the female gender, a part of women's "nature"? A review of the predominantly feminist literature on caring work reveals little agreement on the answer to this question beyond the fact of its vital societal importance. In dispute, however, is how best to conceptualize caring work and how to discover the origins of society's assignment of caring activities to women.

Feminist psychologists have looked to gender socialization for clues. In doing so, some theorists have maintained an essentialist position, arguing that there exists a close affinity between caring work and femininity, that caring work is a prerequisite for all women, a part of their female identity, the organizing principle around which other aspects of womanhood are centred, and the location from where women gain their "different voice" from men (Gilligan, 1982). While men concern themselves with abstract issues of justice, women are socialized to internalize an "ethic of caring." As Carol Gilligan (1979: 440) writes,: "women not only define themselves in a context of human relationship but also judge themselves in terms of their ability to care. Woman's place in man's life cycle has been of nurturer, caretaker, and helpmate, the weaver of those networks of relationships on which she in turn relies." Nels Noddings (1995: 24) makes a similar point, stating that the evidence suggests that women are "better equipped" to give care than their male counterparts, largely due to the deep psychological bond that develops between mothers and daughters during the process of socialization.

Other feminist psychologists, attentive to the ideological context of caring, point out that gender socialization is not universal across time and place, but is tied intimately to the system of male dominance that women play a central role in reproducing (Chodorow, 1978; Baker Miller, 1976). Yet even those psychologists who show an awareness of the male-advantaged underpinnings of modern society continue to conceptualize caring and femininity as closely intertwined. Nancy Chodorow (1978: 190) notes that "as long as women mother, we can expect that a girl's preoedipal period will be longer than that of a boy and that women, more than men, will be open to and preoccupied with those very relational issues that go into mothering."

On the positive side, Chodorow (1979: 11–13) contextualizes her answer as to "why women mother," by pointing to women's inferior status in capitalist society. Baker Miller (1976: 11) makes a similar point in recognizing that women's unique "feminine intuition" is a product of their subordinate location in male-dominated modern society. Yet what both authors emphasize in their scholarship is the apparent "naturalness" of women's mothering role, seen as a product of early sexual identification and socialization, and passed from mothers to daughters. At the same time, both the unpaid nature of women's caring work and the fact of men's control over most societal wealth tend to slip from view. This is made even more manifest in writers such as sociologist Adrienne Rich (1978), who calls for a celebration of women's maternal bonds, which apparently are located in a "separate space," outside of the institutions and laws controlled by men.

Other sociologists have extended these initial explorations into the significance of women's caring work by examining its hidden social and economic value to patriarchy and capitalism. In doing so, they have paid particular attention to the actual *labour* involved when women perform caring tasks, whether in the family, community, or formal economy. Hilary Graham (1983: 28) writes about the work scripts of men and women in a male-dominated capitalist society: "men negotiate their social position through something recognised as 'doing,' doings based on 'knowledge' which enables them to 'think' and to engage in 'skilled work.' Women's social position is negotiated through a different kind of activity called 'caring,' a caring informed not by knowledge but by 'intuition' through which women find their way into 'unskilled' jobs."

Nicky James (1989) also contends that women's caring work is necessary not only for the social reproduction of family members, but as well for the economic success of men and profit-making in general. James (1989: 30) suggests that women's caring work involves the following: 1) *physical work* (preparing meals, bathing children, and ironing clothes, etc.); 2) *organizational work* (planning shopping, homework routines, holidays, and children's weekend activities, etc.); and 3) *emotional work*. The latter may include flexible acts such as taking part in an intimate conversation while preparing the evening meal, "being there" for a family member when she or he is lonely, tired, or depressed, and giving comfort to a sick child. James also illustrates how when emotional labour—undervalued and invisible in the home—is placed in the public realm it is transformed into a *commodity* to be sold and create profit for the employer. Yet emotional labour as a commodity still remains hidden as real work. As James (1989: 31) explains: "in the workplace the employment of emotional labourers is widespread in tasks where close personal attention is required, though the value of what they do is often unrecognised. Instead low-paid, low status women are employed to manage the emotions of others, thereby facilitating the labour of others." The commodification of emotional labour in capitalist societies is, at its core, a *class* and *gendered* process.

Arlie Hochschild's (1983) research on the gendered organization of paid service workers in the American airline industry offers a persuasive analysis of how profitable it is when employees' feelings are commercialized. In *The Managed Heart*, Hochschild argues that many of the jobs assigned by private companies to women, such as flight attendants (she notes that women made up 85 per cent of US flight attendants in the 1980s), are located at the toe of capitalism. While to some extent these jobs require workers to use their physical and mental capabilities, they especially draw upon workers' emotional skills. This involves the suppression of negative feelings towards customers (anger) and the exaggeration of positive feelings (kindness), the ultimate goal being to encourage passengers to patronize the company (i.e., to increase profits). Workers are asked to *feel* sympathy, trust, and good will—to "bow from the heart"—even when customers are disrespectful or rude.

These "soft" service jobs tend to be assigned to women, while men more frequently are appointed service jobs located at the heel of capitalism; "male" jobs (e.g., bill collectors) are based on the "hard" approach, involving duties such as deflating consumers' egos and causing them to feel enough guilt or fear to pay their outstanding debts. It is argued that this gender organization of service jobs in industrial capitalist societies reflects the patriarchal bias, in that the latter type of work—masculine, competitive, assertive—tends to be rewarded by higher wages as well as social prestige. In most instances it is women who are asked to perform emotional labour involving the tender smile and soft touch, and for this they receive lower pay than their male counterparts engaged in the more "manly" activities.

Scholars studying the fast food industry provide another example of the gendered nature of service work in the marketplace. Robin Leidner (1993: 210) contends that "doing gender" in what she calls "interactive service work" is inevitable for both men and women. However, when men "do gender" they do so most often by demanding a position of authority; when women do gender on the job, this frequently means accepting a subservient role. The McDonald's restaurant chain, and the fast food industry in general, are based on a particular gender-work arrangement, with men in upper management positions and women as both the main clientele and primary labour force. Ester Reiter (1996: 155) argues that the same holds true for another fast food chain, Burger King. "How would the expansion of the industry have occurred without the nuclear family to draw from? The work women do within the family unit makes the conditions of paid work Burger King offers the best choice they have. It is not possible to rule out the gender nature of experience."

Such is the underside of gendered work in the market economy and the private sphere. Women's devaluation as paid workers is rooted inside the class system itself; male dominance and capitalism are intimate bedfellows and both depend crucially on women's other work—their unpaid labour in the home. No other economic system so burdens its female population with the bulk of caring work essential to family and community survival, yet refuses to give them adequate economic or social value. This is despite the fact that the second half of the twentieth century has witnessed a sharp increase in women's gainful employment. The fact remains, it is argued, that much of this paid caring work of women remains unappreciated and poorly rewarded, while at the same time women's "second shift" (Hochschild,1989) or "family shift" (Eichler, 1997)—the emotional work and other caring tasks they perform after their paid job is done—is not even perceived of as work. Moreover, it is estimated that unpaid caring activities outstrip the value of paid services by three, perhaps even four to one (Armstrong, 1994: 116).

In brief, much of the psychological and sociological literature on the gendered nature of caring work suggests that whether due to nature, gender socialization, patriarchy, capitalism, or some combination of these, women's work is largely bound up with caring for and about others, that such work is difficult to define and organize, and that it is undervalued in the family, economy, and society. This scholarship leaves us with a rather bleak picture of the future for women workers in capitalist societies: seemingly resistant to contingent forces, the *caring dilemma* remains that women workers "accept a duty to care rather than demand a right to determine how they would satisfy this duty" (Reverby, 1987: 5). Women homemakers are expected to perform their unpaid caring work as a maternal duty, integral to their female identity; altruism is promoted while societal recognition and other rewards are sacrificed. Paid women workers, too, continue to fall short of what Baker Miller (1976:71) views as truly socially valued caring work—"caring without dilemma … a way of life that includes serving others without being subservient."

It is important to note that much of the theorizing about the essentially female character of caring work and its lack of societal recognition is based primarily on US and, to a lesser extent, British research. How applicable are these theories to other times and places? What was the situation of women with regard to their work roles and social rights in Canadian history, for example, and how does the Canadian evidence compare cross-nationally today? How closely does this scholarship fit the situation of unpaid and paid women workers in Sweden, a country with different historical traditions than Anglo-America and at present displaying a more social-democratic form of capitalism than that discussed in the literature reviewed above?

There is no single definition of caring work, just as there is no single definition of women's reproductive and productive work in general. The phrase "women's caring work" holds no intrinsic meaning; it is shaped by social, economic, and cultural processes that differ across time and place. Although in most societies women's work assignments accord with the overriding gender division of labour (along with other social categories, most importantly social class but often also race/ethnicity), different economic systems and gender ideologies, supported by different political structures, tend to value various types of women's work in a multiplicity of ways. Given viable opportunities, women can balance personal autonomy with the capacity to care for others (clients/consumers as well as family members). The job/family conflict so common today—especially for solo mothers—is not inevitable. Women's work is not always and universally devalued, and caring for others is not dismissed in all cultures and times as "non-work." Furthermore, certain social conventions from the past that continue today result in greater male involvement in caring work, approximating a genuine welfare society based on a *shared gender model* of paid and unpaid work, with women and men enjoying equal access to social rights, while at the same time sharing opportunities and responsibilities in employment and family (Dalerup, 1994).

THE PROFESSIONS AND THE COMMON FATE OF THEIR FEMALE MEMBERSHIP

Although classical sociologists such as Karl Marx, Emile Durkheim, and Max Weber acknowledged some workers as more privileged than others, these early social thinkers were focused primarily on the broader picture of the changing nature of work in capitalist societies. By contrast, sociologists writing in the post-World War II period have attempted to distinguish core features of the "professions" that make them distinct from other types of paid work. The abundant literature from the past half century highlights three perspectives on what makes the professions unique—the structural-functionalist, professional dominance, and patriarchal control perspectives.[1] In all three instances, professions are assumed to denote maleness and dominance over both clients and other occupations. Workers who do not make it to the apex of the professional aristocracy are either the women who are located largely at the outer circle of the professions, or those in the "semi-" or "caring" professions.

The Functionalist Perspective

The functionalist perspective actually constitutes a variety of viewpoints. One version presents an evaluative framework on the professions based on their hallmark "traits." A service occupation is warranted a professional designation if it has most of the following: 1) abstract, specialized knowledge; 2) work autonomy; 3) authority over clients and allied occupations; and 4) altruism (Greenwood, 1957). A second version outlines the step-by-step process by which an occupation becomes a profession. The steps include: full-time occupational engagement; establishment of a training school (ideally an academic program); creation of a professional association; government licensure protecting a secure mandate to practise; and development of a formal code of ethics to separate the qualified from the unqualified, to protect the clientele, and to foster collegial relations among the membership.[2]

Talcott Parsons (1951) extends this early scholarship beyond the listing of traits or attributes of a particular group of service workers by highlighting the important *functional role* played by the professions in modern society. Parsons (1968: 545) identifies service professions as being one of the—if not the most important—homeostatic structures underlying the social order. According to Parsons, superior technique and collectivity-orientation of the "professional man" encourages protection "by a series of symbolically significant practices which serve to differentiate him sharply from the businessman" (1951: 464). Parsons maintains that modern society awards the "practising professions" a monopoly over knowledge and its transmission, a high degree of clinical autonomy, and authority over clients and associated occupations in exchange for acceptance of normative constraints on the behaviour of individual practitioners: noblesse oblige is rewarded and exploitation of the public is penalized.

The functionalist perspective also encompasses the professions' neighbouring service occupations, referred to as the "semi-professions." More than any other theorists of the professions, functionalist writers state without ambiguity what the semi-professions are and are not able to attain. Thus, writes Amitai Etzioni (1969: vi), "a significant segment of the semi-professions aspire to a full-fledged professional status and sustain a professional self-image, despite the fact that they themselves are often aware that they do not deserve such a status, and despite the fact that they objectively do not qualify."

The semi-professions are those service occupations that fall short of the defining characteristics of the true professions, in which Parsons includes the clergy, law, medicine, and academia. In contrast, the semi-professional membership is assumed to have a less than specialized body of knowledge; their training is too short and not academic enough; they lack autonomy in their work because they are subject to supervision by a bureaucratic administration; and their status is less legitimized by clients and society at large.

While Parsons and his colleagues drew their conclusions without conducting much by way of actual research in their home country, the United States, Richard Simpson and Ida Harper Simpson (1969) examined the statistical evidence on four groups of service workers they deemed to be semi-professional: librarians, nurses, social workers, and elementary school teachers. They note that all four occupational groups are found primarily in bureaucratic settings (libraries, nursing services, social work agencies, and schools) and that in terms of numbers, all are dominated by women service workers. The Simpsons conclude that the semi-professions are destined to remain in subordinate positions due to the bureaucratic nature of their work, but also because of the predominantly female status of their membership, which "strengthens all of these forces for bureaucratic control in the organizations in which they work. The public is less willing to grant autonomy to women than to men. A woman's primary attachment is to the family role; women are therefore less intrinsically committed to work than men and less likely to maintain a high level of abstract knowledge" (1969: 199).

The Simpsons did not extend their empirical studies of the semi-professions beyond the United States, which leaves the question of whether women in the caring professions elsewhere faced the same constraints as their US counterparts in the late sixties and early seventies. Given the paucity of comparative studies by functionalist theorists, it can only be assumed that they deemed such research unnecessary. An underlying assumption is that the problems faced by the semi-professions are explained principally not by larger social and economic forces, but by psychological or "natural" processes, an assumption that forms the basis of much of the psychological theorizing on women's caring work. Parsons (cited in Simpson and Simpson,1969: 244) states as much when he refers to the apparent submissiveness of librarians: "Sex composition should therefore be considered both a symptom and a partial determinant of the pattern [of semi-professionals such as librarians] with which we are concerned." William J. Goode (1969: 266) draws a similar conclusion, writing that the "four great *person* professions: law, medicine, ministry, and university teaching" remain in a league by themselves .... The semi-professions will never become professions in the usual sense: they will never reach the levels of knowledge and dedication to service that society considers necessary for a profession."

In short, if we are to believe the functional theorists, it seems that occupations considered "semi-professions" (i.e., caring work) will remain only partial professions—time and social setting cannot alter their destiny. How adequate is this depiction? Later chapters will illustrate historical instances where female (numerically) dominated service occupations actually possessed specialized esoteric knowledge, enjoyed autonomy in their daily work, and were held in high esteem by clients. But not all theorists on the professions embrace this perspective.

The Professional Dominance Perspective

The professional dominance perspective challenges the functionalist notion that the professions take part in a mutually beneficial exchange of prestige and authority for rendering unique services to the public. In fact, goes this argument, the professions are far from beneficial for society; professionals exploit their relationship with the public in order to gain power, status, and privilege. Professional dominance theorists question whether the professions' claim of expert knowledge is genuinely helpful or whether it simply serves to bring certain states of affairs under professional dominance by constructing them as, for example, medical concerns or matters of the law.

This critique of the functionalist perspective began in the early 1970s with the work of Elliott Freidson (1970a; 1970b) and other, mainly British, scholars (Johnson, 1972; Parry & Parry, 1976; Parkin, 1979). These writers put forth an alternative perspective on the professions that depicts them as self-interested, monopolizing groups aimed at gaining *professional dominance*. From this viewpoint professionalization has little to do with quality care by empathetic experts; instead it involves the considered attempt by powerful service occupations to attain exclusionary *social closure*. According to Frank Parkin (1979: 45), "the distinguishing feature of exclusionary closure is the attempt by one group to secure for itself a privileged position at the expense of some other group through a process of subordination." If successful in their efforts to achieve closure, professionals gain the much valued privilege of protection from outside evaluation and control by others. The result is extensive freedom to define professional work mandates and organize daily practices (Freidson, 1986).

In analyzing various strategies employed by privileged professionals to gain exclusionary social closure, Frank Parkin (1979) identifies the employment of *legalistic tactics*, which involve using government licensure to acquire a monopoly over a particular mandate to practise. Virtually all professions are protected by laws that make it illegal for professionals to practise without a license, and anyone found to be doing otherwise can be charged and taken to court. *Credentialist tactics* are a second major strategy, and include the specification of formal and informal qualifications for professional inclusion/exclusion. As Anthony Giddens (1975: 186) states: "the most significant type of difference in market capacity is undoubtedly between the capacity to offer marketable technical knowledge, recognized and specialized symbolic skills, and the offering of general symbolic competence." According to Gerard Larkin (1983: 15), professions can become "imperialistic" in this regard, manoeuvring themselves in such a manner that they successfully "poach" skills from neighbouring occupations, "delegating" them to perform less skilled, more menial tasks. Other writers, such as Andrew Abbott (1988), have extended the professional dominance perspective to include the idea of a "system of professions," which he conceptualizes as a complex, dynamic, and interdependent network of professions linked together in specific domains of service work ("jurisdictions") and ceaselessly clashing over areas of expert knowledge and skill. At the apex of the health service domain, for example, medicine exercises extraordinary power, much like a private government (Freidson, 1970b).

While at polar opposites in their views of the functionality of the professions, there is one essential point on which professional dominance scholars agree with functionalist theorists: the location of the semi- or caring professions. Mike Saks (1998: 181) argues, for example, that given the social closure strategies of the archetypical British profession of medicine, "it is understandable that nursing and other professions allied to medicine are still frequently referred to as 'semi-professions'." Saks implies that doctors continue to hold a strong position at the pinnacle of the division of labour in health care; they alone possess an "organised autonomy" that not only allows them extensive freedom to practise as they will, but that at once enables them to dominate related service occupations.

The relationship between medicine and the semi- or caring professions, such as nursing and midwifery, is typically depicted as a "zero-sum power game." The semi-professions are permitted by doctors to inform and advise, but never to directly challenge their omnipotent position (Stein, 1967). The professions are those service occupations that have managed to win the "turf battle" in the power game. Those who do not win—the semi-professions—are allowed to continue to play the game as long as they abide by rules set by the winners. The semi-professions are thus destined to a half-life status; they are not "real" professionals, because they are too weak, not competitive or aggressive enough to win the war over how to divvy up service work.

The above criticisms of the functionalist perspective apply equally to the professional dominance approach: 1) the scholarship involves sweeping conclusions about service workers that are often not verified by empirical evidence; 2) what empirical research there is has an Anglo-American focus, primarily on Britain and the US. There remains a crucial question about the applicability of the professional dominance theory in time and across place. The implicit male bias underpinning both the functionalist and professional dominance perspectives is a third shortcoming, which is raised by patriarchal control theorists.

The Perspective of Patriarchal Control

As with professional dominance scholars, feminists studying the service occupations remain skeptical of the functionalists' view of the professions as experts working in the public's best interest. However, feminists are quick to point out that both perspectives overlook the essentially "masculine project" that has framed the professions historically and continues to do so today. This masculine project initially entailed the legal obstruction of women from the professions altogether. More recently it has involved the subordination of those women who make it into the professions—as well as their counterparts in the adjacent caring professions—to the interests of professional men. As Celia Davies (1996: 669) points out about the exclusion of women in once all-male professional clubs, "work that traces women's struggles to enter the professions in the late nineteenth and early twentieth centuries have suggested that these were not just a matter of doors and minds being closed to women, but of the values that were embedded in the notion of the practice of a profession reflecting a masculine project and repressing or denying those qualities culturally assigned to femininity."

Feminists argue that, at their very core, the professions *profess* gender. The examples of medicine and law are paradigmatic in their initial absolute exclusion of women from their ranks, followed by gradual inclusion on inequitable terms. Women's struggles to gain access to the requisite medical and legal training have been long and difficult and, for the most part, carried out with zealous opposition from male physicians and lawyers (Hagan and Kay, 1995; Walsh, 1977). It is only since the 1960s—and due to the persistent call for change by the women's movement—that better representation is enjoyed today by women in the medical and legal professions.

However, even this inclusion has been on the basis of an unarticulated set of gender terms. Despite noteworthy strides in gaining access to medical schools and hospitals, for example, evidence suggests that patriarchal strategies continue to keep women near the bottom of the profession's internal hierarchy. Women physicians cluster in areas that draw heavily on the worker's feelings and emotions—the "feminine" specialties of general practice, family practice, and primary care. Yet it is in these domains that women physicians lack the professional power to provide quality care to clients (Butter et al., 1987; Elston, 1977). Women physicians are forced below a "glass ceiling" of what remains in many ways a dual medical market. There is a favoured male medical sector based on monopoly over the development and transmission of esoteric knowledge and special techniques, autonomy in health work settings, and authority (male dominance) over the practitioner-client relationship and allied (mainly female) caregivers. Then there is a less advantaged female medical sector characterized by exclusion from the knowledge strata, limited work autonomy, and little authority within the occupational health structure and vis-à-vis clientele (Lorber, 1992). According to Judith Lorber (1993), women physicians will *never* be true equals in the American medical profession. John Hagan and Fiona Kay (1995) report that women in the legal profession also confront formidable difficulties.

Feminist scholars tell a similar story about the fate of other women service workers. Female nurses are an obvious case in point. Like women in medicine, recently nurses have taken steps to overcome their historical subordination (Reverby, 1989; Bullough, 1975). Despite their achievements, the overall picture of nursing care remains largely under patriarchal control—they remain a semi-profession (Elzinga, 1990). As Rose Weitz (1996: 269) states: "the increased educational qualifications of nursing has enabled it to achieve semi-professional status, achieving some but not all the hallmarks of a profession. Although most nurses consider themselves professionals and although nurses have more autonomy and status than in the past, they remain subordinate to medicine."

Midwives appear to face a similar destiny. Over the course of the last three centuries, medical men increasingly have encroached on "midwives' affairs" (Donnison, 1977; Witz, 1992), so that by the "mid-nineteenth century the occupational boundaries between midwifery and medical practice had been constructed around a division between assistance in the process of 'normal' labour, constructed as a natural process and remaining within the sphere of the midwife, and intervention (frequently with instruments such as forceps) in the process of 'abnormal' labour, which was the exclusive prerogative of men" (Witz, 1990: 683). Medical men emerged as "policemen" in the birthing process, in control not only of the instruments but of the ultimate authority to define what is "normal" and "abnormal," leaving midwives de-skilled and their work under continuous surveillance, even when doctors are not present in the birth chamber. Some feminist writers have gone so far as to allege that medical men have "stolen" childbirth from women (Rich, 1975), "captured their wombs" (Oakley, 1984), forcing midwives to "act as spies," reporting to male physicians the intimate details of women's reproductive lives (Hearn, 1982: 196). While midwives have not been excluded from serving birthing women—although this has indeed been the case to a large extent in North America until recently—their inclusion has been on terms set by men. Midwives' own "professional project" was one of accommodation, "conceding to medical men's restrictive definition of the midwife's sphere of competence, as well as concurring with the limited knowledge base and programme of training set down and provided by doctors" (Witz, 1990: 685).

In short, women doctors, nurses, and midwives have had to engage in a long struggle simply to be permitted within the outer circles of the male profession. Even when they have been "included" in the professional division of labour they have not been seen as autonomous workers. As Celia Davies (1996: 661) puts it, "the key issue for consideration is not so much the exclusion of women from work defined as professional, but rather their routine inclusion in ill-defined support roles." The female professionals and their semi-professional counterparts work as "adjuncts" to men, "facilitators" of men's power. Jeff Hearn (1982: 191) writes about the latter: "activities and experiences formerly performed privately or controlled by women became in this way brought into public control by men, and so subject to the expertise of experts. As such, the semi-professions are symptomatic of a later stage of capitalist patriarchy than that which spawned the traditional professions."

While contributing a useful analysis on the gendered structure of the professions—and how they are intertwined with the forces of patriarchy and capitalism—as with functionalist and professional dominance theories, the perspective of patriarchal control nevertheless remains problematic due to the scanty evidence in support of the concept, much of which is gleaned from US and British studies over the past few decades. Especially bothersome is the common conclusion that the semi- or caring professions, regardless of aspirations, strategies, and professed beliefs, can never attain genuine professional power, prestige, or status.

A central problem with scholarship on the professions is its tendency to use old categories and concepts to explain historical and cross-national data on service workers in such a way that the same dismal conclusions about the fate of women and the professions can be drawn. The result is similar to what E.P. Thompson (1978: 228) terms "self-evident mystification": "if we suppose that bad harvests and famine are caused by the visitation of God upon us for our sins, then we cannot escape from this concept by pointing to drought and late frosts and blight, for God would have visited us through these chosen instruments." Thompson argues that we need to break with worn concepts and devise new ones before we can hope to analyze the data that has always been there.

This apparent duality between men and women in the professions and semi-professions needs to be problematized rather than accepted at face value. Only through historical and cross-national examination of the situations of the midwife, nurse, physiotherapist, librarian, teacher, doctor, and lawyer, only by investigating them *at work*, can we know what concepts best describe the social conditions within which they find themselves. Everett Cherrington Hughes (1958: 7) argues that understanding a person's work is "as good a clue as any" to understanding the course of his or her life, social being, and identity. "This has been so," writes Hughes, "longer than we sociologists, with our love of stereotypes" are usually willing to allow. Chapter 5 offers my research on midwives to illustrate that the semi-professional label for midwifery does not hold true for all times and societal contexts. Fundamental to women's inclusion in the professional division of labour as autonomous workers is their opportunity to access social rights to formal education and childcare, as well as opportunities for public employment. However, as is shown in the next section on the gendering of welfare states, there remains controversy among scholars on the role of the state in furthering or entrenching women's status as workers in society.

WELFARE STATES AND SOCIAL RIGHTS

What is the relationship between women workers and the welfare state? Three theoretical perspectives stand out in attempts to answer this question. *Mainstream* scholarship[3] on welfare states offers historical and cross-national perspectives, but nevertheless has been criticized for excluding women as central actors. Mainstream writers on the concept of citizenship have been challenged for basing their analyses on the average "citizen worker," which essentially has meant the male worker. *Early feminist* work on welfare states sought to correct this implicit male bias by underlining the patriarchal nature of welfare state provision, arguing that the welfare state functions essentially as a "silent partner" of men and the ruling classes. More recent feminist cross-national research has attempted to blend and further these two perspectives by offering a *gendered welfare states* perspective. While acknowledging the male bias of some types of welfare states, this third perspective also recognizes the emancipatory potential of other types of welfare states in fostering women's equality in unpaid and paid work. Below is a brief examination of these three perspectives.

Mainstream Perspectives

The core concept upon which mainstream analyses of welfare states is based is that of *citizenship*. T.H. Marshall's concept of citizenship customarily serves as the starting point from which to map the historical changes in individual rights as capitalist countries developed. According to Marshall (1965: 92), "citizenship is a status bestowed on those who are full members of a community .... All who possess the status are equal with respect to the rights and duties with which the status is endowed." Marshall (1965: 91) demarcates three categories of rights of citizenship: civil, political, and social. Each classification, in his view, is a site of struggle between individual actors and the state over how the boundary of inclusion/exclusion of citizenship is determined. In general terms, *civil citizenship* refers to individuals' rights before the law, and dates back to the eighteenth century with the development of the modern judicial system. *Political citizenship* refers to individuals' rights to enter into democratic processes, including the right to vote, and dates for men from the middle of the nineteenth century, and for women from the early decades of the twentieth century. *Social citizenship* is a development peculiar to the twentieth century, and refers to individuals' rights of economic welfare, universal education, and social security conferred by the state in order to minimize the negative effects of capitalism.

It is in regard to social citizenship that Marshall discusses the formation of the welfare state and its important role in promoting social democracy in capitalist societies, arguing that a comprehensive welfare state would make available to citizens a broad assortment of social rights. The outcome, according to Marshall (1992: 33), is a "general enrichment of the concrete substance of civilized life, a general reduction of risk and insecurity, [and] an equalization between the more and less unfortunate at all levels—between the healthy and the sick, the employed and the unemployed, the old and the active, the bachelor and the father of a large family."

Marshall is especially interested in members of the working class, particularly wage earners or breadwinners, who in the first half of the twentieth century were extremely vulnerable to exploitation by capitalist employers. His chief concern is thus with enlarging citizenship entitlements for working-class men, since women were only marginally attached to the economy (see Chapter 3) and tended to hold subordinate positions to their husbands in matters regarding law and politics.

More recent mainstream analysts of welfare states (Gough, 1979; Offe, 1984; Esping-Andersen and Korpi, 1987) also place the economically independent citizen—i.e., the gainfully employed worker—central to their analyses, and attempt to develop typologies or cross-national comparisons of welfare state regimes in regard to social provision. A range of approaches typically are included under the umbrella of more recent mainstream scholarship, and some writers have revised their approach over time. There is some research on specific countries in regard to the distinctive features of individual welfare states. A second approach has searched for differences between two contrasting ideal types of welfare states, typically employing levels of public expenditure as a means to measure growth. A third approach develops welfare state typologies along two axes of dissimilarity.[4]

A more recent approach, examined below as informing the perspective of gendering welfare states, classifies national governments on the basis of a convergence of characteristics. This approach is represented by the typology of welfare state regimes and social policy variations developed by Gösta Esping-Andersen (1990) and Walter Korpi (1985). These authors work within a *power resource model*, and propose three dimensions that form the core of welfare states: 1) the state-market relationship, "the extent to which needs are to be satisfied through the labor market or, as an alternative, through political mechanisms"; 2) the impact of welfare states on economic stratification, "the status relations among citizens within the framework of social policy"; and 3) the constitution of social rights, "the range, or domain, of human needs that are satisfied by social policy" (Esping-Andersen and Korpi, 1987: 40–41). On the basis of these three dimensions of variation, three types of welfare state regimes are distinguished, each founded on very different underlying principles of stratification and social rights for citizens: the liberal market regime; the conservative corporatist regime, and the social democratic regime.

Liberal market regimes are most concerned with the commodification of human labour and least concerned with its *decommodification*. This means that liberal welfare states are the least focused on reducing workers' dependency on cash wages, or in increasing their security through universal entitlements (Esping-Andersen, 1990). Relatively few social policies get enacted in liberal market regimes, and those that do tend to be meagre in regard to worker entitlement. Although Esping-Andersen notes that "there is no single pure case" of a liberal welfare state, he nevertheless indexes Canada, Australia, New Zealand, the United States, and possibly Britain as liberal market regimes. These countries are seen to rely principally on means-tested programs, modest social insurance benefits, market answers such as "corporate welfare" (company sponsored social benefits), and private insurance.

Conservative corporatist regimes are those European countries (including France, Germany, Italy, and Austria) that built their welfare states on the cornerstone of the classical insurance model introduced by Chancellor Otto von Bismarck to Germany in the late nineteenth century. In this welfare state model, citizens' social benefits depend on their previous contributions as workers and their present employment status. With some variation, the welfare states of Continental countries have arranged social programs around occupational groups, and "labor market status tends to condition benefits, which implies that large groups are typically excluded and heavily reliant on public assistance, private charity, or the family" (Esping-Andersen and Korpi, 1987: 42). In this respect, conservative corporatist regimes retain some elements common to liberal welfare state regimes (e.g., means-tested benefits), while at the same time embracing other, more comprehensive, social policies (e.g., universal access to some form of health insurance). While better able than liberal market regimes to meet the needs of marginalized citizens, conservative corporatist regimes nevertheless preserve status and class distinctions, as Ramesh Mishra remarks about Germany:

> Although a big spender and a generous provider of income security, especially pensions, Germany emphasized security and hierarchy rather than equality, linking benefits to occupational status …. Germany did not seek to promote income equality or gender equality through social welfare policies. Nonetheless, the welfare system has been large and redistributive enough to ensure that Germany has one of the lowest rates of poverty in the world. (1996: 321–22)

Although differences in the degree of social provision exist, the Nordic countries (Sweden, Finland, Denmark, Norway, and Iceland), have gone furthest along the road to developing welfare states that fit the model of the *social democratic regime*. This assessment is based on three distinct features of this type of welfare state: 1) *comprehensiveness* in social policy (i.e., a wide scope of public intervention geared towards assuaging an assortment of social needs); 2) *institutionalization* of social entitlements (i.e., citizenship or residency rights include a very large spread of social services); and 3) *universalism* in regard to social provision (i.e., inhabitants have equitable access to available social welfare benefits). Welfare state social policies in Nordic countries serve as a major means for heightening solidarity among social groups and strengthening egalitarianism. The Swedish welfare state is seen as a prototypical social democratic welfare regime: "Sweden's welfare state, besides being universal and comprehensive, has also been the world's most redistributive" (Mishra, 1996: 321).

The model of welfare state regimes outlined above has been challenged within mainstream camps for a number of reasons, including its omission to take account of change over time when categorizing particular countries (e.g., does Norway's welfare state have the same essential form it had in the early 1970s?). This model has also been criticized for its inadequacy in analyzing variation in regard to social policies among countries falling within a particular welfare state regime. A third and more immediately relevant criticism of this perspective is its failure to address the underlying male bias in the research informing its central concepts. It is to this latter criticism we now turn.

The Feminist Critique

Implicit in mainstream perspectives on welfare states is the assumption of *gender neutrality*, or that social provision has a similar bearing on men and women. Also assumed in this perspective is that the higher public expenditure and the greater the redistribution of resources in society, the greater the level of equality among inhabitants. Those countries that spend comparatively more on social welfare and have developed universal social security programs are speculated to have advanced further along the road to genuine social democracy.

However, the fact that there is very little information about the impact of social policies on women (or indeed on other social categories, including racial and ethnic minorities) causes concern about the actual effect of welfare state social policies on women as separate from "individual wage earners" or "family heads." Many feminist writers maintain that the wage earner/breadwinner/citizen discussed in mainstream perspectives, whether stated explicitly or implied, is almost always considered to be male (Pateman, 1988a). This holds true for the most recent contributions to the mainstream approach focusing on comparative welfare states (Esping-Andersen, 1990; Esping-Andersen and Korpi, 1987). The assumption remains that economic independence is essential for full citizenship and that employment is the chief distinctive feature of the [male] worker. As Helga Hernes (1988: 190) states: "the social-democratic citizen is the citizen worker, a male family provider, a working-class hero. *His* identities and participation patterns were determined by *his* ties to the labour market, and by the web of association and corporate structures which had grown around these ties."

Feminist scholars highlight sexuality, reproduction, and physical bodies when discussing gender differences that shape the concept of citizenship, arguing that women face unique hazards to their bodies in the private and public spheres of capitalist countries, which have hampered their full participation as autonomous individuals in the economy and civil society (Jones, 1990).

In short, the welfare state affects women and men differently. Furthermore, even when the welfare state decreases women's dependency on men, women remain dependent on the state for economic support (e.g., in the form of social assistance). Once women become dependent on the welfare state for income, the welfare state gains public control over women's lives (Pascall, 1986). To the extent that more women are reduced to the dependent status of "wards" of the state, the welfare state can hardly be seen as gender neutral, but rather as reinforcing a deeply ingrained sexual division of labour based on gender inequality.

Both mainstream and feminist approaches to understanding the welfare state have methodological limitations. On the one hand, mainstream theories have been comparative, but their analyses exclude differences in women's and men's relationship with the state. On the other hand, feminist theories of the welfare state recognize these differences, but have not attempted to take their research cross-nationally. A third perspective, discussed below, has attempted to overcome these conceptual problems.

Gendering Welfare States

Cross-national scholarship that attempts to advance the mainstream approach by gendering welfare states, argues that women's citizenship rights—civic, political, and social—are premised on correcting two major obstacles to women in capitalist countries, as identified by feminist writers: inadequate wages and unequal access to jobs; and economic dependence on others (men, state officials) due to women's inordinate caring responsibilities for children and dependent others. As Ann Shola Orloff (1993: 309) contends, "relations of domination based on control of women's bodies in the family, the workplace, and public spaces undermine women's abilities to participate as 'independent individuals'—citizens—in the polity, which in turn affect their capabilities to demand and utilize social rights. The ways the state intervene—or refuse to—are critical to women's situation."

This third perspective calls for an extension of the mainstream welfare regime approach to take into account actual gender differences in employment and family life so that social policies not only aid decommodification—making it possible for a person to "maintain a livelihood without reliance on the market" (Esping-Andersen, 1990: 21–22)—but at the same time result in positive changes that promote women's economic independence, a prerequisite for their equality with men.

From this it follows that focus needs to be placed on those welfare state social policies that enhance women's position in paid work and at the same time grant them recognition for their substantial non-paid caring work, so that they are neither forced into dependency on male partners nor stigmatized as "welfare mothers" reliant on social assistance. *Equality in wages and employment* concerns whether and to what degree welfare states enact strategies to promote women's equality with men in regard to paid employment, pay equity, freedom from workplace harassment, and access to employment-related benefits (O'Connor, 1993). This necessarily challenges the (male) breadwinner model of employment and accompanying social benefits that have been the principal focus of labour movements in earlier stages of capitalism. By emphasizing the need for a "family wage"—as was the call of unions throughout the early twentieth century, and is still in some quarters today—women's waged work generally has been viewed as secondary and less valued than that of the male wage earner or family breadwinner. Social policies provided by welfare states to enhance women's entitlements to higher education and occupational training, access to jobs, and gender equity in wages, are examples of "women friendly" social policies that feminists argue promote women's equality in the public sphere and enhance their independence as wage earners.

Social provision to form and sustain an autonomous household is the second dimension of a gendered welfare state approach. This involves examining social policies with an eye to distinguishing between women's entitlements as a) wives/family dependents and b) mothers and carers. Social policies that enhance recognition of women's valuable (if unpaid) work as mothers and carers of dependents—and aid women's independence in performing these vital societal tasks—also tend to be women-friendly welfare state policies. On the contrary, women's entitlements based on their status as wives/family dependents are viewed within this third perspective as regressive in regard to equality in employment and family life, since they leave women vulnerable to poverty in times of marital breakdown/desertion, and at the same time ignore (leave invisible) women's caring activities in the home.

The more that welfare states base their social policies on the *principle of caring*, the closer they come to championing gender equality in employment and family life, one in which men's involvement in caring work is encouraged and where there is an equal balance between paid and unpaid work for both women and men, sharing opportunities and responsibilities in employment and family (Sainsbury, 1996; Orloff, 1993; O'Connor, 1993). Important social policies to consider in this regard include family leaves and benefits and public childcare services.

This book endorses this perspective to a large extent, although I seek to highlight differences as well as similarities within types of welfare state regimes in regard to women-friendly social policies. However, as is discussed in the final section of this chapter, a new body of scholarship on the nature of work in what has come to be called the post-Fordist era maintains that the welfare state is no longer a viable institution and that work itself, in the sense of secure employment, is at an end.

POST-FORDISM AND THE NEW WORLD OF WORK

Market economies around the world are said to be undergoing fundamental restructuring with the dawn of the twenty-first century. The globalization of finance and the application of new information technologies to the production of goods and services are believed to be behind the demise of Fordist capitalism. Characteristic of earlier decades of the twentieth century, Fordist capitalism has involved some or all of the following: industrially-based centralized production; national economies supporting domestic mass manufacturing; Keynesian economic policies; collective bargaining; strong unions; full-time employees with job shelters; and welfare state policies such as progressive tax systems, unemployment benefits, and pension rights (Reich, 1991; Krahn and Lowe, 1998; Jenson et al., 1988). The argument is that a "new world of work" has arrived, a *post-Fordist* era characterized by opposite trends that include: deindustrialization; transnational corporate linkages; international trade agreements; weakened unions; limited labour contracts; contingent work; increased self-employment; and retrenchment of welfare state social policies (Jessop et al., 1987; Barley, 1996).

Scholars adopting the post-Fordist perspective have described the emerging globalized economies of high-income countries as segmented into three distinct employment sectors: 1) the *innovative sector*, a small elite of "sky workers" in entry-port jobs that offer possibilities of further training, career ladders, greater pay and fringe benefits over time, and worker participation (Reich, 1997); 2) a much larger *marginal sector*, mainly located in the peripheral/secondary market, occupied by "ground workers," who are without access to secure employment, performing non-standard jobs that include short-term contracts and self-employment along with other forms of contingent work accompanied by few if any employment benefits and rarely leading to greater responsibility or higher pay, social security, or career ladders (Harrison and Bluestone, 1988; Reich, 1997); and 3) an emerging *third sector* comprised of workers doing voluntary/community-based work, which is largely devoid of either pecuniary reward or employment rights (Lewis, 1994; Armstrong, 1994).

Some writers have described these developments in the form of a "polarization of the labour market" and the "shrinking of the middle classes," with fewer and fewer workers in secure employment and many occupied in marginal jobs, voluntary activities, or no employment at all (Reich, 1991). Economic forecasts for the early decades of the twenty-first century predict an entrenchment of this post-Fordist economy, a downward spiral of secure workers, who join the ranks of an enlarged "disposable workforce" (Moore, 1996). The emerging brave new world of virtual companies is predicted to involve transnational corporations (TNCs) shifting their operations around the globe, irrespective of union contracts and national political boundaries, moving about in a "borderless world" (Ohmae, 1991). Some post-Fordist observers see these developments as a new form of global exploitation, as Miyoshi (1993: 748) writes: "TNCs are unencumbered with national baggage. Their profit motives are unconcealed. They travel, communicate, and transfer people and plants, information and technology, money and resources globally. TNCs rationalize and execute the objectives of colonialism with greater efficiency and rationalism."

A possible solution to this ominous prediction is suggested by the popular writer, Jeremy Rifkin (1995), who calls for public valuation of work now performed outside of capitalist markets and welfare state bureaucracies, neither of which, in his view, is likely to offer secure employment for most people in a future society characterized by lean corporations without frontiers and downsized government organizations. Rifkin envisions instead the growing importance of the "third sector"—i.e., voluntary workers providing services to needy individuals, families, and communities, perhaps rewarded for their efforts with a minimum monetary payment. What we need, in short, is support for a new "social economy," as Rifkin (1995: 249–50) explains: "today, with the formal economy receding from the social life of the nation and the government retreating from its traditional role of provider as last resort, only a concerted effort spearheaded by the third sector and adequately supported by the public sector will be able to deliver basic social services and begin the process of revitalizing the social economy of every country."

Feminists writers examining the post-Fordist perspective have argued that it is a gendered process, noting that the demise of the welfare state is affecting women directly in at least three ways (Armstrong and Armstrong, 1988; Oakley, 1994). First, it results in a reduction of transfer payments to households, and this is especially detrimental to disadvantaged households, among which the most vulnerable are female-headed families. Second, contraction of the welfare state also means an end of secure public sector employment, where comparatively large numbers of women workers are located. Third, a leaner public sector results in the loss of important health and social services, including public childcare provision, that make it possible for women to undertake gainful employment in the first instance (Armstrong, 1994; Baker, 1996).

Feminist writers point out that it should come as no surprise that a decline in public sector jobs for women compels a decline in public services for all women (and their families). Nona Glazer (1993: 5–6) has labelled this latter component of post-Fordism the *work transfer*, "the redistribution of labour from paid women service workers to unpaid women family members, but one that maintains a connection between the work .... The work transfer exemplifies the capacity of capitalism to shape even the most intimate details of social life, in this case even the tending work that women do as family members." Pat Armstrong et al. (1994: 106) make a similar point after examining the transfer of nurses from hospital to "home care" in recent health care cutbacks in Canada. Although this move has been championed for its less expensive but higher quality of care, "people do not necessarily receive even decent care at home, in part because women are already so overburdened. Moreover, there are a whole range of hidden costs which may, in the end, serve to increase both the social and economic expense, especially for women."

Mainstream and feminist scholarship on welfare state regimes discussed earlier in this chapter largely parallels this scholarship on post-Fordism and its gendered undercurrents. There is a general tendency by both feminist and mainstream scholars to assume that welfare states in the late twentieth century are "in transition," that nation-states are being forced to adapt to global economies, and that the "golden age" of the welfare state is over (Esping-Andersen, 1996; O'Connor, 1996). Other scholars state that we have now entered an era "after the welfare state" (Collier, 1997). While this scholarship recognizes that national institutional traditions mean that differences between countries will remain, the conclusion is that their markets have become increasingly deregulated, the division of labour polarized between core and periphery workers (the latter including a growing voluntary sector), and that welfare states have reduced public provision even more so in recent decades (Armstrong and Armstrong, 1988; Lewis, 1994; O'Connor, 1996).

Yet there are critics of the post-Fordist perspective who show that this model hides as much as it reveals. Diana Sainsbury's (1996) recent study of significant variations within types of welfare state regimes along a number of gendered dimensions even in the 1990s, challenges the notion of the reduction of all welfare states to a lowest common denominator. Janet Gornick et al. (1997), in their multi-country analysis of social policies promoting employment for mothers in the 1990s, make a similar point by highlighting significant variations in welfare state policies across a select number of countries.

This alternative framework of analysis, one that focuses on highlighting differences as well as similarities between countries along time and place dimensions, helps to frame this book. Subsequent chapters seek to show that significant cross-national variation in women's work situations and access to social rights persists, both prerequisites to women's economic independence and overall equality with men in family and society. To understand such variation, it is argued that a glance back in history is crucial to discovering the forces that came to shape women's inordinate caring burden and unequal access to societal resources.

SUMMARY AND CONCLUSION

This chapter has examined four areas of scholarship that attempt to conceptualize the nature of women's work and social rights in the modern era. It has been shown that each domain of inquiry offers useful concepts whereby to understand the gendered underpinnings of women's unpaid caring work in the home and its continuing gendered shape in paid work, including professional employment. The underlying premises of feminist literature on caring work have been questioned, not least because of the paucity of research that examines the social organization of women's caring work in historical and cross-national perspective. It has been argued that there is no single definition of caring work, that it possesses no innate or inherent meaning in and of itself. While caring work is assigned in accordance with the reigning gender system, different economic structures and cultural ideals about what is appropriate for either sex, supported by different types of institutional formations, tend to organize and reward caring work in an assortment of ways.

In short, the social organization of women's work, in general caring activities as well as in the professions, is the product of a complex mesh of factors. It is a central premise of this book that the particular formation of the state and the specific social construction of the "public" and "private" spheres of society play consequential roles in this process. A comprehensive social democratic state is important to women workers today in that it tends to recognize the unpaid labour that women perform, while also acknowledging the essentially important work performed by women in the professions. At the same time, the welfare state, even in its most ideal (women-friendly) formation, is only one step forward in the direction of gender equality, which is also dependent on change in the organization of capitalist relations and in the intimate ways that men and women relate. Finally, although the welfare state is under restraint in all high-income countries, significant variation remains across countries such as Canada, the United States, and Sweden in regard to women's status as unpaid and paid workers, and thus in regard to their economic independence.

ENDNOTES

[1] A fourth perspective on the professions, *de-professionalization* or *proletarianization*, is not discussed here since it is premised on the notion that the professions are no longer an important workforce in capitalist societies. This is said to be due to either a "client revolt" or "corporate takeover" of the professions. See Benoit (1994) for more detail on this perspective.

[2] See also the "taxonomic" approach, which is not discussed here (Millerson, 1964).

[3] The term "mainstream" is employed here not to suggest that all writers included under this umbrella embrace a similar approach to understanding welfare states. The intent is to distinguish scholarship that fails to gender its subjects from feminist scholarship that strives to do so.

[4] For details on all four approaches see Sainsbury, 1996: 9–12.

WOMEN'S WORK AND SOCIAL RIGHTS IN THE PRE-CAPITALIST ERA

"Woman was made specially to please man; if the latter must please her in turn, it is less a direct necessity; his merit consists in his strength, he pleases by that fact alone. This is not the law of love, I grant; but it is the law of nature, which is antecedent even to love. If woman is formed to please and live in subjection, she must render herself agreeable to man instead of provoking his wrath; her strength lies in her charms." (Rousseau, Emile*)*

INTRODUCTION

One of the most remarkable features of human societies is their great variety of social organization. There is no pan-historic system of a privileged class free from work, with an underclass doomed to endless toil. Nor indeed—Rousseau notwithstanding—is there an immutable gender contract across human societies that devalues women's work and places their social rights secondary to those of men. Work activities that seem indigenous to one or the other sex are shaped by complex societal factors.

Some pre-capitalist societies are organized *horizontally*, with the social norm of generalized reciprocity encouraging mutual sharing among members of both sexes, and where social stratification is virtually non-existent. Other societies, usually those with greater over-all wealth in the form of an "economic surplus," tend to be organized *hierarchically*, with social stratification or *vertically ranked systems* based on wealth and prestige. Such societies tend to distinguish particular classes of persons; one common arrangement includes a chief/head family, nobles, commoners, and sometimes slaves. Ranked societies also rely on both inter-societal trade and warfare. Slaves and booty are the main "prizes" awarded to conquerors. In most instances slaves perform the society's most menial and physically de-manding work. They also tend to have little or no access to disposable resources and some-times are prevented from having families of their own. Because slaves are without any social rights, they are at the mercy of their owner's whim. Should the owner be displeased with a slave for reasons beyond the latter's control—perhaps he or she cannot work in the capacity expected—then his or her death can be demanded without the owner having to answer to any higher authority.

As with men, the social situation of women depends upon the type of society in which they live. In horizontally organized societies, where social divisions are minimal, inequal-ities among women—apart from those based on individual characteristics—are slight. Women and men enjoy a relatively equal division of work assignments; women's work—including productive activities, care of others, and household maintenance—is both socially visible and honoured; and women, children, and men enjoy comparative access to societal resources. This is the case even though there tends to be a division of labour along lines of gender (as well as physical ability).

However, in vertically ranked societies, marked by social ranking and frequent war-fare, women are destined, as are men, to be socially stratified, both in regard to the work they perform, as well as to their access to material resources. Elite family position separates privileged women from commoners, and they in turn from slaves. The latter are forced to sur-vive on the fringes of the former's social world, along with enslaved men and children, car-rying out much of the work required for the maintenance and reproduction of the privileged, with little opportunity to enjoy the fruits of their labour beyond the sparse resources of min-imal survival (and this is never guaranteed). Slave women are sometimes even robbed of motherhood; a child still at the breast may be taken away from its mother and given body and soul to a "legitimate" mother, a white woman perhaps, who henceforth decides the child's fate (Polakow, 1993: 16).

Historically, the US Constitution accorded blacks with less than human status, as they were deemed as three-fifths of a person (Gordon, 1976: 3). Much the same perspective was held about slaves among some northwest coastal Aboriginal peoples in Canada prior to European contact, as well as in colonial Canada before the mid-nineteenth century. However, slavery existed not only between different racial/ethnic groups. Poor white immigrants came as slaves to the New World from Europe until they could buy their freedom. They were part of the *indentured class*, legally permitted to work their way to freedom but, due to cruel treatment by their masters and interminable debt, often remaining enslaved all their lives. Many in-dentured servants who came to Canada and the United States were children and widows.

Further complicating matters, all women—regardless of rank—tend to share a common heritage in regard to their reproductive capacity. Women are the actual bearers of children in every society and, at least until recent times and the invention of artificial substitutes, a woman's nursing capabilities (sometimes children other than her own—hence the role of the "wet nurse") was the decisive factor determining whether a child lived or died in early life. These primary functions of all societies—reproducing and nourishing—have also left women vulnerable. In both horizontally organized and vertically ranked societies, women's reproductive or caring work determines their other "productive" work tasks. The productive activities that women perform are those that make a direct contribution to economic subsistence, which are organized around their equally fundamental caring and domestic work. Hence, as is shown in this and the following chapter, it is women who tend to be the food gatherers in hunter-gatherer societies, the gardeners in small-scale agricultural societies, the fish preservers in fishing societies, and the domestic servants, secretaries, and caring professionals in capitalist societies. Yet this gendered division of labour need not be oppressive for women. It is only in vertically ranked societies, especially those marked by competition over resources, wealth, warfare, and plunder, that women's reproductive and productive activities tend to leave them vulnerable to exploitation.

Capitalist societies are a contemporary example of vertically ranked or stratified social organizations. Yet existing capitalist societies vary in their degree of stratification. Some exhibit greater equality between men and women (and among women themselves), and thus tend to be more horizontal in their organization. Much depends on the shape of the polity, especially its institutional processes aimed to redistribute societal wealth and grant public recognition and reward to women's paid and unpaid caring work.

The United States, a frontier society that gained political independence in the aftermath of war with Britain, later engaged in civil war, and has been a major geopolitical power in more recent times, remains in key respects a highly stratified society. It is the chief aim of this book to show that US women, especially those fated with poverty or the "wrong" race or ethnic status, are by and large left to their own devices, without access to necessary economic and political resources.

Once a vertically ranked society marked by warfare and empire building, in the last century and a half Sweden changed its historical path towards one of peace with its neighbours and redistributive justice within its borders. While no longer a "great power," Sweden is nevertheless attractive sociologically because of its comparatively low degree of economic ranking and its significant gender equality, albeit still male-advantaged in some respects. Social and economic policies of Sweden's comprehensive welfare state, most evident in the post-World War II period, have not only enhanced equalization of societal resources, but have also politicized women's reproductive role. The result for Swedish women is increased economic independence from men, yet lingering economic dependence on the welfare state itself.

Canada, a frontier society like its southern neighbour, but one that gained independence by peaceful means, stands somewhere between the US and Sweden along the horizontal/vertical axis. Warfare marks Canada's history too, both against its Aboriginal peoples and between the two colonial powers, resulting in the "two solitudes"—French and English Canada. Individual competition amidst social solidarity distinguishes Canada as a country to this day. Similarly, Canadian women find themselves in an ambivalent situation in relation to the welfare state, with more extensive social rights than their US sisters, but less public recognition for their unpaid and paid caring work than Swedish women.

This chapter focuses on the pre-capitalist period, outlining the situation of women at work and in society beginning with the Aboriginal peoples of Canada and tracing the changes up to the mid-nineteenth century, at which stage capitalism emerged as an important economic system in urban areas. The chapter also opens windows on the United States and Sweden in the pre-capitalist era. Before beginning the historical overview, a methodological point is in order.

METHODOLOGICAL ISSUES IN EXAMINING WOMEN'S HISTORICAL SITUATION

Although a literature is gradually emerging, we still know amazingly little about the work of women (and to a lesser extent men) in times predating capitalism, especially that of the vast majority of women whose work and thoughts about their work were not considered worthy of historical note. Here can be mentioned peasant women, indentured servants and slaves, single mothers, widows, domestics, prostitutes, disabled women, and countless others whose toil and ways of coping across the centuries have remained in the shadows of time. Historians of "civilization" offer meagre information about the everyday lives of women, and to whom they looked when food supplies dwindled or misfortune struck. The records available are virtually exclusively concerned with public events deemed important to the record-keepers themselves—scribes and clergy, who were nearly always men and usually closely associated with those in power (Applebaum, 1992). Hence the focus has been on the *grand narrative*—the rise and fall of ruling families and dynasties, wars, and conquests—but little about the everyday events of lives that can be known only by listening to the "voices from below," the dispossessed of the past whose labour and survival strategies have most likely varied significantly from that of the ruling elite (Samuel, 1981).

The majority of women, doubly prejudiced against due to their "weaker" sex and their disproportionate (lack of) access to formal education and economic resources, are virtually absent from the chronicles. Until recently, official history has been all but devoid of description of them, their work, interests, needs, and worries. At most, readers can glimpse what things might have been like for a tiny minority of high-ranking "important" women, what is sometimes called *compensatory history*, the history of great women who recorded in their diaries events significant to their own lives. However, it must be kept in mind that these women tended to be the exception rather than the rule. By focussing on the lives of privileged women, biographers have overlooked (whether unconsciously or by design) the lives of ordinary women (Errington, 1995: xiv).

Given the scanty historical writings on women's work activities and their coping strategies for economic hardship and ill-fortune, attempted here is, at best, a series of vignettes about the situations of our earliest and not so distant female ancestors, who lived before Canada experienced its own "great transformation" in the last decades of the nineteenth century, gradually recasting the country from a largely rural economy to a urban market economy by the early decades of the twentieth century (Polanyi, 1957). The central focus during this historical voyage is on "common" women, whose work lives are sketched using an assortment of secondary sources.

The main section of this chapter, centred on pre-capitalist Canada, is divided into two subsections: 1) the *pre-contact* period, the long timeline before the arrival of Europeans to the New World, a stretch of human history characterized by tremendously varied economic and cultural arrangements and gender systems; and 2) the *contact* period, beginning in the late fifteenth century, a time marked by European exploration and trade, and eventually colonialism, warfare among Aboriginals, the French, British, and Americans, and a revamped vertically ranked society (see Table 2–1 for a summary of each societal type).

TABLE 2–1	Societal Types: Pre-capitalist Societies			
Categorization	**Hunting and Gathering (Band)**	**Small-scale Agricultural (Gardening)**	**Fishing**	**Large-scale Agricultural (Farming)**
Technical Change from Earlier Society		use of hand-tools, digging	use of boats, nets, and traps stick, and hoe	use of animal-drawn plows
Economic Characteristics	hunting game; gathering roots and berries	clearing and planting of small gardens; tending of animals for food	catching and preserving fish; some gathering of roots and berries	clearing and plowing; tending large tracts of land
Control of Wealth and Income	equal sharing of income; no surplus wealth	rough balance between the sexes in sharing income and surplus wealth	men enjoy a greater amount of income and wealth—they tend to dominate as fishers, warriors, traders, and clan heads; women's work activities become undervalued	men completely dominate income and wealth—they own most of the land, tools, and weapons, and dominate in the military, trade, and the crafts
Inheritance	no wealth to inherit	shared (mainly via matrilineal kinship)	tends to be patrilineal	almost exclusively patrilineal
Women's Societal Status	relatively equal	decreasing, but still relatively high	decreasing lower	lowest

Source: Based in part on Lorber (1994).

PRE-CONTACT

> When we speak of the drudgery of the women, we must note the equal division of labour; there is no class of women privileged to sit still while others work. Every squaw makes the clothing, mats, moccasins, and boils the kettle for her own family .... Compare her life with that of a servant-maid of all work, or a factory girl—I say that the condition of the squaw is gracious in comparison, dignified by domestic feelings, and by equality with all around her. (Anna Jameson [1838] quoted in Prentice et al., 1996: 28–29)

Beginnings

When European explorers voyaged to the New World at the end of the fifteenth century, they were in a quandary to explain the presence of people making a living in what was for Europeans alone the "New World." Who were these Aboriginals?[1] Were they humans and, if so, from where did they originate? The Bible provided no clue; nowhere in its pages was there even a hint that human beings lived in this land.

It is unknown from where, when, by what means (land or sea), and how many immigrants initially came to the part of the New World where Canadians now reside. There is evidence, however, that there were well over one million inhabitants north of the Rio Grande at the time of European contact (Jaffe, 1992). Nine-tenths of this population were probably "American Indians," with Inuits and Aleuts making up the remainder. The earliest immigrants who came by sea must have possessed a fairly developed maritime culture, including knowledge about the ocean's food sources and the skills involved in building watercraft, fishing gear, and harvesting techniques. These water-bound immigrants probably bypassed Alaska altogether and landed at various points along the coast of the Pacific Ocean, including what is today British Columbia in Canada, as well as California in the United States. Evidence suggests, for example, that 8 000–9 000 years ago inhabitants of Heceta Island off the coast of BC possessed a sophisticated maritime culture, including a diet of fish, birds, sea mammals, molluscs, and crustaceans. Other "data suggests that the northwest coast was initially settled by peoples with a maritime tradition who were experienced in the exploitation of off-shore resources and who made extensive use of water transportation" (Ackerman et al., 1984: 7).

Even less is known about precisely when and how these original inhabitants spread themselves across the western hemisphere, since their movement was largely affected by changing climatic conditions, marked by periodic glaciation and thus variance in the availability of game and vegetation. Much as has been noted about twentieth-century hunter-gatherers (Lenski et al., 1995), the founding peoples of Canada and the US migrated depending upon available food sources, which were in turn determined by climate and at times competition from other hunter-gatherer bands. Given the large land masses, abundant natural resources, and small populations, Canada's hunter-gatherers appear to have lived relatively autonomous and peaceful lives (Dickason, 1992). This finding agrees with the general evidence on hunter-gatherer populations: perpetual warfare is found in none of the hunter-gatherer societies about which there are social-scientific data, and in nearly three-quarters of these societies warfare is rare or absent. By contrast, vertically ranked and capitalist societies exhibit frequent, sometimes continuous, warfare with large death tolls.

The importance of climate regarding population size and geographic distribution for Canada's Aboriginal peoples is evident when examining the situation at the onset of the sixteenth century, shortly after the first Europeans set foot in the New World. The distribution and density of the Aboriginal population reflected the availability of natural resources and climatic conditions. The Arctic areas of Canada, where the Inuit still reside, were sparsely populated, as were to a lesser extent the northern forested lands, where small autonomous bands likewise survived largely by hunting fur-bearing animals and foraging for wild foods. The arid western areas between present-day Ontario and BC were without fertile and naturally irrigated farmland or access to sea life, and were at that time much less inhabited, mainly by the Plains Indians living nomadically in search of buffalo. The greatest density of population in Canada was on the northwest coast, renowned even today for its relatively warm, moist climate, rich assortment of wild vegetable matter, and bountiful (although dwindling) fishing grounds, all of which helped to sustain an exceptionally large Aboriginal population. The comparatively rich fishing beds off the east coast also made for a relatively large population. Southeastern Canada, just north of today's US border, was also able to sustain a large Aboriginal population because of its fertile soil and extensive system of glacier lakes. As discussed below, Aboriginal populations living in the more fertile areas of pre-contact Canada tended also to experience the greatest competition from European settlers over the "free" land promised them by colonial powers, who had by then taken control of key areas of the country.

Evidence suggests that Aboriginal peoples at the beginning of the sixteenth century belonged to 12 distinct language families, of which 6 were exclusive to present-day British Columbia. As many as 50 languages belonging to one or other of these 12 language families were spoken (Dickason, 1992: 64). Reflecting their wide geographic distribution, at the time of European contact the population of Aboriginal peoples in what is today Canada ranged between 500 000 to 2 million people, scattered across a wide variety of climatic zones and subsisting in 3 relatively distinct ways: hunting-gathering, horticulture, and fishing. The following section will examine the gender organization of work in these different societal types, and attempt to answer these questions: How was work organized among Aboriginal peoples before the arrival of the Europeans? How were work activities allotted between women and men? Was the gender division of labour horizontal or vertical? How were resources distributed between the sexes so that they could meet the challenges of their physical and social environment?

The Hunter-gatherers

If the length of life of the average woman or man is taken as the single measure of societal success, then hunter-gatherer societies would have to be seen as unsuccessful compared to all others. Evidence suggests that hunter-gatherers in pre-contact Canada lived short lives, and that women lived even shorter lives than men. It is estimated that the length of life at birth for male New World hunter-gatherers was not greater than 20 to 25 years, with females living 2 to 3 years fewer (Jaffe, 1992: 58), due largely to risks associated with childbirth. Compare this to the life expectancy at birth of the average population in high-income countries today—over 75 for Canadian men and 81 for women—and note the gender reversal, with higher life expectancy for Canadian women (Macionis, Benoit, and Jansson, 1999: 355).

However, two points regarding life expectancies should be considered. First, the invention of agriculture in the Old and New Worlds and even the onset of merchant capitalism (see Chapter 3) did not drastically improve life expectancy for the average person, nor reverse the gender expectancy rate. Life expectancy at birth for agrarian Europeans in 1760–69 ranged from 27.7 in France, to 34.6 in England, and 36.3 in Sweden (Livi-Bacci, 1991: 70).[2] For Canada's settler population in the mid nineteenth century the figure was 39 years (Clarke, 1996: 66). Mark Cohen (1989: 102) argues that life expectancy at 25 years for pre-contact hunter-gatherers "would approach that for much of Europe as late as the eighteenth and early nineteenth centuries and for many urban European communities well into the nineteenth."

Second, on its own, life expectancy at birth tells very little about the *quality of life* of hunter-gatherers—their nutrition, the difficulty of their toil, their levels of social equality, the support systems available to vulnerable members, and the social relationships between men and women. A longer average life does not necessarily mean a higher quality of life. It can even mean the opposite: greater relative poverty for many, who manage to survive, but with a low quality of life. These other factors affect the health and well-being of a society's members, allowing us in particular to understand the situation of women as gatherers, their caring activities and ways of coping that in many respects appear attractive from the lens of late twentieth-century Canada.

With few exceptions, hunter-gatherer societies tended to be very small—40 persons was the average size, contracting and expanding depending on the seasons (Lenski et al., 1995: 111). Hunter-gatherers were nomadic; they exhausted the available game and wild vegetation in one area before migrating on foot to another. Two advantages of this precarious lifestyle were that hunter-gatherers were not encumbered by transporting extra foodstuffs from place to place, and they did not have to worry about protecting a surplus from others. Hunter-gatherers, in fact, had no notion of private wealth, whereby a privileged social group, race, or gender owns more "goods" than others. Rather, game and wild plants were nature's "gifts," available for all to reap through their daily labour.

In a similar manner, hunter-gatherers did not perceive "work" to be a separate sphere of human activity. Their language contained no term for work per se, although many had elaborate vocabularies for the various kinds of activities and objects involved in hunting, gathering, and the making of tools and clothing. Work appears to have been such a natural activity—akin to breathing and sleeping—that it did not require a distinct name. The hunter-gatherer Aleut carried out activities such as berry collecting in small groups of women. The work group might spend as much as a day out gathering different kinds of berries, socializing with each other as they went about their task (Udy, 1967: 20).

This is not to suggest that the subsistence economy of hunter-gatherers was without social organization. Horizontal divisions by gender and age were commonplace. All healthy adults—women and men alike—contributed to the survival of the group, typically by men pursuing hunting activities and women gathering wild plants and berries. There were no other differentiated occupational groups as such, although younger adult men and women performed more tasks than their elders. Does this then mean that there was no *gender hierarchy*, with males in a more powerful economic and social position than females? Those gender inequalities that did exist were probably fluid, and dependent upon regional resources and band culture. On the one hand, while healthy adult men and women tended to perform different economic activities, both types of contributions were valued. However, hunting did seem to be more highly valued, and studies show that in addition to their equal economic contribution, women typically performed more domestic and childcare activities (Prentice et al., 1996). As Pastore (1978: 3) notes, "in common with many other Indian people, Micmac women did one sort of work and the men another. While comparisons of this sort are risky, it would appear as if the women worked harder and longer than the men. In addition to making all the clothing, they had to cook and preserve food, carry game from the site of the kill back to the wigwams, move and set up camp, and care for the children."

On the other hand, in these early societies, where healthy children were deemed crucial assets of the group's survival, in addition to women's subsistence activities, childbearing and rearing awarded them respect and honour. Respect was also forthcoming for women who "adopted" an orphaned child, who was subsequently integrated into the extended kinship group. Indeed, virtually every band member was related in some way—either by blood ties or socially via marriage relations (Anderson, 1991).

These various features of hunter-gatherer societies were premised on a general ethic of mutual sharing or *generalized reciprocity*, the exchange of goods and services free from consideration of their material worth, with the expectation of a "gift exchange"—"I give to you so that you may give to me" (Dickason, 1992: 78). This is not to argue that hunter-gatherers were morally superior in this respect to their counterparts in ranked societies. The sheer struggle for survival of these small bands encouraged hunters to share their game with other members of their extended kinship, to "spread the risk," so to speak. Not only was a hunter's success dependent upon cooperation from other hunters, but he was also dependent upon their generosity whenever his own hunting efforts proved fruitless. Thus it is said of the Canadian Inuit that "he knows that the best place for him to store his surplus is in someone else's stomach, because sooner or later he will want his gift repaid" (Farb, 1969: 43). A hunter who refused to share his kill might be excluded for a time from all social activity, imperilling his own health and well-being and that of his immediate family. Given the relative ease of finding wild plants, roots, and berries (which provided 50 to 70 per cent of subsistence), women in hunter-gatherer societies were under less group pressure to share the products of their labour. Nevertheless, even in the case of collected foodstuffs, the nomadic lifestyle itself discouraged hoarding. Better to share now than to have to carry an extra load, even if this meant not always having food for the next evening's meal. The end result was that "people ate or went hungry together" (Hodson and Sullivan, 1995: 8).

The absence of wealth in the form of an economic surplus provided other benefits for women that those in vertically ranked societies go without. Hunter-gatherers were not concerned about passing on family names, titles, and property, and hence were largely free in regard to sexual partners, marriage liaisons, and places of residence. There were no structural reasons for parents to be concerned about the paternity of their children or to attempt to control their sexual relationships, beyond the need to strengthen group cooperation (Prentice et al., 1996: 19–25). Karen Anderson describes what was believed to have been the flexible organization of social life among the Montagnais of the Quebec-Labrador peninsula:

> During the winter the tribe broke up into small bands, the members of which comprised several nuclear families. About ten to twenty persons lived together for the entire winter in conical lodges that served as a base camp from which the men left to hunt. Residence rules were flexible and the people moved on the basis of personal choice and the need to keep a balance in the working group between young and old, men and women. (1991: 77–78)

Such adaptable elements of family life, combined with the relatively high societal value placed on women's gathering and caring work, meant that these early societies provided an extensive safety net, in many respects analogous to the role played by comprehensive welfare states in capitalist societies of the late twentieth century (see Chapter 4).

To view hunter-gatherer societies as "uncivilized" or, as Thomas Hobbes (1588–1679) put it over three centuries ago, a life "poor, nasty, brutish, and short," appears to miss much that was attractive about these social organizations in the New World and elsewhere (Shostak, 1981; Lenski et al., 1995). Women gatherers, in particular, were esteemed as primary providers in ways that were lost to women in vertically ranked societies. Egalitarianism rather than hierarchy was the general rule, in personal relationships as well as within kinship networks. All members shared in the multifaceted work activities, and women as well as men were able to access available material resources.

Of course, there were less than ideal aspects of hunter-gatherer societies. Work was often arduous, particularly among hunter-gatherers residing in less fertile or cold environments, including Canada's northern regions. Even after a successful hunt, men would more often than not be occupied with a range of other activities—chipping an arrowhead, shaping a scraper, or crafting an object for religious ceremony, while at once socializing among themselves or with their children and female kin. Women too worked in their "leisure time," performing activities that spanned both production and reproduction.

Hunter-gatherers were also without the benefits of an outside agency—a church, monarchy, or welfare state—to assist individuals facing misfortunes beyond their control (Cohen, 1989: 20). While egalitarian along gender lines, hunter-gatherer societies were not always egalitarian towards weaker members. Very young children, the frail elderly, the disabled, and ill persons were dependent upon the good will of the band's able-bodied women and men.

Small group sizes enhanced sharing between the strong and the weak, yet in times of food shortages or foul weather, dependent persons were vulnerable to being deprived of food and water, or to simply being left behind as the healthy adults moved on to replenish their food supply. The data shows that abortion and infanticide were comparatively high in these societies, and that anywhere between 15 and 50 per cent of all live births ended in infanticide (Lenski et al., 1995: 111).

In short, among the positive aspects of hunter-gatherer societies was the absence of a *leisured class*, a class of persons exempt from toil (Veblen, 1943 [1899]). Nor was there a privileged patriarchy, or a male elite absolved from daily toil to engage in warfare, plunder, and the mastery of women. These were to become distinctive features of vertically ranked societies, which although wealthier in material terms, were in many ways regressive for the majority of women (and perhaps even men).

The Newfoundland Beothuk and their Extinction

The origins of the Beothuk people of Newfoundland, who in their heyday numbered anywhere between 500 and 1 200, remain uncertain. It seems likely, however, that between 800 AD and 1 500 AD they lived an undisturbed migratory existence, travelling freely in small bands across much of the Island without contact with other groups, Aboriginal or otherwise.

Evidence also suggests that the status of women was high among these "Red Indians" of Newfoundland. Even male historians such as J.P. Howley (1974: 261) are inclined to agree: "amongst the Beothuk the women seem to have been held in greater esteem and been treated more in accordance with civilized notions of what is due the weaker sex."

From the 1500s on, the Beothuk way of life became challenged by a complexity of outside forces, ultimately leading to their extinction as an indigenous population. While contagious diseases were the chief cause of the depletion of many Aboriginal populations, recent evidence suggests that competition for resources with other Aboriginal groups and the newly arriving English and French settlers restricted the Beothuk migratory movements so that severe malnutrition and eventually starvation decimated their numbers (Waldram et al., 1997). Other factors worked against them too. Unlike many Aboriginal peoples, the Beothuk played a marginal role in the fur trade, and Europeans were unwilling to intervene on their behalf. Thus "there was no missionary to plead for their souls, no trader anxious to barter for their furs, no solider to arm and use them as auxiliaries in his wars, no government to restrain the settlers" (Upton, 1978: 153). Shanawdithit, the last surviving Beothuk, was taken into captivity by European settlers in 1823 and died six years later in St. John's, Newfoundland. A once viable hunter-gatherer society became extinct.

Increased material wealth did not necessarily result in either the undervaluing of women's work or inequitable access to obtainable societal resources. An examination of the situation of women workers in the early agricultural societies that emerged at different times in more fertile regions of the globe, including the fecund southeastern areas of Canada, is instructive in this respect. It is to these early agriculturists that we now turn.

The Small-scale Agriculturists

The key difference between hunter-gatherer and small-scale agricultural societies is that the latter has the means to store a stable and dependable food surplus. The first small-scale agricultural societies (also known as gardening or "horticultural" societies) emerged somewhere around 9 000 to 3 000 BC.

In fact, even before the emergence of the first agricultural societies, some hunter-gatherer groups, including the Huron and the Five Nations of the Iroquois (Mohawk, Seneca, Cayuga, Oneida, and Onondaga), had begun to harvest, grind, and store wild rice and other naturally occurring grains, including wheat, barley, and maize. Moreover, it is likely that hunting free-roaming game and gathering wild vegetable matter continued as the main food sources for many of these groups after they began to experiment in farming. Concerning the Iroquois, James B. Waldram et al. (1997: 32) note that "the consumption of animal protein remained quite stable and the subsistence base of pre-contact Iroquoian villages involved mixed swidden horticulture, hunting, fishing, and collecting from the fifth century to the contact period." Eventually, however, these overlapping productive activities tipped the balance towards small-scale agriculture, with more than 50 per cent of the food supply being provided in this manner (Dickason, 1992).

Typically gardens were created by cutting and then burning existing vegetation, especially shrubs and small trees (the "slash-and-burn" or "swidden" technique). The resulting layer of ash provided fertilizer for the planted crops. Yields were high for the first few years, but declined as the nutrients in the ash were consumed. Because they had no way to dislodge robust weeds, early agriculturists were forced periodically to abandon their garden plot and clear more land for a new plot (Lenski et al., 1995: 138–39). Early agricultural societies were able to sustain larger populations, averaging 20 times as many people per mile of territory as hunter-gatherers. Advancement in their subsistence technology—from wooden digging sticks to metal hoes and other tools—led to far-reaching changes in the social organization of this new type of society, not least of all in regard to its gender system.

Greater permanence of settlement emerges as one significant change. Planted gardens necessitated periodic weeding as well as the secure storage of surplus. Stored foods were too heavy to be moved easily from place to place. Small-scale agriculturalists were forced to remain year-round more or less within the vicinity of their planted fields and storage areas. According to Mark Cohen (1989: 23), in small-scale agricultural societies, "permanent villages become the rule, and the relatively flimsy dwellings of temporary or seasonal camps may be traded for more substantial and permanent houses."

Other changes gradually resulted. Greater productivity per acre led as well to greater productivity per capita, thereby releasing some workers from full-time food production and enabling them to specialize in other types of activity, such as handicrafts, religious ritual, trading, and warfare. Though very few persons could enjoy such privilege in small-scale agricultural societies with little by way of an economic surplus, those with larger surpluses were able to free greater numbers for roles separate from gardening.

In fact, small-scale agriculturalists eventually became dependent upon items traded with neighbours, not least of all because of the reduced variety of foodstuffs available through subsistence activities. Health was an important consideration, since research indicates that, for example, bone lesions from infections were highest in those societies where maize consumption was high (Waldram et al., 1997: 33). So for reasons of diet, among others, early agriculturalists found themselves increasingly relying on a small number of individuals who served as "dealers," bartering a portion of the village's economic surplus in, for example, maize, for other foods and basic necessities.

Two further changes of crucial importance accompanied these developments. In virtually all small-scale agricultural societies the gender balance of food production tips in the direction of women. Precisely why gardening work tends to fall on the shoulders of women is not known, but scholars link the gendered system of food production—men clearing the land for new gardens and women planting, tending, and harvesting the crops—to the original division of labour between women and men in hunter-gatherer societies, where women gathered most of the vegetable foodstuffs (Boulding, 1976). Or as Deckard (1979: 199) puts it: "since men had been hunting, men were the inventors of systematic herding. Since women had been gathering plants, women were the inventors of systematic agriculture."

Men in small-scale agricultural societies continued to engage in hunting wild game, although increasing less so as human populations increased and wild areas dwindled. The end result was that the "men's contribution to subsistence [was] often much less than that of women in horticultural societies and require[d] less time" (Lenski et al., 1995: 140). On the one hand, this indicates a depreciation of men's social status in the horticultural village, leaving them little to do with their time apart from clearing the land and periodically hunting to distinguish themselves as important contributors to their family and community. However, at the same time, trade in foodstuffs and other items not produced locally led to the need for another new specialist: the male warrior who could handle tensions among villagers over land for gardens, while protecting the village's stored surplus from maundering neighbours.

Recruitment for male warriors was through extended kinship. Group identity was now based on membership in kin-based *clans*, which performed a number of key functions, "above all ... mutual aid associations, providing individuals with protection from enemies and with economic support" (Lenski et al., 1995: 149). Clans often were subdivided into lineages, which in small-scale agricultural societies tended to be organized along lines of *matrilineal descent*, reckoned through the mother's extended family. Putting aside the consequences for women, tracing kinship through either the female or male lineage (*patrilineal* descent) required that members adhere to solemn obligations to their lineage, not least of all protecting its property and its honour. Members of a lineage cooperatively owned territory and goods, and were headed by a "big man," who was partly or fully removed from subsistence activities. Lineage big men were answerable to a clan head. Larger villages might have a number of clans, which were themselves joined together under a tribal chief residing in one of the villages. Further alliances across tribes were also possible (nations, alliances of nations, and so forth).

Lineage heads played important roles in trading matters, the organization of feasts and rituals, and the negotiation of marriage arrangements between their members and those of other clans, a practice called *exogamy*, or marriage outside of one's kin group. This marriage system helped to keep intra- and inter-village peace, since kinsmen were less likely to launch an attack on a rival clan group if their sister, daughter, or other blood relative had married into it: "The "Great League of Peace," another of the appellations for the Iroquois confederacy, was governed by a council of fifty chiefs representing participant tribes .... The aim was to keep peace between them and to co-ordinate their external relations, which had to be by unanimous decision" (Dickason, 1992: 71).

In brief, due to their sedentary lifestyle and need to protect their economic surplus, small-scale agricultural societies gradually became more rigid in their overall societal organization.

Mutual gift giving became less common across villages, and individual needs increasingly were superseded by the needs and concerns of the individual's lineage and clan, organized along lines of segregation and exclusion. "In addition, the resources of societies become diverted more and more from immediate application to individual needs and toward celebration of community membership and defence of the community, celebration of privilege and authority, and, perhaps, privileged consumption by leaders" (Cohen, 1989: 26).

What were the consequences for women in small-scale agricultural societies? In regard to the distribution of tasks, it was probably the case that women did the bulk of subsistence work. This is not to say that men's subsistence activities were of minor importance; new gardens had to be cleared and new homes built periodically, tasks almost always assigned to males. However, as among the Iroquois, "the wealth of the community consisted chiefly in its cleared lands, but also in the food stored and controlled by the women" (Prentice et al., 1996: 15). Matrilineal descent also meant that while gardening and domestic tasks, including childcare, were "women's work," the children belonged to the clan into which the mother was born, and to which she remained attached and obliged even after marriage. While such an arrangement did not always make for happy marriages (divorce was frequent in matrilineal societies), it gave women an important source of life-long protection and security.

Nevertheless, certain features of small-scale agricultural societies, including that of the matrilineal Iroquois, suggest serious dysfunctions that appear to have had comparatively negative effects on women and children. Women's fundamental work in food production and in the domestic sphere left them largely confined to the boundaries of the village or, at best, the planted fields beyond. Men, by contrast, controlled the territory beyond the community—trading, negotiating, and warring when it was deemed necessary. Furthermore, although women sometimes were involved in the selection of their chiefs (as was the case for the Iroquois), chiefs were almost always men. Unarmed women and their children were vulnerable to attack from other clans and were the most likely to be taken as prisoners of war and subsequently adopted, sacrificed, enslaved, or used as pawns in negotiations between powerful chiefs.

In these many ways, small-scale agricultural societies, when compared to hunter-gatherers, were both progressive and regressive in societal terms. They made it possible for greater numbers of people to survive and, for those who did survive, to live slightly longer lives on average (Donald, 1997). However, possession of a stable economic surplus also encouraged the beginnings of vertical ranking, constructed a more rigid gender division of labour, and created an underclass of (mainly) women and children captured in war, some of whom were subsequently taken as slaves and cut off from their own kinship. The incidence of warfare in small-scale agricultural societies was frequent: in 55 per cent of these societies warfare was common (Leavitt, 1977, Appendix B); slavery was present in a minority (Lenski et al., 1995).

These emergent inequalities in small-scale agricultural societies became even more pronounced in the comparatively wealthy fishing societies that developed on Canada's northwest coast, particularly but not exclusively those arranged along patrilineal descent systems, enhancing the status of some high-ranked women, while at the same time making women in general more subordinate in regard to food production and domestic life.

Gender Relations among the Matrilineal Iroquois

An Iroquois man's concern, then, seems to have been a constant search for a household that would provide him with food and shelter—a household of mother, wife or clan member who might be induced to provide these necessities, perhaps in return for such goods and services as he could provide. Women's concerns would seem to have centred on keeping the household running. One task involved obtaining stores, the women of the household often working together to provide the basic provisions (the household held these in common). It was the women who planted, cultivated, and harvested the crops—corn, beans, and squash—that constituted the basic diet. Such food as was furnished by the men supplemented that provided by the women. Nonetheless, the women needed

the help of the men, particularly in clearing the land for cultivation and in building houses ....

The matrilineal clan system was not so much a means of distributing property or of organizing life in the village as it was a means of relating to people in other villages beyond the surrounding forest. Men typically dealt with matters beyond the clearing, including political affairs. Hence, the chiefs who did so were men, but their names indicated that they had been designated by women as worthy to speak for them and the people generally. On the other hand, visitors to the village needed only to know the name associated with a particular role to be directed to the proper individual and the name of his own clan to be provided with food and shelter. (Tooker, 1984:123)

The Fishers

The designation of *fishing society* in a sense is misapplied, for no fishing society has been able to depend entirely on harvesting the ocean and rivers to meet the subsistence needs of its population (Lenski et al., 1995). However, some areas of pre-contact Canada where fishing was a major subsistence activity were also very fertile. Indeed, more that half of the pre-contact Aboriginal peoples of Canada resided in what is now the province of British Columbia. Anthropological studies of the area show the importance of the sea and its inhabitants to coastal tribes, which often adopted the names of coastal birds and animals to denote different clans, such as Killer Whale, Eagle, and Raven.

Fishing is simply a form of hunting on salt or fresh water. The gender division of work in fishing societies, not surprisingly, reflects the patterns of hunter-gatherer or small-scale agricultural societies. Just as men were the hunters in these, so were they the main harvesters of the rivers and oceans in fishing societies, while they continued to hunt on adjacent lands. Yet there were differences: the subsistence activities and physical environment of fishing societies supported much larger populations, which had cultural and social characteristics more in common with historical large-scale agricultural societies. This is not to say that there were never times when local resources failed to provide for fishing populations, leaving some villages unable to meet their basic needs. However, overall the anthropological research suggests that "intensive harvesting of almost the full range of marine resources, but with particular emphasis on the salmon, provided the economic foundation for social organizational complexity, dense, sedentary village populations, and diverse forms of artistic expression" (Waldram et al., 1997: 40).

Despite the advantages of greater economic wealth and larger populations, fishing societies disadvantaged women in key respects. As in other pre-contact forms of society, women in fishing societies performed activities essential to subsistence as well as biological and social reproduction. Their work included the preservation of harvested fish, food gathering and preparation and, equally important, caring for children and other dependents—all activities that could be carried out relatively close to or at home. Yet it was the fisher*men* who were celebrated as "primary producers"; bountiful fish catches awarded men a special status as the chief providers of their families. Women's no less vital—but less publicly observable— work activities were seen as supportive (i.e., *secondary*) activities. Granted, among some coastal tribes women were more directly involved in the fishery and sometimes hunted small-game land animals. But these were exceptions to the general division of labour in fishing societies.

Celebration of the male as primary producer in fishing societies did not necessarily place women in an economically dependent position. Although northwest coast fishing societies were primarily patriarchal, there were exceptions. Among the Nishga and Coast Tsimshian, for example, kinship ranged along matrilineal lines, and even after marriage women were awarded protection and economic security by their own kin. Members of a matrilineage cooperatively

> ... owned territories such as fishing sites and hunting grounds, and these resources were shared according to rank. Membership in a matrilineage was lifelong. Although a woman joined her husband's residential group at marriage, she never abandoned her membership in or loyalty to her own matrilineage. In addition, at birth her children automatically assumed their mother's clan and lineage affiliation. (Cooper, 1996: 90)

Women in matrilineal fishing societies were recognized for their contributions to clan potlatch ceremonies and controlled the distribution of food supplies. Furthermore, in those cases where women were not full participants, they were held in high esteem nevertheless, because of their intimate knowledge of the secret societies (Cooper, 1996: 95).

Yet matrilineage in northwest coast fishing societies did not grant women an equal voice in matters involving politics, trade, marriage, or war. In one matrilineal society, the Haida, women had little choice regarding their marriage partners, and were expected to accept the authority of their husbands. Widows were compelled to receive a new partner chosen by their deceased husband's relatives (Prentice et al., 1996: 23–24). Warfare, almost always a male activity, was frequent, and one of the major prizes of war was *slaves*. Anthropological evidence indicates that, compared to its rarity among hunter-gatherers and its infrequent occurrence in small-scale agricultural societies, slavery was found in slightly over 50 per cent of fishing societies (Lenski et al., 1995). Fishing societies in pre-contact Canada were no exception. The Haida, for example, frequently raided the Salish of southern Vancouver Island and enslaved members of its population. Warfare was also common among the ranked societies of the Tlingit and Tsimshian (Dickason, 1992: 69).

Women in patrilineal northwest coast fishing societies, such as the Salish, had even less economic security and fair access to essential resources. Fishing gear, sites, and hunting grounds were owned cooperatively by patrilineal clans, and property was passed on through the male line. Upon marriage, women resided with their husband's kin, and their children, in the event of divorce, continued to live within the patrilineage. Men in patrilineal fishing

Northwest Coast Women and Slavery

The majority of pre-contact fishing societies on Canada's northwest coast counted slaves among their numbers. The wealthy elite—"big men"—were the main slave owners (Donald, 1997). As in other pre-contact societies, women and children in fishing societies were most commonly taken as slaves by marauding tribes. Perhaps the men were away fishing or hunting, while unarmed women and children were isolated within or near the village compound, making them easy prey for warriors. Men were believed to be more difficult to enslave than women and children, creating problems for future slave owners (Dickason, 1992). But men were enslaved, as Leland Donald notes:

> Many slaves were women and obviously available to supplement the labour of free women. In addition, male slaves were available for all kinds of labour, including female labour, because their slave status had already demeaned and degraded them and prevented them from resisting performing tasks usually associated with women. (1997: 6)

While in some cases individuals might look favourably on their slaves and even regard them as family members, generally the status of slaves was very low, and the tasks they performed menial. According to Carol Cooper (1996: 102), the slave population of the northwest coast Stikine Tlingit were banned from marrying or taking part in any activities considered central to the tribe's social and religious life. Slaves, including women and their children, were kept hostage by their masters unless a trade deal was struck with a neighbouring tribe.

Despite—or perhaps because of—their low station in fishing societies, slaves were a vital resource to these economies even in the pre-contact period. Receiving little in return for their labour, slaves provided wealth in the form of preserved fish and other foodstuffs, which awarded prestige to their individual owners and the entire lineage, enabling them to purchase even more slaves. Fishing societies would have been very different without the labour of their predominantly female slave populations.

societies held most positions on the governing councils and, as in other fishing societies, weapons and warfare were male prerogatives (Prentice et al., 1996: 24). In addition, virtually all slave owners in patrilineal fishing societies were male (Donald, 1997: 88).

Regarding women's economic independence and social rights, fishing societies were at best inconsistent. In these larger, better-off societies, wealth enabled high-ranked women to enjoy (along with men of their station) some freedom from the work required of all women of lower rank. In the lowest rank of all were those women condemned to slave status; they were to all intents and purposes "outside of society," given heavy workloads and denied the capacity to establish households of their own or to have any control over the fate of themselves or their children. Ironically, slave women played an essential role in the preservation of the salmon, the primary economic resource of many BC coastal tribes. The fruits of their labour also increased the prestige of the chiefs, who often were able to display bountiful supplies of preserved fish during potlatches or other clan ceremonies. Given that slaves in some of these fishing villages comprised a third of the population—and that the majority were women and children deprived of all social rights, including life itself—caution must be observed when generalizing about women's position in societies predating European contact.

The arrival of Europeans, and the imposition of colonial rule, provided new opportunities for some Aboriginal women, but left many more economically dependent and vulnerable to exploitation by members of their own communities, as well as by Europeans and their even less egalitarian institutions.

THE CONTACT PERIOD

> I have as yet said nothing about my wife ... she is not indeed exactly fitted to shine at the head of a nobleman's table, but she suits the sphere she has to move better than any toy, in short she is a native of the country. (Charles Ross, Factor of Fort McLoughlin, near Bella, BC, in a letter to relatives in Ontario, 1943)

Explorers and Fur Traders

At the beginning of the sixteenth century, what is now Canada was home to amazingly diverse societies of Aboriginal peoples. Some of these societies possessed little by way of material wealth, yet fostered comparatively gender-egalitarian social systems. Others, such as the fishing societies of the northwest coast, were economically prosperous, but more hierarchical, ranked by gender, among other designations. Still others, for example the small-scale matrilineal agricultural societies of the Iroquois, fell somewhere between these extremes.

Despite their many differences, Aboriginal peoples at the time of European contact shared some principles about social relationships and the place of human beings in the natural order of things. All of them held the larger kinship group, rather than the nuclear family, as the basic social unit. Careful attention was given to cultural rules surrounding gift giving and hospitality, especially towards members of one's extended kin or larger clan group. Material possessions were not considered forms of "personal property," but were acquired mainly to be given away to those in need, or as a display of wealth with subsequent redistribution within the extended family, lineage, or clan. Aboriginal people also shared a view of humans as part of a transcendent universal system that included all other life forms. All things in nature were believed to possess a spiritual character and were shaped—and in turn did shape—the lives of human beings.

The Europeans who travelled to the New World had a different view of nature and understanding of social relationships. They perceived economic matters as the concern of free individuals entering into exchange relationships without the social obligations of kinship (but also without its protective mechanisms). They were in search of the "enormous treasure house of resources" that was apparently free for the taking (Lenski et al., 1995: 242).

European exploration was also comprised of men—explorers and traders from France, England, and other areas of Europe—whose travels often were financed by the rising European merchant class interested in expanding their wealth through the acquisition of land and natural resources. It was said of the east coast of present-day Canada, which first attracted Europeans at the beginning of the sixteenth century, that "no part of the world has ever been so rich in edible fish and other products of the sea as the Newfoundland Banks, the coast of the Labrador, and Gulf of the St. Lawrence" (Morison, 1971: 470).

Along with the demand for fish, furs had become a highly desirable trading item in Europe. Canada, with its rich abundance of fur-bearing animals, was considered a prime location for what was to become over the next century a flourishing fur trade. Given their expertise in hunting, the Aboriginal peoples were of major interest to European explorers interested in establishing trade. Some tribes, already avid traders with other groups, were attracted to the goods that the Europeans were willing to barter. Iron axes were especially prized items (Dickason, 1992: 101).

It is only recently that history has recognized and acknowledged the vital role that Aboriginal women played during the initial stages of European contact. It had been long believed that the fur trade between Europeans and Aboriginals in Canada was an entirely male enterprise. Recent evidence suggests, however, that Aboriginal women are a "missing link" in the success of the fur trade (Van Kirk, 1980). Despite stipulation by trading companies that fraternization between European agents and Aboriginals be kept to a minimum, many explorer-traders depended in no small way on relationships they engendered with Aboriginal women. Susane Merritt (1994: 17) tells the story of the Chipewyan woman, Thanadelthur (d. 1717), who when just a teenager was enslaved by the Cree. Thanadelthur and another slave woman eventually escaped, but were unable to find their nomadic people. The two women headed for York Factory, a Hudson's Bay trading post where they hoped to find protection from the Cree. Their search took them the better part of a year. Her companion died along the way, but Thanadelthur eventually made it to a hunting camp and travelled with the hunters to York Factory. Thereafter she served as a chief negotiator between the Fort traders and her people.

Similar accounts are given of Aboriginal women who married traders in early nineteenth-century British Columbia: "Indian women were used to isolation and could accept a simple life; they were willing to move wherever the [trade company] men were posted, they accepted company rules which forbade men to eat with their wives. They bore their children easily and devoted their time to childraising. The women sometimes spoke several languages since they often came from other areas" (Gould, 1975: 43).

To the displeasure of colonial officials, some early Europeans traders were willing to adopt Aboriginal customs and traditions. Yet this situation was not to last: cooperation turned to competition once colonial settlement began in earnest. Neither French nor British were willing to treat Aboriginal peoples—devoid as they were of white European traditions of God, aristocracy, and word of law—as rightful inhabitants of the vast land Columbus once thought to be the Indies (hence his naming Aboriginal peoples as *Indians*) (Dickason, 1992: 83).

Once contact was fully established, the autonomy and economic independence of Aboriginal peoples in Canada were decimated. At the beginning of the eighteenth century there were about 10 Aboriginal persons per single European in Canada; by 1881 there were about 40 Europeans for each Aboriginal person. But this changed ratio was not due primarily to a natural increase in European immigration (Jaffe, 1992). Traders and later settlers to New France and British North America held a conqueror's attitude towards the non-Christian "savages" who resided in the New World, and used technologically advanced military might against those unwilling to be colonized. Europeans also brought with them an unexpected weapon. Smallpox and other epidemic diseases, including measles, influenza, and tuberculosis, had pervaded Europe in previous centuries (Cohen, 1989). However, in the New World, these contagions ravaged Aboriginal populations, who were without immunities:

In the 85 years between Captain Cook's visit in 1778 and the Royal Fellowship census in 1863, the Nootka nation was decimated. The Nitinat once numbered more than 8 000 people; less than 35 remained. Yoquot, once home of 2 000 men, their multiple wives, children and slaves, was less than 200. In Clayoquot Sound more than a thousand warriors, their multiple wives, children and slaves, had been reduced to a total of 135. Tahsis, with more than 2 000 fighting men, their multiple wives, children, and slaves, was shrunk to a total of 60 people. (Cameron, 1981: 12–13)

These "diseases of civilization," combined with the deleterious effects of adulterated whisky, reduced the Aboriginal population of British Columbia by nearly two-thirds before the end of the 1800s (Jaffe, 1992). Aboriginal men, women, and children, high-ranked and slave, died by the thousands, severely reducing their capacity to resist the increasing colonization of their land.

Song for the Dead

We are beating the drums
and singing the songs
having a great feast for the dead
for our children are gone
and none remain.

Come back my nephew we miss you
Come back my daughter we miss you
Come back my son we miss you
Come back our lost ones we miss you….
(From Cameron, 1981: 12–13)

Frontier Settlers

For the earliest colonists, the Atlantic voyage to the New World was a harrowing experience. Many died of scurvy and other diseases en route, and those who survived faced tremendous adversity in the "howling wilderness" that was to be their new home. In order to protect themselves from military attack by other Europeans and inhospitable Aboriginals, settlers built their homes primarily for protection, not necessarily on land adequate for farming. At first food was scarce and disease claimed many. Some who could afford it made the gruelling passage back to more familiar and comfortable surroundings. Others, many of them married women, but also single women from aristocrats to peasants, stayed on and established families of their own. Still others joined the "family of God," sometimes heading charitable institutions for the sick and desolate, such as the French hospital, *Hôtel-Dieu*, originally designated to give health care services to newly arrived immigrants living in the vicinity of Fortress Quebec.

Charitable institutions were also established by immigrant nuns in Ville Marie (Montreal), founded in 1642, as well as in other settlements of New France, now the province of Quebec. Both cloistered and non-cloistered religious sisters shouldered much of the responsibility of sheltering single women who came to the colony with the intention of marrying—most likely a trader or soldier. At first, men far outnumbered women immigrants to New France, but by 1760 there was a near gender balance in the colony's 70 000 inhabitants (Prentice et al., 1996: 37). Reflecting the stratified system of Old France, women of noble background—and those who married high-ranking men—lived free from toil and in comparative comfort in New France, albeit subservient to their fathers and husbands. The other avenue open to educated white women in New France was "marriage to the church," a career closed to Aboriginal and black women, as were the services offered by nuns to citizens of New France. Aboriginal and black women were at the very bottom of the new settler society: "in Louisbourg, for example, black and Native slaves were clearly the most exploited group of women: one black slave named Marie-Louise gave birth to six illegitimate children during the sixteen years she was owned by a local merchant" (Prentice et al., 1996: 47).

Upon the transfer of Acadia from French to British hands in 1713, Acadian residents were either deported back to France or resettled in the northeastern regions of British North America. York (now Toronto), established in 1793 by Britain, was strategically situated to afford protection from the independently-minded Americans to the immediate south, who had won their liberty in the Revolution of 1775–83. Maintaining loyalty to Britain (hence their title *Loyalists*), many families made their way from colonies in New York and Pennsylvania to the shores of the St. Lawrence, Lake Ontario, and Lake Erie. Some of the immigrants were women from both advantaged and disadvantaged backgrounds, some travelling without families, all aspiring to a new life with continued ties to Britain.

Women in "Upper Canada" had much in common with women in defeated New France. Most settled on farmland distributed by the British Crown, in coastal fishing villages, or in the few small urban areas where commerce, trade, and handicraft production were concentrated. Farm women combined running a household with fieldwork, planting and thinning, harvesting root vegetables, and raking the hayfields. Women in inshore fisheries on the east and west coasts worked the "flakes" (wooden drying racks on which fish were stacked), salted the fish, and often carried it to merchant stores to trade for foodstuffs not grown in their home gardens. It was not an easy existence. One writer reported a fisherman's wife as saying, "If I had but two hours sleep in 24, I could stand the week's labor; but to do without rest for nearly a week is too much for my strength" (Wilson, 1866: 212).

Women's labour also involved milking cows, cleaning, carding and spinning wool, and making and mending family clothing. Every girl learned these *feminine*, home-based activities necessary for family survival. Settler women were expected to bear and raise many children, for a broad labour force was essential to large-scale agricultural production (Errington, 1995; Porter, 1995). Moreover, the importance of the ownership of arable land brought a new significance to paternity. The patriarchal order of frontier settlements was premised on female subordination to husbands, fathers, and men in general. Particularly in Upper Canada, women had no voice in matters of religion or politics: "marital property law was based on the common-law concept of 'legal unity' whereby women's married identity was submerged in that of her husband. Thus all property upon marriage belonged to the husband" (Ursel, 1988: 130). During this period, widows could, however, claim the legal *right of dower*, which awarded a widow one-third of her husband's property upon his death. Yet a husband's will might make no mention of this legal right. Instead, the homestead could be willed directly from father to eldest son, who henceforth had the power to exclude his mother from using the family property. This situation persisted in rural Canada until the beginning of the twentieth century, as Lucy Maud Montgomery pointed out about the situation of her own grandmother:

> Uncle John and Prescott have been using grandmother shamefully all summer. In short, they have been trying to turn her out .... Grandfather's absurd will put her completely in their power—the power of selfish, domineering men eaten up with greed. Grandmother told them she would not leave they home where she had lived and worked for sixty years and since then Uncle John has never spoken to her or visited her. (Quoted in Rubio and Waterson, 1986: 310)

In cases of marital breakdown or desertion, settler women in Upper Canada had no claim to either family property or custody of the children. The loss of child custody was an economic as well as personal blow: "at a time and in a place where children's labour was extremely valuable, the loss of their children constituted more than an emotional loss to those women who endured such separations" (Prentice et al., 1996: 88). Some relationships between individual men and women were no doubt egalitarian ones in which women were treated with respect. Yet generally, men were the family patriarchs and women and children were subservient. In Upper Canada, for example, by virtue of her marriage a woman became a *femme covert* (covered/protected woman). Unless she entered into a prenuptial agreement or maintained a separate estate under the control of an independent trustee, she relinquished both herself and her property to her husband. Most women did not sign such agreements and thus became completely dependent on their husband, required to adopt his name, to love, honour, and obey him until death due them part, and to bear his children. For this, the woman was given food and lodgings (Errington, 1995: 39).

Children in frontier settlements were also expected to live in subservient obedience to their parents and other elders. Young boys followed their father in clearing land, planting, mending fences, and fishing; young girls helped their female kin with gardening, cooking, caring for younger siblings, spinning, and the like. Elizabeth Goudie recalls her role in soap making, a 10-day process that was done at home:

> Mother had me stand at the side of the stove for an hour each day pouring the lye into the fat a cup at a time until the fat was cooked. It took about seven days. When the soap was cooked she took about a half cup of coarse salt and about a pint of water to separate the soap from the lye. Then it was put away to cool for three days and then cut into blocks. After all this work we would get about three pounds of soap. (1983: 10–11)

While young boys might apprentice with a master to learn one of the many trades open only to them, young girls, especially those from small towns, were often apprenticed to families at an early age. Domestic service increasingly became an occupation for single girls from poor backgrounds whose families could not afford their keep. As many as five to eight per cent of the populations of Montreal and Quebec during the nineteenth century were in domestic service. The bulk of them were women. In the city of Hamilton at mid-century, much the same was the case, with girls as young as 13 years of age working as live-in servants in the homes of strangers (Prentice et al., 1996).

In pre-capitalist Canada, sexual exploitation of female domestics by male employers was not uncommon, sometimes resulting in pregnancy, which in turn resulted in dismissal from service, stigma as an "unwed mother," and a life of poverty for the unfortunate young mother and child. Society at large was unforgiving, since pregnancy and childbirth outside of marriage indicated vileness and debauchery. Privileged women themselves tended to share this perspective:

> In 1817, Anne Powell found herself in a awkward and embarrassing situation. A young servant girl of "respectability" in whom Anne had shown particular interest was suddenly taken to her bed .... Out of "Christian charity," Anne Powell gave the new mother and her child her own warm chamber in preference to the drafty servants' room. Anne was nonetheless scandalized by the affair .... Christian charity notwithstanding, a day after giving birth, the girl was dismissed. (Errington, 1995: 55)

Some female servants, finding themselves pregnant, unmarried, and without resources to support a child, attempted abortion, which at times ended in the tragic death of the mother as well. Child abandonment occurred; even infanticide might be attempted as a last resort.

The average number of children born to families in 1851 in British North America was just over seven. All frontier women, regardless of rank, shared the valid fear that frequent pregnancy and lack of medical help would sooner or later result in maternal morbidity or death. Prairie homestead women were perhaps the worst off in this respect, as substantial distances separated farms from roads and railroad links, and kin and friends were often few and far between. Nanci Langford (1995: 281) quotes from the diary of Sophie Puckette about her neighbour's preparation for childbirth: "Then she took me upstairs and showed me all her wedding outfit she had laid carefully out for them to put on her should she die. She imagines so strongly that her life will end for the little life she is expecting in Jan., that she has all her things put in her trunk in order, and each is marked so that Mr. Bond will know what to do with them all."

Loneliness and isolation during pregnancy and childbirth were less of a problem for women residing in towns, provided, of course, they had means. Much depended on their social class and the opportunity for employment in those occupations that were open to their sex. More remunerative work opportunities were available for women in urban areas: either with their husbands or alone, town women sometimes worked for pay as traders, innkeepers, retailers, seamstresses, hat makers, laundresses, and schoolteachers, or by taking in boarders (Prentice et al., 1996: 73–74). Much of this work was done out of women's own homes and provided money to purchase staples that were not produced within the household. Immigrant midwives, many with formal qualifications from their home country, were attracted to urban areas where they were more likely to find women willing and able to pay for their services. However, given the small numbers of middle-class women, it was difficult for most "occupied" women to make ends meet.

Urban centres brought together a wide array of immigrant women, including many escaping from slavery in the American South. As with urban Aboriginal women, these black women faced problems of racial discrimination. Divided by race from their white sisters, they were frequently excluded from the more attractive occupations open to women at the time, forced instead to become domestic servants or prostitutes. They were banished to the edges of the new colonies, where poor white women, especially single mothers and their "illegitimate" children, might also be found living in poverty. In short, frontier Canadian society deprived a category of women of human rights enjoyed by their "privileged" sisters.

Canadian frontier and urban women were diverse in social class, race, and family structure. Apart from the small minority who enjoyed domestic servants and other economic privileges, most women in colonial life spent their waking hours in toil of one kind or other. Their work activities too were astonishingly diverse, ranging from productive to caring endeavours that called for a vast assortment of skills. As was said about the homestead, "everything depends on the mother, who cannot share the responsibility with the shoemaker, tailor and baker, school or priest, and therefore, one stands by oneself, poor and powerless" (Prentice et al., 1996: 149). Despite their valuable contribution, the laws and mores of the day were stacked against them: all women, regardless of status, faced the same legal restrictions placed on their sex by the patriarchal system of the time.

A glance through the window to the United States during the pre-capitalist era indicates that American settler women faced many of the same circumstances.

Settler Women and Feminine Purity

Upper Canadians seemed to be preoccupied with the question of female "purity," a term that included female chastity. Direct and explicit references in local newspapers to the destructive effects of a woman's sexuality were rare. However, the passionate temptress was a familiar image in the Upper Canadian press. Moreover, it was presumed that women could "bewitch" and enslave men with their charms. Short stories in the local press confirmed that an unscrupulous woman could lead an unsuspecting man astray. Didactic tales graphically illustrated that young girls without innocence were brought to despondency and despair. That some, perhaps many, women in Upper Canada did sell their sexuality to earn a living is beyond question. This was never openly acknowledged, however.

Reports from the courts in community newspapers did sometimes include brief mention of women charged and convicted of keeping a house of ill fame, being drunk and disorderly, or keeping a disorderly house. In 1829, the editor of the Colonial Advocate *added a brief commentary to his report of the case of Margaret Tripp, a prostitute who had committed suicide while in prison. The cause of her despair, the editor judged, was her "great distress of mind" at "having lost [her] station and character in society."* (Errington, 1995: 35)

A WINDOW ON THE UNITED STATES IN THE PRE-CAPITALIST ERA

> The shift of the status of the woman farmer may have happened quite rapidly, once there were two male specializations relating to agriculture: plowing and the care of cattle. This situation left women with all the many subsidiary tasks, including weeding and carrying water to the fields. The new fields were larger, so women had to work many hours just as they did before, but now they worked at more secondary tasks …. This would contribute further to the erosion of the status of women. (Boulding, 1976: 161–63)

Canadians share important aspects of their history with their American cousins, including their New World status, customs, traditions, and laws brought from Britain. But the Pilgrims who first settled the US were fleeing the Protestant church that ruled the lives of Britons. The Pilgrims envisioned a "New England," severed from the power of the church, with religious freedom for all individuals. They eventually succeeded in establishing a "republic" with freedom for all, but the gendered system of work and social rights upon which the new society was based was far from women-friendly. Ironically, although many of the colonists were themselves victims of religious persecution, they were still intolerant regarding the freedom of others. Thus John Adams, one of the leaders of the American Revolution and the second president of the United States, wrote that in a "pure" republic, "men must be ready, they must pride themselves, and be happy to sacrifice their private Pleasures, Passions, and Interests, nay, their private Friendships and dearest Connections, when they stand in Competition with the Rights of Society." But as far as women were concerned, "their delicacy renders them unfit for practice and experience in the great business of life, and the hardy enterprise of war, as well as the arduous cares of state" (quoted in Bernhard et al., 1992: 192–93).

The centre of the New England community was the patriarchal household (Demos, 1977: 60). Settler women's work activities ranged from bearing and raising children to tilling the soil. Some urban women engaged in a variety of trades and businesses that took them beyond the household: they were soap makers, brewers, wax workers, tea processors, nurses, and spinners (Queen, Habenstein, and Quadagno, 1985), but patriarchal controls deprived them of economic independence:

> Common law gave the use and profit of a woman's real estate and the ownership of all her personal property and earnings to her husband. Without her husband's consent, a married woman could not engage in business, make contracts, or sue to collect debts. Even if her husband deserted her, a woman had no right to the use of her own property, a regulation that deprived women of the ability to earn their own living. (Langley and Fox, 1994)

If a woman, for whatever reason, deviated from unquestioning obedient service to her husband or from sexual relationships within the bonds of the marriage contract, she could expect a harsh outcome for both herself and her children. Defying the rule of the father or engaging in a forbidden sexual relationship, as did Hester Prynne in Nathaniel Hawthorne's *The Scarlet Letter*, resulted in severe punishment: without husband or father, Hester and her daughter were unable to measure up to the definition of a real family and were abandoned to fend for themselves, with neither respect nor help from those around them (Polakow, 1993: 25). But by the 1800s some patriarchal rulings regarding sexuality outside the confines of marriage, women's "proper place" (as helpmate, not equal), and children's deference to their parents, began to ease. Punishments changed from corporal to monetary, although having a child outside wedlock remained a serious offence against God and country for some time. In brief, the New England colonies developed peculiar and specific notions of gender and women's place that were to shape women's work and social rights.

Gender notions also were embedded in ideas about the nuclear family and its autonomy from central state control. Patriarchal traditions not only survived the Atlantic passage, but were intensified and expanded in New England. Colonial America viewed poverty as a private, *individual* concern, caused by moral shortcomings. The "politics of conduct" rather than the "politics of redistribution" prevailed, and blame for "defective" families was especially placed at the doorsteps of mothers in poverty. Addressing the chapel of the New Almshouse in Portsmouth in 1834, the Reverend Charles Burroughs stated, "Let me repeat it, the causes of poverty are looked for, and found, in him or her who suffers it" (Polakow, 1993: 46).

The organization of American society in the southern states in the pre-capitalist era differed from that of New England, as isolated plantations and farms constituted the main types of settlement. The South was originally inhabited by single males seeking fortune rather than settler families seeking religious freedom. The first waves of Southern women were mainly *indentured servants*, sold to plantation owners for service in the large households. The plantations were rigidly stratified, with indentured servants just above black slaves in the ranked order consisting of "yeomen, a pioneer fringe of poor whites, indentured servants, and black slaves" (Queen, Habenstein, and Quadagno, 1985: 209). Although the statutes of the southern colonies were less harsh than those of New England (there was no death sentence, scarlet letter, or gallows; and some women owned land in their own right), an illegitimate pregnancy for a female indentured servant resulted in a heavy fine, a period of unpaid service for the "trouble" she caused, and the stripping away of her child after weaning, to be sent out to a household in need of labour (Baxandall et al., 1976). The plight of female slaves and their children was equally perilous:

> On the one hand, it was customary to sell or trade slave mothers "with their increase," thereby allowing young children to remain with their mothers, or other kin when the mother was at work in the fields, and to perhaps even live with their fathers as well in a large slave household compound. On the other hand, little or no thought was given to detaching the household unit when "estates were divided among heirs, or when slave traders purchased and sold slaves on their river journeys." (Polakow, 1993: 16)

To summarize, although early American settler society established a value system that held the nuclear family, individualism, and freedom from the state as cultural ideals, patriarchal traditions continued to dominate women's work and family lives. Colonial America showed little concern for those unable to care for themselves, and even less for those who did not meet the strict standards of decency and good behaviour deemed necessary for the new colonies to survive and prosper. Race figured largely as a determinant not only of status, but of individual and group survival. A series of "Indian Wars," in combination with contagious diseases, killed a large segment of the American Indian population. It took a civil war between North and South to finally end slavery, which was banned in 1865 by the Thirteenth Amendment to the American Constitution. By this date, capitalism was already on its way.

A WINDOW ON SWEDEN IN THE PRE-CAPITALIST ERA

> Together with Norway and Iceland, Sweden is in contrast to all the rest of Europe a country where the farmers have always been free and where feudalism never developed as more than a threat. (Myrdal, 1941: 13)

Sweden, while still divided along lines of social class, ethnicity, and gender, is commonly recognized as among the most egalitarian countries of the world, which is the result of an assortment of factors, including a high average standard of living and well-developed system of social security available to all citizens. It may come as a surprise to learn that this progressive aspect of Swedish society is a very recent historical innovation, a result of developments dating largely from the present century, especially the post-World War II period.

Until the early nineteenth century, Sweden shared with Britain, France, and other "empire builders" of the pre-capitalist world a number of distinctive characteristics (Hobsbawm, 1968). At one time Sweden was a major power in northern Europe. Swedish explorers during the Viking Age (800–1050 AD), with the mixed motive of trade and plunder, travelled the globe and established trading stations as far afield as what is today northeastern Canada. Near continuous warfare, internal and external, marked the history of the country during the Middle Ages up until the early decades of the nineteenth century (Klinge, 1993).

The social organization of Swedish society in the pre-capitalist era also reflects in broad strokes the situation found in other European empires. The kingdom of Sweden dates back to 1000 AD, and the crown went back and forth between two rival families, the Sverkers and Eriks. Yet the Swedish monarchy was never all-powerful. Nobles in the provinces, sometimes in alliance with rebellious independent peasants, contested and seized power from the king and central administration. The eventual result was a strong centralized government headed by the Swedish king, who was elected by regional administrators. In the province of Finland, for example, "the right of representatives of the Finnish ... to participate in the election of the (Swedish) King was confirmed in 1362. This legal system, together with the four-estate representation (the nobility, the clergy, the burghers and the farmers) which had developed since the beginning of the 15th century, gave Finland indisputable and full political rights within the Kingdom of Sweden" (Klinge, 1997: 26–27).

In fact, it was later that a provincial nobleman, Gustav Vasa (1523–60), supported by the farmers, seized power from the present king and was himself elected King of Sweden (Heclo and Madsen, 1987: 9). Under Vasa, the Church's property was largely confiscated and taxation and administration came under the control of the central government. At the same time, Protestantism arrived and subsequently became Sweden's national religion. So powerful was Vasa's rule that in 1544 he managed to eliminate the system of elected kings and replace it with one of hereditary monarchs. In the succeeding century, the monarchy and nobles continued to struggle for power, while the Kingdom was engaged in continuous warfare with neighbouring Norway and Denmark. By the mid 1600s and until the Great Northern War of 1700–21, Sweden was a great power in Europe, controlling southwestern areas of Finland as well as northern parts of Germany. In 1814 Sweden fought a last war—against Norway—and henceforth was at peace.

These developments suggest that early Sweden was quite different from the social democracy it became in the twentieth century. However, the inclusion in the Swedish empire of a fourth estate of peasants set it apart from most kingdoms; pre-capitalist Britain, for example, was restricted to the first three estates (Laslett, 1984). This unique feature of early Sweden gave some power to the local parishes, which remain an important feature of Swedish society today. Even in the sixteenth century parishes "assumed, or had thrust upon them, responsibilities of a secular as well as a religious nature: the relief of the poor, the care of the sick and later, education and other welfare duties which still remain in their hands today" (Wilson, 1979: 1).

How did the estate system affect Swedish women in the pre-capitalist era? Compared to their New World counterparts, Swedish women, even those in the poorest circumstances, were spared bondage of slavery and serfdom. Yet in other respects, Swedish women, over 90 per cent of whom worked in rural agriculture even into the nineteenth century, shared with their Canadian and American counterparts a number of disadvantages. Swedish women, even when they belonged to the landed peasant estate, were nevertheless deemed "legally incompetent," permitted only half the rights of inheritance as their brothers. As in the New World, the mediaeval guild system in Sweden during this period excluded women from most trades and their accompanying forms of support. Most educational institutions of the day were also closed to women. Moreover, Swedish women were required to seek the help of a male trustee regarding control of personal income and property. Until 1858 marriage also granted husbands the legal right to beat their wives (Ohlander, 1994).

In the predominantly agricultural society of the pre-capitalist era, Swedish women shared with women of the New World a range of activities from fieldwork and household production, to the care of children, the old, and disabled. Young Swedish women also apprenticed in farming households, where their work never ended: "[she] helped with the harvest out in fields. Then she had to help with cooking the food and washing dishes, taking care of the animals in the byre and the evening milking. Men could rest at midday and were not called upon for any indoor duties in the evening. Judging from her account, women were never free" (Ohlander, 1994: 14–15).

And as with their sisters in the New World (then and today), Swedish women bore the burden of childrearing. Many children died either at childbirth or before age five; high death rates among both men and women in the pre-capitalist period left surviving children vulnerable as orphans.

There was one important respect, however, in which Swedish women and their families were advantaged. In the latter quarter of the seventeenth century a public health system was established across the country (including the then province of Finland), made up of a network of municipal physicians and midwives. The "*Collegium Medicum* was set up in 1763 to certify the qualifications of doctors and midwives and to supervise the pharmacies, duties which it continues to perform to this day" (Wilson, 1979: 2). This early public health system was an example of one of the more positive aspects of a strong central government.

Social and economic developments in the early nineteenth century, however, placed great pressure on local parishes to solve the increasing impoverishment of the overwhelmingly rural population, which comprised 90 per cent of all Swedes. A downward trend in mortality rates created "over population" in the countryside; neither agriculture nor alternative employment in trades could meet the demand for work. What industry did exist (chiefly iron and timber exports) evolved around village workshops that could not absorb the labour surplus. The end result was the rise of a landless, agricultural proletariat of men, women, and children, not unlike what had occurred already in Britain, providing one ingredient for capitalist forms of production that were to transform women's work and ultimately women's lives in Sweden as well as the New World.

SUMMARY AND CONCLUSION

This overview of women's work and societal situations in pre-capitalist Canada, the US, and Sweden has shown that these three countries share commonalities as well as differences in regard to a range of social, economic, and political factors that impacted women in significant ways. The three nations relied largely on women's reproductive and productive labour in the pre-capitalist era, and none viewed women as legally competent during this period. New World countries were advantaged in that their populations were not trapped in the caste-like estate system that characterized Sweden and other empires, allowing North American women freedom from some of the traditional barriers placed on their sex by the patriarchal order of the old aristocracy. On the other hand, patriarchy and oppression were not at odds with the new-found independence of North American colonists; women worked equally hard, but in many respects received fewer rewards than their male counterparts. European New World societies were built without regard for Aboriginal populations and on the backs of a large indentured/slave caste of poor white and black immigrants. As the next chapter explores, capitalism was founded on a different understanding of social relationships and a new gender system. As defined by its intellectual father, the English economist Adam Smith, capitalism is a system of exchange into which the individual enters freely; a free or "open market" of labour, goods, and services exchanged for moveable capital is fundamental. The "private interests and passions of men," Smith believed, would lead in the direction "most agreeable to the interest of the whole society." Capitalism in its ideal form is a self-regulating system, outside of the laws of kinship, church, state, and nature; capitalism functions best independent of these outside forces, as if an "invisible hand" ruled economic life (Smith, 1937 [1776]).

Yet we will see that capitalism has not been a homogeneous economic system. Like the societies that preceded it, capitalism has been shaped by geography, history, politics, and culture, creating different circumstances for women as paid and unpaid workers. It is to this topic that we turn next.

ENDNOTES

[1]The term "Aboriginal" is adopted in this book to reflect the categorization of Canada's diverse Native peoples in the 1996 Census. Approximately 1.6 per cent of people claimed *Aboriginal ancestry* in the 1996 Census, and about 800 000 of these went further and claimed *Aboriginal identity*. Most people in this second group saw themselves as "North American Indians," while some claim to be Metis and a smaller group to be of Inuit (Eskimo) background.

[2]The Black Plague, which ravaged Europe in the middle of the fourteenth century, is reported to have killed 25–50 per cent of the population in a 4-year span (Gottfried, 1983: xiii).

3

CAPITALISM AND WOMEN'S WORK

"Whatever contours of family we choose to trace, whether in Europe or America, the lives of the poor or the privileged, the public or the private sphere, we return to the central ideology of care that burdens women with the 'terrifying assignment' of a mother-child couplet. Mother stands at the center of the private sphere of family and, contingent upon her class and place in the social realm, moves in spreading circles of powerlessness and simultaneous domestic responsibility. As we watch the ideology of care developing in the nineteenth and twentieth centuries, we also note the increasing placelessness of women in the public sphere." (Polakow, 1993: 29)

INTRODUCTION

Capitalism created major changes in the organization of work and family life in traditional societies, but the consequences of these changes were not the same for women and men. Continuing practices established during the pre-capitalist era, the economic system of capitalism became linked with *masculinization.* As Yvonne Hirdman (1994: 6) explains, economic expansion "created both disorder and new order in terms of women's position in society. The need for (cheap) labor undoubtedly involved a process of (unintentional) integration, while at the same time women's participation in capitalistic development at higher levels, as either capitalists or business professionals, was negligible."

Occupations in such enterprises as banking, commerce, and industry, which formed the backbone of the new economic order, were almost exclusively male; much the same can be said about education and politics. This occupational exclusivity created a very different gender contract than that of earlier periods. Polakow points out how in the nineteenth century "the 'true woman' emerged as desexualized, uninterested in intellectual pursuits, imbued with piety, and devoted to home and hearth ... stress[ing] the 'naturalness' of her condition and construct[ing] the female sphere as irrational and emotional, psychologically primed for motherhood and childrearing" (1993: 30). Protestant evangelicalism reinforced this new ideal of the sexes, maintaining that women's domesticity would help to erect a new social morality, with mothers as the chief moralizers:

> Protestant evangelicalism was a crucial influence in the formation of the ideology of domesticity. The moral and social conservatism of the evangelicals evolved a religion that was compatible with economic competitiveness. Middle-class evangelicalism was concerned with the creation of a new morality. It was a movement to moralise society itself, to inject into it a new code of respectability. Central to the creation of this new morality was a redefinition of woman's position within the family. (Pennington and Westover, 1989: 2)

In effect, the form that capitalism initially took in what eventually were to become many of today's high-income countries undermined the important productive role women had performed in the pre-capitalist period. By narrowing their role to societal spaces deemed "female" and "private," women's economic progress and involvement were impeded. The ideology supporting this new gender system was based on the *doctrine of separate spheres,* a doctrine that "was born among the English upper-middle classes [and] called for the separation of work and family life. It held that a woman's proper place was in the home and not in the workplace; a man's natural sphere was in the world of commerce—or, at any rate— at his job—and not at home" (Reskin and Padavic, 1994: 21).

The notion of "binary oppositions—masculine/feminine, market/non-market, public/-private, waged/non-waged" (Krahn and Lowe, 1993: 152)—placed all women—even the bourgeois woman whose father or husband could afford her maintenance—in indeterminate circumstances should male relatives, for any number of reasons, decide to withdraw economic support (Cohen, 1988).[1] Women from all social groups faced the same "terrifying assignment" of primary responsibility for reproducing the labour force on a daily and generational basis, with few possibilities of economic independence or escape from abusive or unhappy marriages (Badinter, 1981).

Yet social class separated women also from each other. Without recourse to a bourgeois lifestyle, the vast majority found themselves caught between the ideology of women's "proper place" in the private spaces of society, and the economic reality that necessitated whatever employment they could find that fit around their family duties. Capitalism drew on economically vulnerable women as a *reserve army of labour* (Fox, 1981), employing them in work activities defined as insignificant, with commensurately low economic rewards. Women attained more important jobs only when male breadwinners were in short supply (e.g., during wartime), only to be dismissed as "unproductive" when male workers again became available.

TABLE 3-1	Societal Types: Pre-capitalist Societies			
	Mercantilism	**Small-scale Manufacturing**	**Large-scale Manufacturing**	**Post-industrial**
Technical Change from Earlier Society	small machines (sewing machines, hand looms etc.)	inanimate power sources (coal, steam power, rail, telegraph, telephone); mechanization of agriculture	electrical and nuclear power; aviation	Automation; new information technologies (personal computer/Internet)
Economic Characteristics	conquest of the New World; putting-out system; cottage and sweated industry; lingering importance of agriculture; crisis of the craftsmen	mills; factories; mines; domestic service in households	large centralized manufacturing plants organized along lines of mass production; scientific management; modern corporation; bureaucratic administration	dominant service sector; multinational corporations; lean production; internationalization of labour; growth in self-employment and home production
Control of Wealth and Income	mainly men; declining power of male-dominated landowning class and crafts; rising power of class of mainly male merchant capitalists	mainly men; new class of male industrialist capitalists; gradual rise in income of male factory workers	mainly men; increasing economic power of shareholders, corporate managers, CEOs; increase in income of unionized male workers and male dominated professions	mainly men, but women making important economic gains, especially in the public service sector, management, the professions, and social policies
Inheritance	almost exclusively patrilineal	almost exclusively patrilineal	mainly patrilineal	increasingly bilateral
Women's Societal Status	lowest	very low; increasing for bourgeois women	slowly rising	large increase; yet still not on par with men

A major shift in the gender contract of capitalist societies occurred in the post-World War II period. The need for women's special "caring" skills in the expanding service sector resulted in the *feminization* of the labour force of capitalist countries. Indeed, labour requirements were so great that even married women with young children were recruited, a reversal of a trend established in the early part of the century. Thus capitalism first segregated, but then reintegrated women into the new social order (Hirdman, 1994). However, their reintegration was only partial: first, many of the jobs designated as "women's work" were both poorly paid and had fewer social benefits compared with men's jobs; second, much of women's unpaid work in the home remained outside of the public realm—a female assignment, hidden in the household, largely invisible to everyone except the employed mothers themselves. Yet even in this respect there are no universals, as will be shown by placing the Canadian experience in cross-national perspective.

This chapter examines the changes in women's paid and unpaid work under capitalism, a process that can be divided into the general phases of major social organization of production (see Table 3–1 for a summary of each societal type). As in the former chapter, Canada is the main focus of attention, with windows opening on the United States and Sweden.

THE FIRST PHASE: MERCANTILISM (MERCHANT CAPITALISM)

> There are scores, hundreds, of women in this city whose only means of subsistence is by their needle. They are paid starvation wages, viz., 6 cents each for making shirts, 17 cents for making and pressing pants, 75 cents for coat and vest, etc. In the words of a skeleton living on Maitland St. with a sick girl: "I have to work with my needle until midnight to earn the money to buy bread for tomorrow. And this is my hard experience every day of the week, and every week of the year." (McIntoch, 1996: 142)

Until 1920, half the Canadian population still worked in an agricultural "toiler society," in which—aside from those economically privileged—"the role of women was both integral to commodity production and central to economic organization" (Johnson, 1974: 17). In Canada, as in countries such as Britain (where capitalism arrived earlier), agricultural activity was seconded by craft production, based in or near villages or small towns. The crafts were regulated closely by guilds—the forerunner of unions and professional associations—which were associations of skilled workers, artisans, and their apprentices, organized to maintain standards and to protect the economic interests of their members. The craft occupations were engaged mainly by men, although their wives and female children often laboured alongside male apprentices in the family home/workshop. Sometimes widows were permitted to continue their husband's trade (Tilly and Scott, 1978).

Prior to the actual industrialization period of capitalism was an initial phase generally referred to as *mercantilism* or *merchant capitalism*. The economic theory of *mercantilism* includes direct government support of trade. European governments played their part by lending military support to merchant-industrialists intent on accumulating precious metals and indigenous raw materials in distant areas of the globe (e.g., raw cotton from India), and eventually establishing colonies that were to become a primary consumer of goods (e.g., woven garments) made in the home country. Merchant capitalism also involved an attempt by more economically powerful merchants to undermine the craft system. Positioned between artisan and customer, the merchant occupied a precarious economic position in agrarian society. However, beginning in the sixteenth century, some merchants managed to amass considerable capital by investing in colonial exploration and trading desirable items that brought high prices.

In an attempt to improve their profits, many merchants with disposable capital became labour contractors through what came to be called the *putting-out industry*, so called because the merchants (and in some instances wealthier artisans) would "put out" raw materials to workers' homes to be manufactured (Tausky, 1996: 20–21). In fact, the original meaning of manufacture is "make by hand." The merchant capitalist paid only for the finished piece, hence the definition of this type of labour as *piecework* (Tilly and Scott, 1978: 14). These merchant capitalists aimed to undermine the powerful (male dominated) guild system by controlling the markets for raw materials and finished products previously governed by artisans themselves. In essence, a new social class was emerging, comprised of middle-class men or capitalists who were largely free from manual work and instead occupied themselves with overseeing the putting-out industry.

Merchant capitalism in Canada and elsewhere largely relied on women *homeworkers*, a cheap and vulnerable labour supply, especially in the countryside (Pennington and Westover, 1989): "By having cloth woven in the countryside, the merchants managed to escape the control of the guilds, organizations of urban craftsmen, which closely supervised production in the cities" (Tilly and Scott, 1878: 14). Employing less-skilled workers at lower costs enabled merchants to undercut prices charged by artisans for superior products. Ultimately, more and more basic commodities fell under the merchant capitalist system until only complicated luxury and specialty items were left for the craft producers, a situation that tended to pit the skilled against the less-skilled and the male artisan against the female homeworker: "Before this period men and women had been more likely to labor together at home, doing different specific tasks but engaged in complementary work tasks. Indeed, the fact that a separate term for *housework* was not introduced into the written English language until 1841 suggests the continuation of the home as a centre of integrated work activity as well into the period of industrialization" (Hodson and Sullivan, 1995: 16–17). However, the putting-out system was not confined to rural areas. An urban form of cottage industry, referred to as *sweated industry* or *sweated labour* (because workers were forced to labour in hot and cramped places, such as their own attics or "sweat shops" owned by contractors), developed in towns and cities during this period.

In Canada, during the early period of merchant capitalism, variations of the putting-out system were established in both rural and urban areas. Some merchant tailors and established dressmakers began to transform their traditional shops into small-contract shops, placing larger numbers of male apprentices under the control of a foreman. Rather than learning the entire trade of tailoring, increasingly these apprentices were taught one simple task such as sewing, leaving measuring and cutting to the foreman. By 1835, journeymen in Montreal were no longer living on their employers' premises; room and board had to be paid out of pocket (McIntosh, 1996: 144–45). At the same time, labour contracts between apprentice and master worsened: the lengths of agreements shortened, and more and more apprentice-journeymen received payment only by the product piece. Underemployment and unemployment began to plague the tailoring trade; the need for capital and access to credit to establish oneself as an independent tailor meant that many apprentice-journeymen were left in dire straits.

By the middle of the nineteenth century, others determined to profit in ready-made garments entered the growing manufacturing industry—retailers, dry goods importers, and wholesalers. In an effort to avoid overhead costs such as renting premises and providing workers with basic rights, some established wholesalers and manufacturers began to put out work to women in their homes. Traditionally adept with the needle, yet saddled with the responsibilities of childcare and domestic activities, women in their homes were an easy (and cheap) source of sweated labour. By contracting (and perhaps further subcontracting) work to women at home, the small coterie of large manufacturers and wholesalers was able to pass along virtually all labour costs, other than the piece-wage itself, down the line—ultimately to the homeworkers themselves. In fact, it was not uncommon that "the employer or his agent might sell or rent sewing machines to homeworkers; he often deducted the cost of the needles, thread, or material from the women's wages" (Prentice et al., 1996: 126). Women had little choice but to accept the piece-wage given by the employer or subcontractor, to whom they might even become in debt for overhead costs. In Canadian cities such as Toronto, many girls were employed at "wages ranging from $2 per week and up, and the shirts they make are sold at about 60 to 75 cents each" (Rotenberg, 1974: 47).

Underpinning this system was a sex bias—the assumption that women could always depend upon economic support, in part or in full, from a male relative, either a father or husband. Since it was always a man who was the chief *breadwinner*, by definition women's wages were *secondary* family income, mere "pin money" that provided the extras beyond subsistence needs. In reality, many girls in the needle trade were on their own, some of them immigrants from Britain or other areas of Europe, and others migrants from rural Canada in search of employment because their families could not provide for them, or because of personal problems with their parents. Women on their own with children—due to widowhood or marital breakdown—were sometimes so desperate that they forced their children to labour beside them at home in order to make enough money to provide bare subsistence. If unable to meet an order for cloth or garment pieces within the specified time, homeworkers might jeopardize future employment. In addition, they had to contend with the common practice of *fining*:

> When an employee in a factory or contractor's shop does imperfect work, necessitating an alteration, only the time required to make the alteration is lost. On the other hand, a person working at home must carry the goods back again, frequently losing half a day because of having to make an alteration which in actual work only requires a few minutes of time. To avoid this they are often willing to submit to a fine or reduction in wages far in excess of what the making of the alteration would be worth to them. (McIntoch, 1996: 151)

While garment-industry sweatshops were primarily a feature of Ontario and Quebec, female "home sewers" could be found across the country. In British Columbia before 1900, the majority of Chinese women immigrants who worked for pay performed such piecework. The province's garment industry (predominantly controlled by Chinese men) was one of the few sources of employment Chinese women found open to them under conditions that were similar to those of their white working-class sisters in other parts of the country: "Chinese women and girls [in British Columbia] worked long hours for low pay for Chinese tailors in urban centres …. While many women spent much of their time sewing buttonholes, the sewing trade included other occupations such as seamstresses, tailoresses and dressmakers" (Adilman, 1992: 316–17).

Working for a pittance and without employment rights of any kind forced many garment workers in early industrial Canada to supplement their income by other means—some legitimate and some less reputable. Money from "plying the sex trade"—itself piecework of a different sort—often made the difference for the female garment worker between a small surplus and a deficit. However, these garment-trade pieceworkers were not the only ones forced to combine prostitution with other forms of paid employment. The jobs open to women mirrored in many respects their work in the home—i.e., servicing the needs of others, referred to above as "caring work"—and all were poorly paid.

Perhaps most vulnerable of all were women in domestic service, working in bourgeois households. In 1881 "female domestics" comprised nearly 50 per cent of women workers, making it by far the largest category of paid work. Included under this umbrella were charwomen, cooks, housekeepers, laundresses, nurses and nursemaids, and servants. Immigrant women outweighed the Canadian-born population in almost every subcategory (Rotenberg, 1974: 68).

Although female domestics—unlike other unskilled women workers—had free room and board, as well as higher wages, they were also the most likely to work in the sex trade on a part-time and eventually full-time basis. What explains this apparent contradiction? Certainly they were in demand, due in part to the difficulty of attaining and retaining servants:

> The first hired domestics in British Columbia were Indian women, derogatorily "Klootchmen." Considered inadequate by white employers, they were replaced by selected immigrant women. To the chagrin of employers who, in some cases, paid their fares, most of these women either married shortly after arrival or found more lucrative and less binding employment. (Marie, 1980: 5)

One explanation for the rapid turnover of domestic servants was the harsh conditions under which they had to work. The servant most in demand in Canada between 1880 and 1920 was a kind of "Jill of all trades," who could prepare meals, clean house, sew clothes, mind children, and take care of whatever else needed doing (Leslie, 1974: 74). Those in rural areas usually carried out additional tasks, including caring for farm animals, assisting in the fall harvest, and tending to the needs of farmhands employed during peak periods. Even in urban areas domestic servants needed plenty of muscle power, energy, and ingenuity to keep up with their wide assortment of tasks; hours of service often stretched to 16 hours a day, and 6- or 7-day weeks were commonplace. Isolated from their kind, they resided in private households in living quarters that often barely deserved to be called such. Typically they slept in windowless areas such as basements or attics. Their work rights regarding schedules and tasks were virtually non-existent. The major requirement of the female domestic servant (beyond her physical abilities) was that she be able to take orders, to be submissive: "domestic servants were encouraged to model themselves after Christ, the Suffering Servant, and sacrifice their own interests for their employers' without complaint" (Leslie, 1974: 84)

Despite (or perhaps because of) the hard work involved, domestic service was held in very low esteem—in fact, "the closest to prostitution in the social scale of female occupations" (Rotenberg, 1974: 83). In addition to cruel conditions and long hours, domestic servants were vulnerable to sexual abuse by male employers and their sons. Should a domestic servant become pregnant after such an encounter, dismissal by the mistress was in almost every case the result. The domestic's only alternative was to conceal her pregnancy, seek out a back-street abortion, or perhaps resort to infanticide or abandoning her newborn. For those who kept their "illegitimate" baby, marriage prospects were bleak and subsequent domestic jobs extremely difficult to attain. Slipping into prostitution was often the only way to support themselves and their child.

White domestic servants were not the only category of "fallen woman" in the towns and cities of late nineteenth-century Canada. There were both native and black female prostitutes in many parts of the country (Cooper, 1996; Noel, 1996). Other visible minority women,[2] including Chinese women on the northwest coast, sometimes combined prostitution with piecework or domestic service; others worked exclusively in the sex trade. Chinese women in their early teens or twenties were transported from China to what is now British Columbia by Chinese men after paying a "head tax."[3] Between 200 and 300 Chinese women were brought to the province in the last decades of the nineteenth century. Their going price on the local market ranged from $500 to $2 000 (Adilman, 1992: 314). The poorest of prostitutes in the Chinatown of what is now Victoria, BC, during this time were called *crib prostitutes*:

> The "cribs," each of which held up to six women, were slatted crates, often located out of doors, measuring approximately 12 feet by 14 feet with a curtain, pallet, wash basin, mirror, and usually two chairs. A woman forced into crib prostitution would work for six to eight

years; at the end of her usefulness, when she was ravaged by disease, physical abuse or starvation, she was allowed to escape to the Salvation Army, the hospital, or the gutter. (Adilman,
1992: 314)

Apart from the various jobs described above, a small number of women from the lower-
middle and middle classes were able to access work in what were believed to be more "en-
nobling" or "caring" professions that emerged in the second half of the nineteenth century.
Included in these were trained nurses, later known as "ladies with the lamp," made famous
by the English social reformer Florence Nightingale. Virtually all trained nurses were female
and expected to work long hours for very low wages in charity hospitals while still students. Private duty nursing was the only real employment option for graduate nurses and "it
is estimated that 85 percent of all active graduates were engaged in private nursing before
1909" (Coburn, 1974: 145). At this time trained nurses in Canada had no legal mechanism
to distinguish themselves from the untrained "practical" nurses, nursemaids, and others
without formal schooling, roughly one-third of whom were immigrant women, who competed
with graduates for private employment. Wages for trained nurses were in fact so low that even
those graduates with steady employment barely made ends meet. Virtually all trained nurses
remained unmarried (they were said to be "married to their work") and thus depended solely
upon their wages for subsistence. Trained nurses attempting to specialize in a more autonomous branch of health care, such as midwifery, met with strong opposition from physicians, who were trying to carve out a corner of this market for themselves (Benoit, 1998; see
also Chapter 5).

The situation of "schoolmarms," the colloquial term that originally referred to female elementary school teachers, was analogous to that of nurses. It was expected that the female
teacher would instil "some of the saintliness of womanhood into the education system,"
and at the same time allow significant savings in salaries for boards of education, since
"women would have to be paid only half what men demanded, and they could be counted
on not to complain as well!" (Graham, 1974: 181). The annual salary of a beginning female teacher in Toronto at the turn of the century was just above that of the charwoman, and
below that of the street-sweeper and stockyard labourer. Salaries for rural female teachers
were lower still, sometimes only one third of their urban counterparts. The following is an
excerpt called "The Country Teacher," from an early newspaper in Alberta:

> The requirements of the country teacher are many. She must be a primary, intermediate,
> grammar grade, and high school teacher combined, she must be able to build fires, adjust
> fallen stove pipes, put in window panes, sweep, dust, split kindling, drive a horse, keep out the
> neighbouring quarrels, know how and where to whip a bad boy, raise money for libraries,
> and pass an examination in the branches of modern education. For these accomplishments, she
> receives $45.00 a month. Out of this she pays her board, buys her clothes, buys educational
> paper and books and furnishes slate pencils for pupils. (*The Pincher Creek Echo* 25 Nov.
> 1909)

Such were some of the employment options for women in Canada during the first phase
of capitalism. The rigid ideology of separate spheres was used to justify women's exclusion
from the centres of power in the emerging market economy, confining bourgeois women to
a sheltered life of relative comfort and restricting the employment opportunities for less
privileged women, including those with male partners unable to bring in a family wage, as
well as for others forced to provide for themselves as single women, widows, and solo
mothers.[4] For the vast majority of women, whether employed as pieceworkers in the cot-
tage/sweated industry, domestic servants, or prostitutes, working conditions were poor and

pay was meagre. For those women slightly more advantaged in terms of pay and working conditions, the ideology of separate spheres shaped their occupational positions in private nursing and school teaching, justifying their low salaries and lack of autonomy.

These and other lines of employment (not discussed due to lack of space) continued for Canadian women into the next century. At the same time, a new form of paid work in centralized workplaces or *factories* became commonplace, and we turn now to this type of women's work.

THE SECOND PHASE: INDUSTRIAL CAPITALISM AND THE RISE OF THE FACTORY

> One should see them coming into the town every morning and leaving it every evening. Among them are large numbers of women, pale, starving, wading barefoot through the mud … and young children, in greater numbers than the women, just as dirty, just as haggard, covered in rags, which are thick with the oil splashed over them as they toiled by the looms. (Kuczynski, 1967: 59)

The shift from mercantilist small-scale manufacturing to centralized factory production resulted from the development of innovative technologies, new sources of energy, and a new way of organizing labour, which taken together immensely increased labour efficiency and profits (Hedley, 1992). The invention and subsequent commercialization of increasingly efficient technologies in the textile industry, to take one example, beginning in England with the flying shuttle in the 1730s, the *spinning jenny* in the 1760s, the *mule* in 1768, and spinning machines powered by James Watt's steam engine, enormously magnified productivity.

The latter technological developments produced machines that, compared to those employed in the putting-out system, were massive in size and weight, and so required a centralized location—a *factory*—with workers gathered under one roof. Spinning was now mechanized. Manual weaving initially kept pace through a proliferation of hand looms in weavers' home-workshops. But eventually the loom was mechanized as well (the power loom was invented in the 1780s), and the livelihoods of manual weavers were profoundly imperilled: "thereafter the weavers who had been attracted into the industry before were eliminated from it by the simple device of starvation, and replaced by women and children in factories" (Hobsbawm, 1968: 59).

These developments, which historians refer to as the first *Industrial Revolution*, had results that were indeed revolutionary, not only in regard to the organization of paid and unpaid work, but also to the rhythm of daily life, the size and geographic distribution of population, the relationship between men and women, the nature of politics, and the ideology of productive work and domesticity. Social revolutionaries such as Karl Marx and Friedrich Engels were horrified, not by the technical progress underway, but by its exploitative system of organizing labour. As Eric Hobsbawm states:

> The "factory" with its logical flow of processes, each a specialized machine tended by a specialized "hand," all linked together by the inhumane and constant pace of the "engine" and the discipline of mechanization, gas-lit, iron-ribbed and smoking, was a revolutionary form of work …. Workers were reluctant to enter them, because in doing so men lost their birthright, independence. Indeed, this is one reason why they were filled, where possible with the more tractable women and children: in 1838 only twenty-three per cent of textile factory workers were adult men. (1968: 68)

Compared to Britain, much of Continental Europe, and the United States, Canada was a late starter in developing the factory system (Laxer, 1985). Nevertheless, by 1871 women and children comprised 30 to 40 per cent of the industrial workforce in Toronto and Montreal. By the 1880s the majority of Toronto's labour force working in so-called "light industry"—clothing, shoes, tobacco, furniture—were women and children. Similarly, in the Quebec cotton industry in the early part of this century, women operatives made up nearly half of the factory labour force. Whenever unemployment increased in Canada during a downward trend in the market, women from various pockets of the country would migrate to the industrial heartland of the US to obtain those kinds of work no longer available at home. Between 1880 and 1921 more than 165 000 Maritime women made this journey in search of factory jobs, but also for work as "shopgirls," telephone operators, stenographers, and the like, many never before having been away from their farming or fishing villages (Prentice et al., 1996: 130).

Girls entered textile mills in Montreal and Toronto in the last decades of the nineteenth century as young as 11 and 12 years of age, and typically remained there until they married. And "by the turn of the century two-thirds of the 200 confectionary workers employed by the [Ganong Brothers factory in St. Stephen, New Brunswick] were female, mostly young and single, a pattern not disturbed until the Second World War" (Philips and Philips, 1993: 17). It was assumed that single women would reside with their families, contributing to family maintenance by paying room and board. According to the doctrine of separate spheres, the assumption was that upon marriage, women would want to give up their factory jobs and devote themselves to their husbands and children (Krahn and Lowe, 1993: 152–53). Although "staying at home" was possible for bourgeois women, as well as some working-class married women whose husbands had steady employment and good wages, the majority of women could not organize their lives to reflect this ideology of "women's place." Women without a male breadwinner, or with one frequently underemployed or unemployed, often sought home-based work to make ends meet, while others undertook domestic service or, should all else fail, prostitution. Factory employment was attractive in comparison, and many married women, even those with very young children, sought such work.

The early northwest coast fish-canning industry in the mid to late nineteenth century relied heavily for a time on Native women to perform the most repetitive low-paying tasks that men refused to do—cleaning and packing fish, and soldering cans. They often had their infants in tow, "strapped onto the mothers' backs while the women proceeded with their tasks. Obviously, the conditions of the canneries, which were damp and poorly ventilated, were not always conducive to the health of the infants, but the efficiency of the women cannery workers indicates that the infants' presence did not interfere with their mothers' work" (Cooper, 1996: 111). After the 1870s, Native women were replaced in the canneries by Chinese and Japanese immigrant women. Surviving photos reveal that many immigrant women also brought their infants to the canneries, often working with young children around their feet (Marie, 1980: 10).

Regardless of their age, marital status, whether alone or accompanied by their young children, female factory workers put in long, physically draining hours working with extremely noisy machinery. Managers ran the factories with quasi-penal authority, and were especially prone to penalizing women and children for the most minor infractions. Pay reductions were routine and health and safety rules virtually absent.

The *Factory Acts,* passed in Canada in the late nineteenth and early twentieth centuries, reflect that era's sexist views of women factory workers. Some of the legislation was intended to improve the working conditions of all factory employees: the Workman's Compensation Act of 1886 required that employers provide protectors on hazardous machinery, minimum ventilation on the shop floor, lunchrooms and toilet facilities, and for female factory workers, hairnets to prevent their hair from being caught in machinery (Prentice et al., 1996: 130–31).[5] The Ontario Factory (1884), Shops (1888), and Mines (1890) Acts attempted to deal with another major problem of early capitalism: "the indiscriminate consumption of labour power regardless of age or sex" (Ursel, 1988: 118). These Acts established 14 years as the minimum legal age at which a girl could become gainfully employed in a factory (12 for boys), and restricted the working day of women and girls to 10 hours per day or 60 hours per week, with a one-hour break for the noon meal. Women and girls were also barred from jobs in factories and mines that might endanger their "reproductive health." Similar legislation was enacted subsequently in other parts of Canada (1885 in Quebec), although it was not until well into the twentieth century that such laws took hold in Newfoundland and Labrador.[6] While intended to create cleaner and safer work environments for women working in factories, the new legislation also seriously constrained their employment opportunities. One such act in BC, for example, restricted women from lifting more than 39 pounds, essentially barring female fish-plant workers from less stationary and higher paying "male" jobs involving toting fish from one work station to another (Stainsby, 1994: 68). The situation worsened after minimum-wage laws were passed for female but not male workers. The first of such gender specific minimum-wage laws was passed by Alberta in 1917. Subsequent legislation was passed in British Columbia and Manitoba (1918), Saskatchewan and Quebec (1919), and Nova Scotia and Ontario (1920) (Prentice et al., 1996). Though it was not always put into practice, the minimum-wage legislation had the unanticipated consequence in many provinces of reducing the attraction of female workers to employers, who instead looked to male employees to work longer hours at cut-rate (below the female minimum) wages. Increasingly factory jobs for women were narrowed to the light industries, leaving the higher-paid, more secure heavy-industry jobs to men, who ultimately improved their (male) worker rights by organizing unions.

Seemingly humanistic in intent, these various pieces of legislation were based on a constricted view of womanhood that favoured both employers and working-class men. Moreover, social reformers who called for legislation to protect women and children in factory jobs did not examine the other kinds of paid work women pursued at the time, some of which were even more poorly paid and equally (if not more) exploitative, including home-based work, domestic service, and prostitution. Perhaps the answer is found in Jane Ursel's argument that "it appears that the closer work and the working environment approximated women's traditional place in society, the less appropriate legislators felt the need for state regulation and intervention, regardless of how exploitative the conditions of labour were" (1988: 125).

In hindsight, it is interesting to note that of those expressing concern for the predicament of the "factory girl," few thought to ask women themselves how they conceived their employment conditions and what tactics they might suggest as progressive. Had women factory workers been given a voice, undoubtedly the most serious omission of the protective legislation—the wage disparity between themselves and their male counterparts in the same or similar job—would have been exposed. Census data from the early twentieth century indicates that women factory workers in eastern and central Canada earned between 55 and 60 per cent of male wages. When the cost of living was taken into account, it was clear that most female factory workers without dependents barely made ends meet (having a calculated surplus of $2.43), and that those on their own with dependents *did not* do so, but faced a deficit

($14.23) (Rotenberg, 1974: 48–49). Even working-class men in the trade union movement, caught between their pledge to the brotherhood of men and society's view of women's role, were unwilling to extend help to their working-class sisters. One male social reformer writing in the BC working-class newspaper *Western Clarion*, went so far as to reprimand women wage earners for pursuing equal pay for the same or similar work, regardless of gender:

> The wage of the male is in the main fixed by the requirements of the head of a family, upon whom is dependent the future supply of the wage slaves. Your [the female industrial worker's] wage is based upon the requirements of the individual …. You are helping to cheapen him. You intensify his struggle to live, and, ironical though it may seem, insofar as you crowd him from industry you aggravate the poverty of your own sex, the wife and daughters dependent upon him. (Quoted in Creese, 1992: 372)

Jewish Women and the Labour Movement in Ontario

The Canadian labour movement in the early part of the twentieth century was dominated by the "craft unions," and heavily controlled by men. "Early in this century, craft unions lobbied with middle-class reformers to keep women out of the industrial labour force (allegedly to protect them). Such efforts discouraged union initiatives by women, thereby defining the union movement as a male institution" (Krahn and Lowe, 1998: 346). Yet women's union involvement also varied by industry and ethnicity. While Jewish women in the needle trades faced formidable barriers to equal participation with unionized male workers, for example, at times women garment workers were found to be quite militant, to the extent that "the clothing industry was arguably the most important sector of women's strike activity" (Kealey, 1991: 6). Nevertheless, the chief complaint of male workers in the cotton industry was that their women counterparts were "an element which it is very difficult to organize" (Frager, 1992: 101). Yet as Ruth Frager notes:

> what was needed was an informed analysis of the barriers women workers faced. Such an analysis could have formed the basis for developing special policies to recruit women in particular. In fact, however, male union leaders seem to have had little insight as to why it was difficult for women to participate fully in union and strike activities. Yet women workers' difficulties stemmed not only from their vulnerable position on the shop floor but also from the ways in which household obligations restricted their ability to participate fully in the labour movement. (1992: 101)

It would be a long time still before the reality behind Canadian women workers' apparent lack of commitment to union activities was unveiled.

The "brotherhood of men," it seems, meant something different than equality for all; it meant employment privilege for white working-class males and discrimination against the majority, who were non-white and female (Klein and Roberts, 1974: 220–21). Asian wage earners in BC, for example, were banned from membership in the labour movement until 1927. Employed women were granted union membership earlier, but only as a sort of second class to their white male counterparts, even in unions in which women formed the bulk of the membership, such as the garment industry, packing-plant industry, retail clerks, laundry workers, food industry, cannery workers, and sugar refinery workers. A lengthy strike at the Vancouver Sugar Refinery in 1917 resulted in a wage settlement of "a 10 cent wage increase for male workers but nothing for the women, even though the women earned only $.17 to $.20 an hour, while men already earned a minimum of $.32 an hour" (Creese, 1992: 371).

By marginalizing or excluding women or those from minority ethnic and racial groups from unions, and supporting employers' differential wage schemes for work of the same or similar value, unionized male workers kept wages generally low, often below the rate of inflation, even the family wage itself. Because many women did not have a male breadwinner to support them, and other women sought employment outside of the home regardless of economic need, the male wage earner was placed in a precarious position: a "reserve army of labour" was ready and willing to take his job for a reduced wage, thereby lowering his bargaining power. But by then capitalism in Canada was entering a new stage of its early phase, with new demands for women's employment. The result was once again a revision of the gender contract underlying Canadian society's views on women's paid and unpaid work.

THE THIRD PHASE: MONOPOLY CAPITALISM

> Most of the new clerical jobs created in manufacturing and service industries between 1911 and 1931 were fundamentally different from the craft-like bookkeeping jobs typical of the nineteenth-century office .... Women were considered more suitable for this new stratum of clerical jobs than men. Lower female wages, the higher career aspirations of male clerks and the stereotypes of women as better able to perform monotonous, routine work underlay this shift in clerical labour demand. (Lowe, 1986: 101)

The twentieth century heralded a shift in leading-nation status from Britain to the United States (and to a lesser extent Germany), the rise of the joint-stock corporation, the bureau-cratization of administration, and a new phase of monopoly capitalism. The invention of the internal combustion engine, and of technology efficient in generating and transmitting large amounts of electricity at reasonable prices, promoted industrial production on a large scale. One of the most commercially successful inventions of the period, the automobile, gen-erated an industry that progressed from the annual production of 20 000 cars at the turn of the century to 6 million by 1929. Eighty-five per cent of the cars manufactured by this date were produced in the United States, with the great American industrialist, Henry Ford, dom-inating the surging market. Ford's success was based on a combination of increased mech-anization with assembly-line methods:

> With assembly-line production, jobs become increasingly specific to the technology used in a given plant. Such jobs were considered *semi-skilled* because they required a specific skill but one that could be learned in a relatively short time, often one or two weeks. A smaller portion of workers were required to have more generalised skills, such as those of the machinist, electrician, or tool and die maker. (Hodson and Sullivan, 1995: 26–27)

The assembly-line production base of the Ford plants was rationalized by the introduc-tion of principles of *scientific management* contrived by the innovative industrial engineer, Frederick Taylor. Based on his experience on the shop floor of a steel mill, Taylor noted nu-merous inefficiencies on the part of management, as well as employee laziness or "soldier-ing," and recommended scientific techniques to rectify the situation. The resulting strategy became known as Taylorism: "the managers assume ... the burden of gathering together all of the traditional knowledge which in the past has been possessed by the workmen and then ... classifying, tabulating, and reducing this knowledge to rules, laws, and formulae .... All possible brain work should be removed from the shop and centered in the planning or lay-out department" (Taylor, 1911: 39, 63).

By the early decades of the century, the foundations of modern industry had been laid in the US with the stopwatch and the time-and-motion hallmarks of the scientifically managed mass production process (Hodson and Sullivan, 1995: 190–91). The resulting efficiency proved to be highly attractive to industrialist giants such as Ford, providing relatively cheap mass-produced goods for the growing domestic (and eventually international) market. Although workers resisted the dehumanizing effects of mass production, they nevertheless made gains, often through their newly formed unions, that negotiated for their membership not only attractive wages, but also statutory holidays, shorter workdays, job security, and other fringe benefits.

In brief, a new phase of capitalism (sometimes also referred to as *Fordism*) had arrived— "the rise of an economy composed of a handful of giant lumps of rock—trusts, monopolies, oligopolies—rather than a large number of pebbles" (Hobsbawm, 1968: 177). Compared to earlier periods, optimists such as Daniel Bell (1975: 459–60) viewed the new stage of capitalism as nothing short of revolutionary because of its magical mix of technical efficiency and capital accumulation. Canada also took this route, although comparatively late in its development. In fact, it was not until 1920 that industry had taken over agriculture in economic output. By this time large-scale industrial plants had become dominant features in the urban landscape of Canadian cities, east and west.

Large-scale industrial unions also formed part of the developments of the time. Working-class male wage earners had first organized into craft unions (the first legal union activity in Canada was in 1872); now they represented the skilled trades that made up the so-called *aristocracy of labour* at the national and sometimes international levels. Included were printers, carpenters, bricklayers, masons, cabinetmakers, blacksmiths, shoemakers, and tailors (Krahn and Lowe, 1998). Still virtually absent from the ranks of the emerging labour aristocracy were women wage earners and many immigrant groups employed in the semi-skilled and unskilled mass production industries. It was well into the twentieth century before industrial unions began to dominate working-class labour organizations, eventually absorbing the specialized skilled labour unions organized along traditional craft-like lines.

Not only were women virtually absent from the unionized industrial workforce, but even in those industries where they were employed in large numbers—in clothing and textiles, but by this point also electrical engineering, printing, publishing, and assembly plants— little attention was paid by union organizers to the underlying gender segregation of tasks that assigned women to lower-ranking, lower-paid positions. According to unionists, speaking on behalf of their working-class male constituents, the critical campaign for a suitable *family wage* would be jeopardized if gender equality in employment were adopted as a cardinal union principle. Once again, sexism and capitalism reinforced each other so that both the male worker and the employer benefited at the expense of the underpaid female employee. It made little sense to organize women wage earners, according to many male unionists, as women lacked long-term devotion to their jobs and did not "possess the spirit of solidarity, characteristic of men in industry" (Prentice et al., 1996: 261).

The *administrative revolution* that accompanied the new phase of capitalism was based on a similarly sexist ideology of women's work and place. Management by a few male mid-level supervisors and clerks proved ineffectual as firms and plants grew in size and technical methods became increasingly intricate. Bureaucratization was the answer, whereby pyramid-shaped management systems replaced the foreman and the male clerk "who learned his craft through apprenticeship and carried the office systems in his head" (Lowe, 1986: 101). Rational, formalized procedures supplanted the simpler, more personal administrative arrangement of the early factory system. One positive outcome was employment opportunities for single women in newly created clerical jobs. Like factory employment in the previous era, clerical jobs—stenographers, bookkeepers, secretaries, clerk-typists, bank tellers, telephone operators, and sales clerks—were seen by white lower-middle- and middle-class women as a step up from factory employment and other female job ghettos, where visible minority and Aboriginal women were more often found. Yet these new *pink collar jobs* had the least prestige and lowest pay in the bureaucratic hierarchy. Despite their more attractive physical working conditions, the new clerical jobs open to women shared many of the structural features of women's blue-collar industrial jobs. Both types were shaped by the doctrine of separate spheres that justified women's low wages and subordinate social status, despite the fact that they—even those who wanted to—were often unable to fall back on marriage and the economic support of a male breadwinner.

The apparent shortcomings of the female sex regarding career commitment were temporarily overlooked, however, during wartime, when able-bodied men were called away to battle and workers were needed to "man" heavy industry. Such was the case in Canada during both the First and Second World Wars. During World War I, a severe labour shortage did not occur until 1917, one year before the war ended. It was predominantly single women who were recruited to handle previously male manual jobs in plants producing war supplies, as well as middle-management positions in private industry and government. Steel and cement companies involved in war production also recruited single women for manual employment, as did fire halls and the railroad (for freight handling). Many single women in domestic service were recruited into factory and clerical employment, often occupying high-ranking positions normally held by men. Wages for employed women in a variety of jobs improved, narrowing (although never erasing) the gendered wage discrepancy (Ramklawansingh, 1974).

Traditional attitudes on married women's employment were more tenacious, however, maintaining the assumption that for single women, employment was nothing more than an interlude before marriage and devotion to the full-time duties of being a wife and mother. While single women in Canada were employed in place of men during World War I, this was considered only a temporary measure until the men returned and women could again fulfil their true vocation of marriage and motherhood (Prentice et al., 1996: 144–46). Indeed, following the war, many women saw their new-found employment transferred back to men, and the historic gender division—in which women were viewed as secondary wage earners and dependents of husbands and fathers—reinstated.

Attitudes towards Canadian women wage earners differed little during the Second World War, except that the labour shortage ensued earlier and eventually necessitated the recruitment of young mothers as well as childless women into wartime production. But what were mothers to do with their children? Sidestepping any social responsibility for childcare, both part-time and evening employment were recommended initially, with the expectation that women with young children or other dependents would rely on relatives and other women to manage their double work burden. However, as the labour shortage intensified, mothers were needed as full-time employees. "At the height of munitions production in 1941, which was also the year of conscription, there were at least 35 000 women employed in munitions

Women Workers in a Male Blue-Collar Enclave

Mining in Canada has been carried out by an exclusively male labour force during most of this century. Female pioneers venturing into this male dominated employment in recent decades have had to face numerous obstacles. Yet mining also offers significant advantages to women when compared to many traditional "female" occupations. Leslie E. Martin lived in the Yukon during 1979–80 and spent six months as a "participant-observer" mineworker, which she followed by interviews and further research on the gendered underpinnings of the Cyprus Anvil open-pit mine. According to Martin (1986: 252), women miners of Cyprus Anvil were a small minority of the total labour force, such that their daily work world rarely involved interactions with other women. The men "delight[ed] in symbolic statements of their fearlessness and disregard for danger …. Attention to sexual differentiation [was] articulated daily in work: virtually every time a fe-

male voice [was] heard over the pit radio communications system, prolonged and squeaky kissing sounds filled the airwaves. Through ever recurring sexual banter, women [were] frequently reminded of their presence in a predominantly masculine work culture." Women who had successfully passed their truck-driving job classification were "lady drivers," a label that male colleagues uttered accompanied by laughter. However, according to Martin's interviews with female mineworkers (1986: 260), "when asked to evaluate [their former jobs] in relation to their current work, the near unanimous response was that they infinitely preferred minework. Working conditions, particularly relationships with other crew members and foremen, crew camaraderie, the variety of tasks, the opportunity to learn, the challenges, the high pay and vacation benefits are frequently cited as much preferable to more conventional women's work."

plants located in Ontario and Montreal" (Ramklawansingh, 1974: 276). The situation forced the development of novel government initiatives to aid recruitment. The Income Tax Act was revised after the war so that a wife could retain her "dependent" status despite her earnings. However, her husband could not claim the married status exemption (Pierson, 1986). In fact, given the increased poverty experienced by Canadian families during the Great Depression, which had ended just prior to the war, full-time employment for married women during World War II was as much an economic necessity as a response to the call for patriotic loyalty and service to one's country.

A second major government initiative was the establishment of public daycare centres under the dominion-provincial Wartime Day Nurseries Agreement. This innovative plan shared the cost of institutional daycare for children aged two and over between federal and provincial governments. However, only Ontario and Quebec participated in the accord. French-Canadian Roman Catholics voiced strong opposition to the plan, denouncing government sponsored daycare centres as leading to the destruction of family life (Pierson, 1986). Nevertheless, the establishment of publicly funded childcare was remarkable, as for the first time governments acknowledged women's unpaid reproductive care and made public what had hitherto been private.

This newly created social responsibility for children was not to last. In the period immediately following World War II the government retrenched services created to encourage women's paid employment. Economic support for day nurseries was withdrawn and the Income Tax Act was re-amended so that a husband could no longer claim full married-status exemption if his wife earned more than $250 annually, well below the $750 figure established prior to the war. *Marriage bars* were enacted (as they were during the Great Depression) and married women employed in government bureaucracies were dismissed. At the same time, female industrial employees were steered back into their "natural" lines of employment—i.e., to the most subordinate positions—and others were forced to seek employment elsewhere, including the despised domestic service. Service women who had participated directly in the war were dismissed or demoted to low-ranking positions in the army bureaucracy: "in 1944, at the peak of wartime employment, one-third of all women over the age of 15 had been in the paid labour force. Two years later, only one-quarter were working for pay" (Prentice et al., 1996: 350). Once again, married women employed outside the home were believed to create chaos in Canadian society by transgressing dominant gender "norms." To be a mother and homemaker was the only respectable career for the adult female, as the *gender ideology of difference* reasserted itself and these roles once again defined women's identity and economic location in society. But societal pressure to keep married women at home was interrupted: Canada was on the brink of becoming a service society and women, as skilled service providers, were to remain a central feature of the emerging workforce.

THE FOURTH PHASE: POST-INDUSTRIAL SOCIETY

> A worker needs more than a vague sense of contentment. He needs, let it be repeated, to feel that he is participating responsibly, whether alone or in a group, in an enterprise the overall objects of which he can understand ... the one exception here may be woman workers who, their minds usually being full of subjects out and beyond their chore, are conceivably happier doing repetitive work. (Falk, 1970: 164)

Beginning in the 1950s, escalating in the 1960s, and continuing with a decline only in the recent period of the globalization of production, the employment of women stands out as a distinguishing feature of all high-income countries, including Canada. Virtually all increase in women's employment has been in the *tertiary or service sector*, while paid work in resource extraction and manufacturing (strongholds of male employment) has declined. This increase in women's employment in the new "service society" (Bell, 1975) has included married women with children at home, and even those with children under six years of age.

As indicated in Table 3–2, in 1981 42.4 per cent of women with their youngest child under age 6 were employed; by 1994 this figure had risen to 57.1 per cent. For women with their youngest child aged 6–15 years, the employment change over time was equally significant: from 56.6 per cent in 1981 to 68.6 per cent in 1994.

The numbers of gainfully employed women who are separated, widowed, or divorced (the "other" category) have also shown a steady increase during the 30-year period. The opposite has been the case for single women, as opportunities to pursue higher education have greatly expanded, especially since the 1960s (Statistics Canada, 1995: 64). The percentage of all categories of women in the Canadian labour force increased from 48 per cent in 1981 to 52.1 per cent in 1997, while the percentage for men declined from a high of 73.1 in 1981 to 65.8 in 1997.

As with single women and women on the margins of society (solo mothers, poor married women, divorced, deserted, and widowed women, and women facing economic and racial discrimination), the primary reason for the growth of married women's employment in the post-war period has been *economic*: women's income is needed to maintain families. Average real wages (adjusted for inflation) for paid workers in Canada rose in the decades following the war but then actually declined in the 1980s, so that the purchasing power of workers and their families deteriorated. One of the main reasons that wives and mothers who previously stayed at home entered the labour force was to shore up family income and make ends meet.

TABLE 3–2	**Percentage of Employed Women with Children (by age of youngest child): 1981–1994**					
	Youngest child less than age 3	Youngest child aged 3–5	Youngest child less than age 6	Youngest child aged 6–15	Youngest child less than age 16	Youngest child less than age 16 living at home
1981	39.4	47.1	42.4	56.6	49.7	45.8
1982	39.5	46.8	42.3	55.7	49.1	45.2
1983	42.0	48.1	44.4	55.4	50.0	45.3
1984	44.1	49.2	46.2	57.4	51.9	45.8
1985	46.7	52.1	48.9	59.1	54.1	46.4
1986	49.2	54.5	51.3	61.9	56.7	47.1
1987	50.3	56.4	52.8	64.0	58.4	47.9
1988	51.8	58.4	54.4	66.8	60.7	49.3
1989	53.0	59.5	55.6	69.1	62.5	49.8
1990	53.5	59.5	55.8	70.3	63.27	50.6
1991	54.4	60.1	56.5	69.0	63.0	49.7
1992	53.7	59.4	55.9	68.1	62.1	49.5
1993	54.6	59.6	56.5	68.7	62.7	49.6
1994	55.7	59.2	57.1	68.6	62.9	49.9

Source: Statistics Canada, *Women in Canada* (1995) 72.

Despite the greater likelihood in recent decades of women to remain attached to the labour force, there are still numerous barriers to their equality with male employees. Canadian women face two forms of labour market discrimination that echo earlier problems: occupational sex segregation and wage disparity. Although increasingly in recent decades the concentration of men and women in the labour force has converged, the occupations performed by each sex have remained relatively distinct.

The majority of women today are still employed in occupations where men were concentrated in earlier stages of capitalism. In 1994 70 per cent of all employed women worked as teachers, nurses, in allied health care positions, clerical jobs, sales, and service positions—the so-called "pink-collar" occupations. The figure for male workers was just 31 per cent. In all of these occupational categories except for sales, women also account for a large majority of the total employed: in 1994 86 per cent of nurses and health-related therapists were women, as were 80 per cent of clerks, 63 per cent of teachers, 56 per cent of service personnel, and 46 per cent of salespersons (Statistics Canada, 1995). This data indicates that occupational sex segregation has eroded very, very slowly. In recent years Canadian women have increased their comparative standing in several professional fields from which they were previously excluded or marginalized. Women in 1994 made up an impressive 43 per cent of managerial employees (29 per cent in 1982), and 32 per cent of all physicians and dentists (18 per cent in 1982). A landmark change also has occurred in the last decade regarding the occupation of midwifery (discussed in detail in Chapter 5).

Yet in the prestigious fields of natural science, engineering, and mathematics, women remain very much the minority, and in those occupations in which women have made significant inroads (such as management, law, and medicine), there persists the *glass ceiling* (a hurdle that is most difficult to see and to climb above). Though the term suggests that one is unaware of the glass ceiling until it is confronted head-on, the fact is that the "glass ceiling is not transparent. It is visible and apparent, particularly to those who experience it" (Auster, 1993: 49). Furthermore, the ceiling is not located "in one spot. It is a gender bias. It occurs all the time and takes many forms" (Auster, 1993: 48). In management, for example, "women are clustered in the least responsible and lowest-paying jobs ... women managers are concentrated in predominantly female enclaves within organizations such as office administration, personnel, and sales" (Krahn and Lowe, 1993: 168). In 1994 70 per cent of all corporate managers were male. Moreover, the few women in management who "make it to the top" risk their careers if they have children, as do women in university positions and other high-ranking occupations. Felice Schwartz (1989) points out that women executives who are also mothers are, from the company's point of view, not serious workers. Their male colleagues, regardless of family status, tend to take the *glass elevator* to the top of the organizational hierarchy, occupying top management positions even when they are a minority of the workforce in occupations where females are prevalent (Williams, 1992). It is worth noting that 90 per cent of male executives aged 40 have both children *and* continuous employment. Schwartz calls for corporations to create a "mommy track" (i.e., more flexible, less-demanding work tasks) for women in top management positions when they have young children. Feminists voice mixed reactions to the development of a mommy track, because although it may help women to cope with their double burden, it allows for the continuation of intra-occupational sex segregation (Reskin and Padavic, 1994: 159).

Gender segregation persists within the prestigious profession of medicine, with female physicians located in the less eminent and lower paid specialities, working shorter hours, and occupying fewer administrative positions in hospitals and other health organizations (Blishen, 1991). One explanation for this gender disparity may be that female physicians lack both the services of a full-time "wife" (enjoyed by most married male physicians) and adequate social benefits to help them meet their childcare and domestic tasks (Apter, 1993).

As Table 3–3 reveals, *wage discrimination* also has persisted in the service society. Women and visible minorities who perform work of equal or similar value to men earn still earn less. There has been slow, incremental progress in wage equity over the past few decades for both the highest paying and lowest paying occupations. In 1980 women in

TABLE 3–3	Number and Average Earnings of Full-year, Full-time Workers in 10 Highest-paying and 10 Lowest-paying Occupations (by sex): Canada 1995				
	Number of Workers		**Average Earnings ($)**		**Women's Income as a Percentage of Men's**
	Men	**Women**	**Men**	**Women**	
All Occupations	4 514 850	2 998 940	$42 488	$30 130	71%
Total—10 Highest-paying Occupations	158 795	38 940	$99 605	$64 716	65%
Judges	1 360	405	$128 791	$117 707	91%
Specialist Physicians	9 345	3 220	$137 019	$86 086	63%
General Practitioners and Family Physicians	16 055	5 615	$116 750	$81 512	70%
Dentists	6 995	1 535	$109 187	$71 587	66%
Senior Managers—Goods Production; Utilities; Transportation; and Construction	32 625	2 880	$102 971	$58 463	57%
Senior Managers—Financial; Communications Carriers; and Other Business Services	19 190	3 860	$104 715	$71 270	68%
Lawyers and Quebec Notaries	32 305	12 080	$89 353	$60 930	68%
Senior Managers—Trade; Broadcasting; and Other Services	24 610	4 060	$84 237	$48 651	58%
Primary Production Managers (Except Agriculture)	6 670	405	$78 421	$48 479	62%
Securities Agents; Investment Dealers; and Traders	9 640	4 880	$90 391	$47 323	52%

(continued on p. 74)

full-time employment averaged 64.2 per cent of male earnings; by 1991 the figure was 70 per cent and had increased to 71 per cent by 1995. There has been further decrease in the gender wage disparity so that by 1996 Canadian women working year-around and full-time earned $30 717 or 73.4 per cent of the male comparison group ($41 848). Canadian males in full-time, full-year employment in 1996 still earned an amazing $10 000-plus more per

TABLE 3-3	Number and Average Earnings of Full-year, Full-time Workers in 10 Highest-paying and 10 Lowest-paying Occupations (by sex): Canada 1995				
	Number of Workers		Average Earnings ($)		Women's Income as a Percentage of Men's
	Men	Women	Men	Women	
Total—10 Lowest-paying Occupations	49 810	181 105	$18 640	$15 146	81%
Sewing Machine Operators	2 490	27 750	$20 664	$17 340	84%
Cashiers	9 025	47 110	$20 557	$16 977	83%
Ironing, Pressing, and Finishing Occupations	990	2 375	$19 297	$16 499	86%
Artisans and Craftspersons	2 840	3 040	$20 555	$13 565	66%
Bartenders	7 080	8 495	$18 899	$14 940	79%
Harvesting Labourers	525	605	$18 683	$14 465	77%
Service Station Attendants	8 630	2 175	$16 520	$14 947	90%
Food Service Counter Attendants and Food Preparers	5 550	16 680	$17 912	$14 681	82%
Food and Beverage Servers	11 940	38 250	$18 192	$13 861	76%
Babysitters; Nannies, and Parents' Helpers	740	34 625	$15 106	$12 662	84%

Source: Statistics Canada, *The Daily*, 12 May 1998c; and author's calculations.

annum than female counterparts (Statistics Canada, 1998c). In sum, across all major occupational categories in Canada even today, women continue to earn less than men. This inequity applies no matter the level of education attained: in 1993 women with some secondary schooling earned 64 per cent of the earnings of men with the same level of education; female university graduates employed full-time earned 75 per cent of what their male counterparts did (Statistics Canada, 1995: 87; see Chapter 4 for more detail on the gendered underpinnings of educational policies).

The gender wage gap lingers not merely because of outright discrimination on the part of employers. Union membership also plays a role. Canadian women's union membership rates have been low compared with those of men. However, the gap has closed slowly over time. Between 1966 and 1992, the *gender union rate gap* has narrowed consistently, so that by 1992 30 per cent of female employees in Canada were union members, which is a substantial increase from 16.4 per cent in 1962. At the same time, the 1992 figure for males was 36 per cent, a slight drop from the 38 per cent unionization rate in 1962 (Akyeampong, 1998).

These figures indicate that the rapid growth of the female labour force in the past few decades has been accompanied by similar growth in union membership. In fact, by 1992 women comprised 42 per cent of all union members. Given that unions tend to win higher relative wages, greater job security, and more fringe benefits for workers, increased levels of female membership should be seen as a major breakthrough. However, most of the unionized female employees tend to be located in the public sector for different levels of government, Crown corporations, schools, and hospitals. They form a privileged category among paid women workers, a *female labour aristocracy*. Indeed, women employed in the public sector, such as government service workers, teachers, nurses, and social workers, register a greater rate of unionization than any other occupational group.

In 1992 42 per cent of female workers were employed in the public sector, 95 per cent of whom were located in five industries: government services, transportation and storage, communication and other utilities, education, and health and social services (Akyeampong, 1998: 3). In 1989 56 per cent of women in public employment were union members, while only 11 per cent of women in other industries were unionized. Between 1989 and 1992, women's union rates in the public sector increased even more, partly because of the overall growth in women's employment in the public sector, but also because of the growth in women's union density in that sector. Between 1992 and 1998, the Canadian public sector declined, and only beginning in early 1999 was it experiencing new employment growth. On the other hand, while women employees outside of the public sector and in part-time employment record relatively low rates of union membership compared to their counterparts in the public sector, since 1992 there has been a growth in union membership for women in male dominated industries, as well as in part-time employment. The recent downsizing of the public sector (and hence women's union rates in these industries) has been compensated by the growth of women's union membership elsewhere, although the latter remains much lower even today. Meanwhile, the union rates for women employees have remained at a virtual standstill over the decade (Akyeampong, 1998).

Not all women in Canada have equal access to even those jobs available to their gender. Aboriginal women, like other non-white women, are doubly disadvantaged, by gender and race. Although such disadvantage is not unique to capitalism, it must also be noted that in the twentieth century Aboriginal women have been marginalized in Canadian society to a greater extent than any other category of women. Prior to 1985, under the sexist provisions of the 1874 Indian Act, an Aboriginal women who married a non-Aboriginal man automatically lost her official designation as Status Indian, including band membership, as did her children. However, Aboriginal men who married non-Aboriginal women not only retained their Indian status, but were able to claim it also for their wives. Under the federal government's Bill C-31, the original Act was finally revised to grant official Indian status to every Aboriginal woman, irrespective of her marital status.

Yet discrimination by race and gender continues to affect Aboriginal women across Canada, placing them in an uncertain position on reserves (lands "reserved" by treaty for status Indians), as well as in the urban areas where most of them live today. In 1991 47 per cent of Aboriginal women were in the labour force, compared with 54 per cent of non-Aboriginal women. While about the same proportion of Aboriginal and non-Aboriginal women are employed part-time (30 per cent in 1991), Aboriginal women record twice the unemployment as other women. Much like other women in Canada, Aboriginal women are largely located in traditional female ghettos, but occupy fewer professional and managerial positions. The average income of Aboriginal women is also comparatively low: in 1990, for example, 33 per cent (compared to 17 per cent of non-Aboriginal women) lived below Statistics Canada's "Low Income Cut-Offs"[7] (the figure for Aboriginal men was 28 per cent, and 13.8 per cent for other men).

Similar findings have been recorded for visible minority women in Canada. In 1991 an estimated 1.3 million Canadian women—9 per cent of all Canadian women—belonged to a visible minority group, up from 800 000 in 1986. Most visible minority women are immigrants to Canada and have arrived in substantial numbers during recent decades. Ironically, although they are more likely than other women in Canada to hold a university degree, visible minority women have somewhat lower employment rates and are less likely to be employed compared to visible minority men. Like other women in Canada, visible minority women are concentrated in traditional female occupations—clerical, service, and sales. However, visible minority women are less likely than other women to hold comparatively attractive professional and managerial positions; in 1991 13 per cent held these positions, compared with 16 per cent of other women. Moreover, visible minority women experience higher unemployment rates than other women in Canada. In 1991 13.4 per cent of visible minority women who qualified for the labour force were unemployed, compared to 9.8 per cent of their non-minority counterparts. Visible minority women also report lower incomes: in 1990, 28 per cent had incomes below the Low Income Cut-Offs, compared with 16 per cent of other women (and 12.9 per cent of non-minority men).

Canadian women chafing under the most precarious economic circumstances of all are those who head families on their own, a situation that the historical record indicates has been the case since the inception of capitalism, and even before then, in the patrilineal societies that predated the arrival of Europeans. In 1931, for example, 13 per cent of families were headed by a solo parent. In 1998 the figure was not much higher at 14.5 per cent. One distinction is that in the 1930s couples tended to separate due to death—fathers were killed during wartime and mothers died in childbirth or of contagious disease—while today most families of this type are the result of separation, divorce, or childbirth outside of legalized marriage. A second major difference is that most solo parents today are women. In fact, 83 per cent of solo parents in Canada in 1994 were female.

Female solo parents are less likely to be employed than women in two-parent families, as Table 3–4 shows. In 1994 27 per cent of female solo parents with a child under 3 years were employed; the comparable figure for mothers in two-parent families was 56 per cent. In 1995 63 per cent of female solo parents with children under age 16 living at home were gainfully employed, compared to 73 per cent of mothers in two-parent families. At the same time, 85 per cent of solo fathers were in the labour force and 94 per cent of men in two-parent families were gainfully employed. When solo mothers do find employment, it is usually part-time and excluded from benefits mandated under employment standards legislation (Duffy and Pupo, 1992: 250).

The 1995 data shows that the age of children is related closely to the labour participation rate of single parents and probably explains much of the distinction between lone mothers and mothers in couples. When there is at least one child under age three, the participation rate of solo mothers is little more than half of that of mothers with a partner. The difference between mothers with older children is much smaller and both labour participation rates are close to 75 per cent. Is this determined by the fact that older children go to publicly financed schools, while lone mothers have much more difficulty juggling family and work responsibilities in our privately financed daycare system? This topic is taken up in Chapter 4.

TABLE 3–4 Labour Force Participation Rate (by gender, family status, and age of children): 1995				
	Women		**Men**	
	in couples	**solo parents**	**in couples**	**solo parents**
At least one child under 3	65	38	94	83
Youngest child 3–5	72	57	95	73
All children 6–15	78	73	94	87

Source: Statistics Canada, *Work Arrangements in the 1990s, 77.*

Despite gains made by Canadian women in the post-industrial period—labour force participation, earnings, employment opportunities, and union membership—barriers continue to hinder their overall equality in Canadian society. As well as occupational sex segregation and wage disparity, women must contend with increased part-time employment[8] as their only choice. While many women workers, especially those with young children, actually prefer to work part-time, it is revealing that in 1994 34 per cent of female part-time employees (compared with 22 per cent in 1989) indicated they would like full-time employment, which was not available to them (Statistics Canada, 1995: 66). Furthermore, as Figure 3–1 reveals, although the proportion of men who work part-time has increased over the decade, women still make up over 70 per cent of all part-time workers in Canada.

Part of this disproportionately high part-time employment status for women stems from the fact that they are still responsible for housework and childcare. While men and women in Canada put in roughly the same amount of labour per week, men are far more likely to receive a wage for their hours of activity, while a substantial proportion of women's work hours are unpaid and invisible in the home (Che-Alford et al., 1994: 39).

One final form of work worth mentioning is self-employment, defined in Canada as including incorporated, unincorporated, and unpaid family members. Self-employment comprised 18 per cent of total Canadian employment in 1997 and almost one-fifth of employees (19 per cent) worked fewer than 35 hours on average per week. Self-employment has been one of the main engines of employment growth in Canada over the last decade, especially with the recent downsizing of the public sector. Women's rate of self-employment has increased to comprise 34 per cent of all self-employed persons working for themselves and 24 per cent of those in self-employment who also employ others (Gardner, 1995). While some women view self-employment as a welcome opportunity to work independently of a boss in a large bureaucratic organization, and others see self-employment as a temporary measure while their children are young, there are difficulties that accompany this line of work. First, self-employment is seldom accompanied by a steady paycheque or fringe benefits, which are taken for granted in full-time, full-year employment. Second, it is often difficult to organize self-employment around family responsibilities, especially when offices are located in private homes. And third, "despite the lower bankruptcy rate among female owners of small

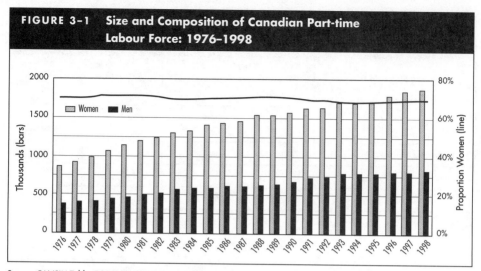

FIGURE 3–1   Size and Composition of Canadian Part-time Labour Force: 1976–1998

Source: CANSIM Tables D984857, D984857, D984862, D984873, D984878, and author's calculations.

businesses … women generally experienced more difficulty than men in securing the credit they needed to start up their enterprises" (Prentice et al., 1996: 358).

In sum, although there is evident progress respecting women's paid and unpaid labour during the latter stages of capitalism in Canada, gender inequality persists for many categories of women, albeit to a greater extent for some than others. Aboriginal and visible minority women, as well as those with a disability, face double discrimination due both to social status (race, ethnicity, and disability) and gender.[9] For similar reasons, solo female parents are also economically disadvantaged. How have women in twentieth-century America and Sweden fared as capitalism developed within their borders? The final sections of this chapter open windows on these two countries in order to place the Canadian experience in perspective.

A SECOND WINDOW ON THE UNITED STATES

With respect to the United States, the emphases on individualism and achievement orientation by the American colonists were an important motivating force in the launching of the American Revolution, and were embodied in the Declaration of Independence. The manifestation of such attitudes in this historic event and their crystallization in an historic document provided a basis for the reinforcement and encouragement of these orientations throughout subsequent American history …. Friedrich Engels, among other foreign visitors, noted that as compared to Europe, the United States was "purely bourgeois, entirely without a feudal past." (Lispet, 1986: 114–15)

The United States industrialized earlier than Canada, and by the turn of the twentieth century was a leading capitalist nation and one of Britain's major economic competitors. In the early decades of the century, many of the innovative developments associated with large-scale manufacturing grew out of American business enterprises, including the assembly line, mass production, and the modern corporation (Lenski et al., 1995). This prosperity grew into the second half of the century: "in the years immediately following the Second World War the United States dominated the world economy. Its domestic market was eight times as large as that of Great Britain, the second leading industrial nation .... American productivity and incomes were the envy of the rest of the world" (Moore, 1996: 53).

Despite the differences between the American and Canadian industrialization experiences and comparative levels of productivity and prosperity, broad elements of women's work and place in American society nevertheless reflect those of Canada. Working-class women in the US undertook home-based work and factory employment in order to contribute to their family's survival and, as in Canada, protective labour laws in the later nineteenth and early twentieth centuries prohibited women from factory work in heavy industry and blocked married women's employment in general (Baxandall et al., 1976). American unions and social reformers argued that women and children needed protection from the ills of industrialization. As in Canada, the doctrine of separate spheres shaped the thinking of the day; American women's proper role was to bear and raise children and care for the private domestic unit; men's rightful place was in the public sphere, in the role of breadwinner (Skolnick, 1991: 30–31). Even sociologists writing during the early part of the century had extreme difficulty conceiving of women combining motherhood with paid work:

> It is generally conceded that in the case of all families having young children and modal incomes—in America this might well mean under fourteen or fifteen—the absence of the mother in wage-earning work operates to the serious physical and moral detriment of the children .... It is here assumed that, as stated before, society cannot well expect or even permit non-domestic "full-time" wagework for women after marriage and during the time when children are still young. (Snedden, 1919: 541, 546)

The result, as in most societies entering the industrial capitalist phase, was the increasing masculinization of the American labour force, with men controlling the centres of economic power and political influence.

However, some features of the emerging economy were distinctive to America. For one thing, labour was readily available and cheap for entrepreneurs, due to government open-immigration policies. Poor women without the support of a breadwinner were available to perform marginal jobs for low wages (Baxandall et al., 1976). African-American women and female immigrants also served as a reserve army of inexpensive labour: "in 1920, for example, only 7 percent of married European-American women were in the labor force, compared to one-third of married African-American women and 18 percent for married Asian-American women" (Reskin and Padavic, 1994: 22). Similar discrepancies in labour force participation rates existed for unmarried American women.

It was not until after World War II that the male-breadwinner/housewife gender contract was undermined, and even then not completely: remnants of this ideology remain, as Americans (like Canadians) continue the assumption that domestic work is women's responsibility, regardless of their employment status (Polakow, 1993: 38–40). In 1975 55 per cent of US women were participating in the labour force; the comparable figure in 1994 was 75 per cent, just slightly below that of Canadian women (OECD, 1995). Many of these US women were mothers, some with young children. Similarly, in 1940 husbands with stay-at-home wives accounted for 67 per cent of all American families; by 1992 comparable figures dropped drastically to only 18 per cent of all families (Reskin and Padavic, 1994: 144). Yet despite American women's increasing labour force participation, a number of indicators suggest that gender inequality lingers in American society, in many measures to an even greater extent than that found in Canada.

In 1997 slightly more than 15 per cent of paid workers in the US worked in part-time positions (defined there as fewer than 35 hours of work in the main or solo job), which is in fact lower than the Canadian part-time rate of 18.9 per cent (Statistics Canada, 1998b). Likewise, while just under 30 per cent of employed women in Canada worked part-time in 1996, the figure for their American counterparts was 26.9 per cent (OECD, 1998; OECD, 1998c). On the other hand, the US rate for women part-timers compared to all part-time workers inched up over the 1990s, while the rate for their Canadian counterparts has decreased slightly (OECD, 1998). And the latter group of part-time workers, although vulnerable in both countries, have a greater likelihood of working enough hours to be eligible for unemployment insurance and vacation pay as well as higher wages, largely because the unionization rate for part-time workers in Canada is over three times that of the rate south of the border: 23.9 per cent of women in part-time employment in 1997 were unionized in Canada, while the comparable US figure was 7.1 per cent (Akyeampong, 1998). In the US, part-time workers have no fringe benefits and—because that country has no national health care system (see Chapter 5)—they also tend not to have health insurance. Furthermore, the average American part-time worker in 1989 earned only 58 per cent of their full-time counterparts (Tilly, 1991); part-time workers in Canada earned about 75 per cent of the wage of full-time workers (Duffy and Pupo, 1992: 166).

A second major difference in the situation of paid female workers between the two countries concerns public sector employment, where women in both countries are strongly represented. Yet in regard to their comparative size and degree of unionization, the US public service is less attractive than its Canadian counterpart. Although among the lowest in the industrial capitalist world even before recent reductions, US public sector employment dropped notably (a full percentage point) between 1989 and 1995, and only recently has seen a slight increase. The trend in Canada has been a very gradual increase in government service employment between 1968 and 1990, followed by a small drop in the size of the public employment sector until the mid 1990s (OECD, 1992; OECD, 1998). Until 1998 the downsizing of Canadian public employment has been heavier, although once again this trend is being reversed with new spending in health, education, and some other government services. Moreover, the public sector in Canada has a relatively high unionization rate—73 per cent in 1997, while the US figure was much lower at 37.2 per cent (OECD; 1998; Akyeampong, 1998).

However, the US appears more impressive in regard to its relatively low levels of *occupational sex segregation*, the degree of concentration of women and men in different kinds of jobs (Charles, 1992). While employed women in the US, like their Canadian counterparts, tend to be concentrated in traditional female job ghettos (clerical, sales, and service occupations), American women nevertheless are more likely to be found in "high status" (male) occupations, especially in management positions in the private sector. US women comprised 18 per cent of all managers in 1970, 30 per cent in 1980, and 40 per cent in 1990 (Reskin and Padavic, 1994: 82). These figures are moderately higher than those in both Canada and Sweden (Charles, 1992: 490; Table 1).

At first glance this finding suggests that the US is more "open" towards women's occupational mobility than Canada or Sweden—and other advanced industrial countries for which there are comparable data. On closer inspection, however, the lower rate of occupational sex segregation in the US can be explained largely by its small public sector (Ginsburg, 1983). Much of women's invisible "caring work" has been transformed into *public sector employment* under the auspices of the welfare state in Canada (and much more so in Sweden, as discussed below). In the US much of this caring work remains invisible in the home or is carried out by voluntary associations administered by philanthropic organizations. There are fewer American women working as paid public sector employees than in many other countries, so that American women's unpaid labour is less socialized (Nermo, 1996).

Also noteworthy is the definite female hierarchical ranking in occupational sex segregation in the United States. African-American and other minority women face the problem of the glass ceiling, or what is otherwise termed the *sticky floor*—non-white women are trapped in low-wage, low-mobility jobs (Berheide, 1992). Affirmative action programs notwithstanding, "being a 'twofer' (a term that personnel directors sometimes use for people who fill two Equal Employment Opportunity categories) may help some minority women get jobs, but it hurts them in promotions because it undermines their credibility" (Reskin and Padavic, 1994: 83). In brief, while American women have done relatively well in attaining management positions in recent decades, it has been primarily a white woman's phenomenon. And even this privileged female category continues to face a "promotion gap" compared with white males. It is worth noting that only two per cent of Fortune top executives today are female—and only half this percentage are minorities.

Similar findings are reported regarding the gender wage gap in the US. In 1992 median earnings for women employed full-time in the US were $22 167 (US dollars), while comparable earnings for men were $31 128; women in full-time employment averaged 71 cents for each dollar that a male employee earned. In 1994 the figure was 72 cents for each dollar. By 1995 median earnings for women working full-time had risen to $23 777, while that of men in full-time employment was $32 199. Women in 1995, then, made 74 cents for every dollar men made, indicating, as in Canada, a very gradual reduction in the gender wage gap for full-time earners over the long stretch (US Bureau of the Census, 1996).

Yet there exist tremendous variations among American women in their relative earnings vis-à-vis men. The share of US workers who were members of unions was 20 per cent in 1983, but had declined to 14.1 per cent of waged and salaried employment in 1997 (US Bureau of Labor Statistics, 1997). American women represented by unions earned 35 per cent more than women in non-unionized work (Chang and Sorrentino, 1991: 48). The gender wage gap also varies widely among American women of different racial and ethnic groups. Hispanic women employed full-time in 1992 earned 78 per cent of the wage of white women; African-American women earned 87 per cent of white women's wages. At the same time, all women earned less than the men of their own ethnic or racial background, and all earned less than white men. For example, among full-time employees in 1995, an amazing 63 per cent of females earned less than $25 000 annually, while the figure for males in this category was only 43 per cent (US Bureau of the Census, 1996).

In the redistribution of non-paid work, the US lags behind most other countries. The primary reason for this discrepancy, as suggested above and discussed in detail in the following chapter, is that the American government assumes little responsibility for the economic well-being of a family, or for the provision or care of its dependent members. In this culture, a parent (in most cases a mother) is responsible for the unpaid labour involved in maintaining a family and raising children (Baker, 1995). In terms of unpaid labour, American women put in more hours of paid and unpaid work per week than both their male partners and their female counterparts in other countries, including Canada, where publicly subsidized childcare and social benefits are more readily available (Sainsbury, 1996).

The plight of solo mothers in the US reveals even more about the entrenched gender inequality in employment and family. There were 12 million families maintained by women in the United States in 1992—double the number of 1970, when there were just 5.6 million solo-parent families. In other words, 3 out of 10 American families with children under 18 years of age have only one custodial parent, the highest rate of all advanced industrial capitalist countries in one recent survey (Baker, 1995). Women in the US are four times more likely to be a solo parent than men. Solo-mother families comprised 14.8 per cent of all US families in 1980, and 17.6 per cent in 1992 (US Department of Labor, Women's Bureau, 1993: 1). Broken into race and ethnic divisions: 14 per cent of all white US families in 1992 were headed by solo mothers, with 47 per cent of all African-American families and 25 per cent of all Hispanic families. On the positive side, the majority of solo mothers in the US are employed: in 1992 the rate was 56 per cent. But their poverty rates—whether employed or not—are substantially higher than those of solo mothers in other industrial capitalist countries (Baker, 1995).

It appears that labour market participation alone cannot advance women's economic standing and capacity to maintain a household. According to Joseph H. Pleck:

> Women's employment patterns in the United States show many commonalities with those in other advanced industrial countries. But one way in which the experience of women's employment in the United States differs markedly from that of other societies is the limited and uneven social policy response to that experience expressed in legislation, collective bargaining, and employer practices. (1992: 248)

As discussed in the following chapter, of crucial importance in this regard is the role that welfare states play in redistributing societal wealth from the rich to the poor—and from men to women—both through taxation and by providing social benefits to 1) reduce gender inequality in paid employment and 2) socialize women's caring work in the family. But first a second window on Sweden.

A SECOND WINDOW ON SWEDEN

> In Sweden the feminization of the paid labor force has been almost complete, resulting in the transformation of family daily life and the lives of women. This transformation has been powerfully shaped by state policy. The archetypal figures of industrial capitalist society have changed. No longer is there a worker and a housewife with their separate but interdependent roles. Instead there are two workers—the classical, male-defined worker and the new worker in whose life the tasks of reproduction and production are intertwined. (Acker, 1994: 38)

Like Canada, Sweden was a late starter along the road to industrial capitalism (Laxer, 1985). Although signs of a market economy were evident as early as the 1870s, at the turn of the century Sweden—once an imperial power of might if not economic influence—had become one of the poorest countries in Western Europe (Heclo and Madsen, 1987: 47). Over 75 per cent of Swedes still worked as peasant farmers or in primary extraction industries such as mining, sawmills, and pulp factories, with the remainder in handicraft production. Wages were low and unstable. Despite the development of large-scale manufacturing by the turn of the century, "in 1900 Sweden still was less industrialized than Britain 100 years earlier" (Alestalo and Kuhnle, 1987: 14).

So precarious were people's lives that as many as 1.2 million Swedes emigrated during 1850–1924, mainly to America, in pursuit of a better life. About one-third of the emigrants were women (Heclo and Madsen, 1987: 47). All told, roughly 25 per cent of the Swedish population resettled during this 75-year period; in terms of population, it was the third largest emigration in Europe. For those who remained, the nature of factory work, including iron, glass, textile, and tobacco manufacturing, was much the same as in Canada and the United States. Women, many of them with small children, formed a substantial part of the labour force at the outset, working long hours for meagre wages: "a survey from a textile factory in western Sweden at the turn of the century shows that the women were often forced to take their children with them to the factory" (Ohlander, 1994: 20). As in Canada and the US, Swedish women's employment problems lead to gender-specific protective legislation that curtailed the number of hours women and children could be employed in factories, and which confined their labour activities to light industry.

Also as in North America, the First World War created new employment opportunities for non-married Swedish women—not in direct war activity (Sweden was a neutral country), but in industries spurred by wartime demand for goods and services. Similarly, following the war, public sentiment reverted regarding employed Swedish women, and the doctrine of separate spheres replaced the more flexible gender contract of the war years. Unemployment remained high throughout the decade following the war. Unemployment rates among union members—the only group of Swedish employees for which data were recorded—was 26.2 per cent in 1921 and continued to rise between 10 and 12 per cent for the rest of the decade, escalating even further in the 1930s (Ginsburg, 1983: 111). Unionized workers engaged in continual industrial action in an attempt to resist employers' moves to cut wages, increase the working day, and aggravate working conditions. Making matters worse, America's increasingly restrictive immigration policy in the 1920s greatly curtailed Swedish emigration.

A series of minority governments offered solutions to the ensuing social crisis, then the Social Democratic Party, which came to power in the 1930s and held office for most of the next half-century, laid the groundwork for what was to become a comprehensive welfare state to guide the country's economic and social development (Wilson, 1979: 6–7). Although the *Scandinavian route* of social democratic capitalism was not unique to Sweden, "the Swedish welfare state with a stronger social democratic party and with a more invisible pattern of welfare spending has, in the absence of strong simultaneous reactions both from the right and from the left, succeeded in preserving a more comprehensive popular support" (Alestalo and Kuhnle, 1987: 37).

However, a collective approach to economic and social matters did not mean gender equality. The Social Democrats' solution, endorsed by female members, to the high unemployment of the 1930s was a society-wide "gender contract" with clearly separate areas of responsibility for men and women: "his responsibilities were wage-earning and financial support and maintenance. Her responsibilities were homemaking and child-raising" (Hirdman, 1994: 15). In reality, however, many Swedish women could not avoid paid employment even if, all else being equal, they might choose to do so. The fact was that all else was *not* equal, that Swedish women's wages were low compared to men's, and that at the same time women were saddled with responsibility for the upkeep of dependent children. "They were forced in their lives to accommodate and, in one way or another, to solve what was basically a social conflict. The deepest roots of this conflict lay in the existence of a social denial of parenthood, care and upbringing, a denial of reproduction. In other words, a denial of the fundamental prerequisites for the continued existence of society itself" (Ohlander, 1994: 33).

Swedish women's response was to refrain from having children at all. The birth rate dropped so low during the 1930s that an impending population crisis was predicted. Rather than barring married women from employment, however, as was the case in North America during the Great Depression (with the passing of *marriage bars*), the Social Democrats chose a path to enable women to combine paid work and family life, as part of a larger social program of reform to enrich "the people's home [Swedish society]" (Wilson, 1979). Nevertheless, beneath the veneer of equal support for women's dual role as mothers and employees, those concerned with the population crisis were far more successful in promoting the former. For example, beginning in 1944 government subsidized home nurses offered respite services free of charge to Swedish housewives, and a universal child allowance began operation in 1948. Swedish married women were not barred outright from seeking paid employment during this period and were even supported in their struggle by the male dominated Swedish unions (Hobson, 1993). Yet it was still understood that Swedish women's careers would be characterized by two employment peaks: before marriage and in middle age—between which they would be occupied full-time with child-bearing and rearing (Myrdal, 1941).

By the mid 1960s, however, a number of social and economic circumstances in Sweden called into question the so-called *conditional liberation of women* that permitted women to seek employment only as long as they assumed full-time care of dependent children and others (Jonung and Persson, 1994: 48). The two-income/dual-career family was promoted, resulting in a new gender contract that acknowledged that the "woman's problem" of combining paid work and family life was in fact a societal problem needing a societal solution. As discussed in the next chapter, this outcome resulted in imaginative policies that both supported the economic independence of women as individuals (rather than as wives) and aimed for equality between the sexes in family life.

Because of the new principal commitment to gender equality in employment as well as family life, Sweden's labour shortages during the mid 1960s to the early 1980's "boom years" were handled quite differently than those of most other industrial countries. Rather than relying on "guest workers" or immigrants to ease labour shortages, Sweden made a concerted effort to employ its already well-educated Swedish female population. Over the next few decades Sweden was clearly a forerunner among advanced industrial capitalist countries in the labour force characteristics of its female population.

From the mid 1960s to the early 1990s, the female labour participation rate in Sweden continued to advance more rapidly than in other countries. In 1983, for example, Swedish women with children under 7 years of age had a labour force participation rate of 82 per cent; in 1990 it reached an all-time high of 86.9 per cent. For Swedish women with or without children the comparable 1990 rate was 90.6 per cent (Jonung and Persson, 1994). By 1995, during a period of deep recession in Sweden, the figure had dropped to 86 per cent, which was still 10 percentage points higher than the comparable Canadian rate and 11 percentage points higher than in the US (OECD, 1998c). Swedish women's portion of the labour force in 1997 at 48 per cent was among the highest of high-income countries and nearly as high as that of Swedish men.

In 1996 24.1 per cent of Swedish women worked part-time, a rate that is closer to their Canadian than US counterparts. Part-time employment is especially common for young Swedish mothers, about 40 per cent of whom are employed in this type of work. However, a number of conditions make part-time work in Sweden less vulnerable than in Canada and especially the US. First, Swedish women's percentage of part-time work as a percentage of total part-time employment has declined significantly between 1986 and 1996. Second, at-work hours for Swedish women over the past decades have also increased, while those for Swedish men have declined relatively. The end result is that there is much less difference in the at-work rates between the sexes in Sweden than in both Canada and the US. Third, while part-time employees in Canada and the US recorded fewer than 20 average hours per week, their Swedish counterparts recorded 24.7 (Sainsbury, 1996). In fact, in the mid 1990s more than one-third of Swedish women in part-time employment worked more than 30 hours per week, which is a rate close to the official standard for full employment (40 hours). One study found that Swedish women have the longest usual hours in part-time work compared to those in Denmark, France, Germany, and the United Kingdom (Rubery et al., 1995). Fourth, Swedish government employment legislation requires that employers provide prorated benefits to part-time employees, including vacation pay, unemployment insurance, and parental benefits. And finally, the vast majority of part-time workers in Sweden (69 per cent) are union members (Sundström, 1993).

In brief, Swedish women in part-time employment are able to remain attached to the labour force and attain economic independence even when their children are small. The profile of Swedish women no longer fits the two-peak employment cycle mentioned above, and they now tend to be continuously employed during their lifecycle. Yet it needs to be pointed out that gender differences in employment hours still persist, largely because women more often than not are the ones to take parental leaves:

> There is still a very marked division of labour between Swedish men and women, with women undertaking a much larger proportion of reproductive non-market work than men. However, it should be pointed out that even if it is still mainly Swedish women who adapt their labour supply to the birth and rearing of children, their situation today is very different that earlier cohorts of women. A low participation in market work because of parental leave is very different from a low participation rate resulting from departure from the labour force. (Jonung and Persson, 1994: 42–43)

Sweden is also positioned favourably internationally in its labour force participation rates for solo parents, most of whom are women (in 1980 they comprised 18 per cent of households and in 1994 just over 12 per cent). The perspective on solo mothers in Sweden parallels that taken on all other women—economic independence (Wilson, 1979: 96–97). In 1997 68.5 per cent of solo mothers with children under 7 years were employed; the figure for counterparts with children aged 7–16 was higher at 82.8 per cent (Statistics Sweden, 1999).

Nevertheless, roughly one-third of Swedish solo mothers are unable to gain economic independence by their incomes alone. But including social entitlements made available through Sweden's welfare state (discussed in the next chapter), the poverty rate of solo parents drops substantially below that of solo mothers in Canada and especially the US.

At first glance it seems that in occupational sex segregation, Sweden lags behind Canada and the US. Yet it is more marked in Sweden than in most other high-income countries because well over half of all employed women in Sweden work in the comparatively large public sector, which in 1997 comprised 31.2 per cent of all employment (OECD, 1998b). In essence, Swedish women's caring work in the home has been far more socialized by local and federal state authorities in education, health, social security, and the like. It should also be noted that from the late 1960s to the early 1990s (the latest date for which data is available), there was a gradual decline in occupational sex segregation in both private and public sectors of Sweden's economy (Nermo, 1996). The decline stems from the changed composition of occupations: more women are moving into male-dominated occupations and vice versa. Especially noteworthy is the increase of women in male professional occupations demanding advanced education, such as medicine, law, and the clergy (Jonung and Persson, 1994: 56).

Mention also should be made of the other major element of gender inequality in employment: the wage gap. Sweden stands out in this area as well, with low pay differentials based on gender (Baker: 1995: 105). Wage differentials persist, reflecting the unfinished nature of Swedish women's struggle for economic equality. However, from the mid 1960s to the early 1980s, the gender wage gap decreased across all employment sectors in Sweden: between 1973 and 1982 full-time female employees in the industrial sector increased their relative wage from 84 to 91 per cent of the male wage ratio; the comparable increase for white-collar workers was from 63 to 73 per cent; for central government employees it was 81 to 90 per cent; and for local state authorities from 74 to 86 per cent (Jonung and Persson, 1994: 57). By the mid 1980s Swedish women virtually had caught up to men in terms of human capital variables such as education and job experience, which partly explains the halt of further reductions in the gender wage gap. Remaining wage differentials between male and female employees continue primarily because of the lingering occupational sex segregation.

Finally, it is necessary to investigate how unpaid caring work is allocated in Sweden. The data, as in Canada and the US, suggests both continuity and change in the distribution of non-paid work, yet in Sweden the "family burden" (housework and dependent care) has deceased more markedly over time than in North America. Like their counterparts elsewhere, Swedish women—married and otherwise—still perform the bulk of household work and childcare. In the early 1990s Swedish males with their youngest child between 7 and 18 years worked roughly 46.5 hours per week in paid work and 20 hours per week in non-paid work. Figures for their female counterparts were 32.5 and 33 hours, respectively (Jonung and Persson, 1994). Despite this lingering division of labour between the genders, there has been a levelling of total hours worked per week by each sex: Swedish women and men work almost the same number of hours per week, albeit in somewhat different activities. There has been some progress as well in the distribution of household work; Swedish co-habiting men doubled the time they devoted to housework between the mid 1970s and the early 1990s; at the same time, Swedish cohabiting women decreased the time they spent on housework. In fact, couples in Sweden have reduced their total housework hours at the same time as there has been a very gradual movement towards gender parity. A similar trend exists in the division of childcare; men are spending more hours taking care of children, and women fewer, although men still spend fewer hours overall. At the same time, total unpaid hours caring for dependent children have decreased due to the rapid growth in recent decades of public childcare facilities.

The "leisure gap" between Swedish men and women has narrowed considerably in recent decades; at the same time both Swedish women and men have increased their leisure time. The former is also the case for Canadians, but not for Americans, about whom most studies indicate that women put in more total hours per week than men, perhaps as many as 15 hours (Schor, 1991; Hochschild, 1989). Moreover, in both Canada and the US, leisure time for either men or women with children is considerably less than that available for their Swedish counterparts, who are less prone to "time-crunch stress" produced by the difficulty of balancing paid work and family responsibilities.

Cross-national differences between Sweden and North America in gendered work can be explained both by the greater equality in all aspects of life (including gender) in Sweden, but also by the comparatively comprehensive nature of the Swedish welfare state, which shares the burden of reproduction with individual families.

SUMMARY AND CONCLUSION

With its focus on women's work under four different phases of capitalism, this chapter has traced continuity as much as change in the gender division of labour in paid and unpaid work. It has been noted that starting dates for particular phases of capitalism differed, with Canada and Sweden being "late starters" compared to the United States in regard to, for example, large-scale industrialization and the arrival of the factory system. Nevertheless, all three countries share a number of characteristics regarding women's employment. At the beginning of the period examined, women performed home-based work for desperately low piece rates and later entered factories, often with their young children in tow, again for low wages and under poor conditions. Protective legislation in all three countries barred married women from many kinds of factory work. During times of high male unemployment, trade unions and governments further curtailed women's employment (except in the case of Sweden between the wars), but during wartime women's labour was in high demand in fields previously closed to them, with relatively higher wages, a demand that was to decline sharply when male claims for jobs recurred.

The rise of the service society in the post–World War II period was accompanied by rapid growth in both non-married and married women's employment across the three countries, with greater growth in Sweden than in Canada or the US. While part-time employment hours vary, Swedish part-timers tend to work longer hours, with higher pay than their Canadian and US counterparts.

In sum, the evidence indicates that, except within occupational sex segregation, Sweden has made the greatest progress in gender equality in both family work and paid employment, with Canada occupying a middle position and the United States bringing up the rear. This progress is especially notable for working-class women in Sweden, as well as for its high percentage of solo mothers. However, without social provision from the welfare state that accompanies these positive economic developments, many more Swedish women would be poor. Lacking similar social provisions, many women in Canada and especially the US experience poverty even when they are employed. The next chapter addresses this topic in some detail.

ENDNOTES

[1] In fact, in some contemporary high-income countries such as Finland, where the market economy became a dominant form only well into the twentieth century, a "housewife parenthesis" never existed. Finnish women were actively involved in agricultural work during the preindustrial era, and when Finland finally industrialized, the wages of working class males were too low to support a family. Much the same holds true today for countries such as China that are only now developing capitalist markets, and where men and women who once worked side by side in agriculture continue to do so in the emerging capitalist economy.

[2] Visible minority subgroups in Canada are derived from the 1986 and 1991 Censuses. They include: Blacks, South Asians, Chinese, Koreans, Japanese, South East Asians, Filipinos, West Asians and Arabs, Latin Americans, and Other Pacific Islanders. See Statistics Canada, 1995: 138.

[3] Chinese immigrants were the only ethnic group required to pay this fee upon entry into the country.

[4] The term "solo" (or lone) parent is adopted throughout rather than "single" parent, because the latter term commonly is used to denote a person who has never married. Solo (or lone) parents include any parent with dependents, who are either separated or divorced, or who have lived common-law and no longer do so, or who have never married or cohabited.

[5]Even this piece of legislation was not without serious shortcomings. Government appointed inspectors were in short supply until well into the twentieth century, and in any case tended to adopt a "blame the victim" mentality regarding industrial accidents, suggesting that it was the worker's own fault that he or she was injured (Krahn and Lowe, 1993: 180–281).

[6]The *Mines Regulation Act* was passed in 1908 in Newfoundland and Labrador, stipulating that no boys under 13 and no girls or women of any age were permitted to work in underground mines. Not until the 1940s was the *Welfare of Children Act* passed, which forbade the employment of women under 17 in restaurants and taverns, and waged work for all women between 9 p.m. and 8 a.m. (Forestell, 1995: 90).

[7]According to Statistics Canada, families and individuals are classified as "low income" if they spend at least 20 per cent more of their pre-tax income than the Canadian average on food, shelter, and clothing. In 1992 families and individuals with incomes below the Low Income Cut-Offs spent on average more than 54 per cent of their income on these items and were deemed thereby to be in straitened circumstances. Family size and urban/rural residence are also taken into account (Statistics Canada, 1995: 86).

[8]Statistics Canada defines part-time work as fewer than 30 hours per week spent in the main or only job.

[9]Due to shortage of space and paucity of comparative data, this book does not explore in depth the situation of women workers with disabilities. See Statistics Canada, *Women in Canada* (1995) for recent statistical data on disabled women.

WELFARE STATES AND WOMEN'S SOCIAL RIGHTS

"A common scepticism toward the state characterized the new Women's Liberation Movement of the 1970s and most Western feminist theory of the 1970s and 1980s. Although time has taken the edge off feminist hostility toward the "patriarchal state" in the West, many women in postcommunist countries, for obvious reasons, today express hostility toward state intervention and public "emancipation" policy .... I argue, however, that women [need to learn] to live with the state." (Dahlerup, 1994: 117)

INTRODUCTION

Welfare states have yet to find a comfortable place in industrial capitalist countries, with either the popular press or with those who study this peculiar feature of the late twentieth century. While few would challenge the idea that some form of state support is essential to society's optimal functionality, the dispute is over the proper mix and extent of social provision. In North America—and in particular the United Sates, which historically has embraced a laissez-faire form of capitalism—the welfare state generally has been viewed as, among other things, intrusive, preying on individual privacy and creating laziness. Attempts in other countries to enact universal social policies have been viewed with suspicion by the main political parties in the US and (to a lesser extent) in Canada. Even today such belittling insignias as *welfare mothers* (referring to solo female-headed households) indicate a deep-seated ambivalence in America, at least among its political leadership, about the role of the state in the welfare of its population.

At the same time, working-class unions and many grassroots organizations have fought long and hard for welfare state policies to reflect the needs of "working families." Yet it has generally been assumed by union organizers that welfare state policies are equally progressive for all family members. The presumption is that social policies developed by the welfare state help to empower [male] breadwinners and their families against the ills of capitalism—that is, "[welfare state social policies] weaken the whip of the market and promote working-class political solidarity" (Palme, 1990: 8).

This book defines the *welfare state* as "a state commitment of some sort which modifies the play of market forces in an effort to realize greater social equality for its population" (Ruggie, 1984: 11). Welfare state provisions are interventions by the state to alter social forces both in the free market and in civil society (Orloff, 1993, fn. 1). Welfare states shoulder responsibility for the well-being of inhabitants, an obligation that cannot easily be consigned to the individual, private business firm, or local community. However, whether welfare state provisions, once implemented, actually promote greater equality between different societal groups is an empirical question. To answer it requires critical investigation of the differential impact of particular social policies on particular social groups.

The need for such a qualifier in regard to the actual success of welfare state policies in meeting their expressed mandate is made especially clear once the situation of women is taken into consideration. While most of the "mainstream" scholarship on welfare states has acknowledged that social policies implemented by different welfare states in the modern era have had important consequences for women *as dependents*, this approach has neglected any attempt to introduce gender to the concept of "citizenship." In brief, social policies need to be examined in regard to their impact on women as *individuals* in their own right, performing both paid and unpaid work activities, not only in their roles as wives and mothers.

Feminist research on welfare states in industrial capitalist countries has been concerned first and foremost with exposing the welfare state's inherent male bias—how it serves to reproduce relations of gender inequality that assign women subordinate status in paid employment and the family and award men special advantage (Hartmann, 1979; McIntosh, 1978; Borchorst and Siim, 1987). Sylvia Walby (1986: 57) thus argues that "the state is a site of patriarchal relations which is necessary to patriarchy as a whole. The state represents patriarchal as well as capitalist interests and furthers them in its actions." Other feminists have analyzed the state in terms of *social patriarchy*, which is defined as "the societal organization of sex-gender relations through rules and laws concerning marriage, property, and child custody" (Ursel, 1988: 112).

Feminist scholarship focussed on revealing the hidden male bias underpinning the welfare state has provided a much-needed corrective to mainstream literature. Yet a major shortcoming has been its oversight of the tangible *variations* found among welfare states in regard to social rights for women and men. Indeed, much of the feminist theorizing on patriarchy/male advantage and welfare states has been based on a small number of case studies, primarily in the United States and Britain. However, as illustrated in previous chapters, the Canadian polity took a somewhat different form than either Canada's mother country or its neighbour to the south, which occasionally translated into distinct social policies. And the Swedish welfare state, due to a complexity of factors, varies substantially from both Canada and the US.

In sum, the two bodies of literature on welfare states—mainstream and feminist—tend to suffer from one or another methodological problem: 1) mainstream theories are comparative but gender-neutral (more precisely, gender-blind); and 2) feminist research on welfare states has suffered from ethnocentrism. As Diane Sainsbury contends:

> [Mainstream] studies tell us little about the impact of the welfare state on women and men or the differences in impact, and they have largely ignored the disparities in welfare provision between the sexes. On the other hand, feminist scholarship … [has] inadvertently reinforced a generic view of both the state and the welfare state. This tendency was also strengthened by a major current in feminist theory which views the state as an epi-phenomenon of patriarchy, thus ruling out both significant variations between specific states and the possibility of variations that might be beneficial to women. (1996: 1)

As outlined in Chapter 1, recent feminist scholarship has attempted to advance conceptual understandings of gender (in)equality and welfare states by joining aspects of both mainstream and feminist perspectives (Gordon, 1990; Hernes, 1987; Orloff, 1993; Sainsbury, 1996; O'Connor, 1993; Skocpol, 1992; Sarvasy, 1992; Dahlerup, 1994). Research conducted by feminists in the social-democratic Nordic countries is especially insightful in this regard since it provides evidence of positive effects of social policies in "carer" welfare states (Leira, 1992) that tend to be more "women-friendly" (Hernes, 1987). In these instances, it is in women's best interests to "learn to live with the state" (Dalerup, 1994). Also helpful is the attempt to note variations even among the Scandinavian/Nordic countries themselves in regard to welfare state policies that impact women (Leira, 1992; Ellingsaeter, 1998). Diana Sainsbury's (1996) recent study of significant variations within welfare state regimes along a number of gendered dimensions, for example, challenges the placement of particular countries that are clustered with others from which they can be shown to differ in ways that are important for women's economic independence and overall social equality. Janet Gornick et al. (1997), in their multi-country analysis of social policies promoting employment for mothers, make a similar point about the limitations of the cluster model that overlooks variation among countries such as Sweden and Norway or Canada and the US. Other researchers as well have highlighted differences between the North American neighbours by focusing on income distribution (Myles, 1996) and access to public services (Olsen, 1994).

This alternative investigative strategy—one that focuses on highlighting differences as well as similarities between countries placed within clusters of welfare state regimes—is adopted below. The aim of this chapter is to show that Canada, the US, and Sweden have common features, but at the same time they differ in important respects. While their governments play a very large role in their economies—1995 government expenditures as a percentage of GDP were 45.8 in Canada, 34.3 in the US, and 63.8 in Sweden (OECD 1998)—significant cross-national variation exists in the degree of government activity. This difference can be explained largely by the greater public support of "big government" (and hence higher taxes) among Swedish citizens compared to North Americans, but also among Canadians in comparison to their southern neighbours.

This chapter takes up a discussion of the particular mix of social policies available to women in Canada, with windows opening on the United States and Sweden, illustrating significant variation among the three countries in regard to women's capacity to enjoy economic independence and gain recognition for unpaid as well as paid work. As has been the comparative pattern in preceding chapters, the Swedish welfare state comes out as the most "women-friendly," its US counterpart least so, while the Canadian welfare state straddles the middle ground. Three categories of social policies are examined in light of their importance for women as employees/mothers performing paid and unpaid work: 1) employment related policies; 2) family leave policies; and 3) childcare policies. This overview does not exhaust the variety of social policies supported by welfare states in the three countries. Rather, the point of interest is the main forms of social provision that support the two added dimensions of welfare state provisions highlighted by feminists examining welfare states in cross-national perspective.

THE CANADIAN CASE

> During this century [Canadian] wives gradually changed their legal status from being their husbands' dependants to being their equal partners. This included, as milestones, the right to make contracts on their own behalf, the right to own and dispose of property, the right to keep their own name after marriage, the determination of domicile on an equal basis for both wife and husband, etc. .... However, socially, emotionally, and economically, this ideal has not been achieved. (Eichler, 1997: 40)

Employment-related Policies

Despite the great advances women in Canada have made in the post-war period in regard to gainful employment, there nevertheless continues to be a gender imbalance in the *commodification* (marketing) of labour; compared to men, women have less access to paid employment, tend to be employed fewer hours, and receive comparatively lower pay even when working in the same kind of jobs for the same length of time. At the same time, women continue to perform much of the non-commodified (non-paid) work that is fundamental to society's functionality. When total hours of work are calculated for men and women in Canada, women do more than 50 per cent of societal labour yet receive comparatively lower economic reward for their efforts (Statistics Canada, 1995: 70). Statistics Canada in 1992 calculated that unpaid work, two-thirds of which is done by Canadian women, was comparable to between 32 and 54.2 per cent of Canada's GNP (Sharma, 1997: 11).

In short, women in Canada continue to be engaged in paid employment under dissimilar conditions from men. Women are more likely to absent themselves from paid work during the early year(s) of a child's life, to exit from employment in times of sickness of an older child or other dependent, to be the main caregiver to children in the aftermath of separation or divorce, and in general to organize their employment schedule around the needs of others. Canadian men generally tend to do the opposite, placing career first and other caring responsibilities second.

This is the case even while Canadian women's *cultural capital* —or formal educational credentials—has improved significantly in recent decades. Due to consequential government support for gender equality in higher education over the past two decades, women now outnumber their male counterparts in undergraduate university enrolment and degrees granted (Statistics Canada, 1997). As shown in Table 4–1, there is now significant overlap in the most popular undergraduate degrees granted to both genders. On the other hand, there are three degrees that tend to be associated with high pay—engineering, computer science, and economics—that made the top-10 list for men but not for women. In fact, neither computer science nor economics appeared in the top-20 list of undergraduate degrees granted to women in 1997.

TABLE 4–1	Average Annual Enrolment for Top 20 Fields of Undergraduate Study (by gender): 1991–1996		
	Women	**Men**	
37 547	Arts/Sciences, General	Engineering	33 419
28 369 33 419	Education	Business, Management, and Commerce	29 792
25 348	Business, Management	Arts/Sciences, General	28 053
19 573	Psychology	Education	9 586
18 379	Languages	Biology	8 673
11 455	Biology	Computer Science	8 637
11 204	Sociology	Not Reported	8 315
10 651	Fine and Applied Arts	Physical Education	8 194
9 930	Not Reported	Languages	6 956
8 083	Physcial Education	Economics	6 899
7 803	Nursing	Political Science	6 670
7 280	Humanities, Other	Humanities, Other	6 576
7 229	Engineering	Fine and Applied Arts	6 433
6 564	Social Sciences, Other	Psychology	6 296
5 819	Law	History	6 285
5 403	History	Law	5 462
5 287	Political Science	Mathematics	5 052
5 062	Social Work	Geography	4 751
4 081	Medical Studies and Research	Social Science, Other	4 422
3 564	Household Science	Medical Studies and Research	4 342
267 876	**Total**	**Total**	**228 313**

Source: Calculated based on data in *Education in Canada 1997*. Catalogue no. 81-229-XIB Statistics Canada (1998).

Despite the advance towards gender balance in university degrees—due mainly to women taking up fields that were formerly considered "male"—a gender imbalance has become even more marked in traditionally female fields such as nursing. In addition, women comprise a minority of postgraduate students, especially at the doctoral level (Statistics

Canada, 1995: 54). Given the trend towards postgraduate certification as a basic requirement for consideration of *good jobs* (those with career ladders, pay scales, and opportunities for personal growth), many women in Canada continue to lose out in attractive employment competitions. Rather than promoting women's greater involvement in postgraduate education (i.e., establishing a woman-friendly educational policy), the federal government has taken the view that post-secondary education is one of the main policy areas requiring budget cuts (social welfare and health are other designated targets).

In April 1996 the federal *Canadian Assistance Plan* (CAP) program was replaced by *Canada Health and Social Transfer* (CHST). CHST redefined the roles of different levels of government in regard to the funding and transfer of social programs. For groups seeking greater independence from federal government—the province of Quebec and Aboriginal peoples in particular—CHST appears progressive in that it allows for the provincial or Aboriginal governmental bodies to gain greater control over their social programs. Yet CHST has been accompanied by an overall reduction in federal social welfare funding for all Canadians, regardless of ethnic background, native language, gender, or geographic location. Equally disturbing has been the transfer of new powers to the provinces regarding how best to divide the block fund among education, social welfare, and health. This allows for increased fragmentation in social policy across and even within the provinces. It is likely that decisions about how to divide the CHST pie among health, education, and social welfare may be made on the basis of political expediency rather than objective evidence of need.

Some provinces have been much more radical than others in cutting their educational budget and raising student tuition fees. Bursaries have been eliminated and tuition fees raised substantially in most provinces. (Quebec remains the most generous in this regard, where, despite modest increases for provincial residents, university tuition fees are among the lowest in North America.) State subsidies, including those for childcare, have been reduced dramatically in Ontario, the country's most populated province, thereby negatively impacting parents seeking higher education (Philp, 1998: A5). Since female students, like women in general in Canada, possess fewer economic resources to begin with and are far more likely than males to be solo parents, the recent educational cutbacks dampen the positive changes in higher education for women that typified earlier decades when the Canadian welfare state was expanding.

University degrees do not exhaust educational achievement possibilities for women and men in Canada. Recent data on employer-sponsored and job-related training indicates that while there is near balance between the sexes in training-program participation, a training time deficit exists in favour of men, whose instruction is also more likely to be funded by employers. Moreover, enrolment statistics in apprenticeship programs in the comparatively high-paying male dominated trades indicate that although recruitment doubled between the mid 1980s and 1990s, women made up only 1 per cent of all apprentices recruited in the 15 major trades (Statistics Canada, 1995: 54). As shown in Table 4–2, women's enrolment in the engineering and applied sciences programs at the community college level increased only marginally over the decade, from 6.2 per cent in 1983/84 to 8.4 per cent in 1995/96. Although women did increase their enrolment in certain trades and vocational programs, the overall picture is not impressive. For one thing, there is no indication of improvement over time. Nor is change likely to occur in the near future, since the funding policies of the federal and provincial governments no longer require reserved seats for a proportion of women in trades and technical programs to ensure that an acceptable number of women are recruited.

TABLE 4-2	Gender Distribution in Full-time Trade and Vocational Pre-employment/Pre-apprenticeship and Special Programs: 1983, 1995-96							
	1983/84		1987/88		1991/92		1995/96	
	M	F	M	F	M	F	M	F
Arts	27.5	72.5	34	66.5	35.6	64.4	30	70.1
Business and Commerce	28	72	22	77.6	27.9	72.1	27	73.5
Engineering and Applied Sciences	93.8	6.2	89	10.9	91.8	8.2	92	8.4
Selected Programs[1] Aircraft Mechanics	98.8	1.2	98	2.4	97.6	2.4	96	4.1
Automotive Technology	99.2	0.8	97	2.6	96.7	3.3	96	3.7
Electrical/Electronic Technology	97.3	2.7	91	8.6	95	5	90	10.5
Heavy Equipment Mechanics	97.7	2.3	95	4.8	96.3	3.7	97	3.2
Machinist	97.3	2.7	92	8.1	93.9	6.1	94	5.9
Marine Mechanics	99.6	0.4	98	2.1	97.3	2.7	97	3
Small Engine Mechanics	93.7	6.3	94	5.7	92	8	93	7.2
Welding Technology	98.7	1.3	96	4.3	96.4	3.6	95	4.6
Woodworking and Carpentry	94.9	5.1	86	13.7	87.7	12.3	90	10
Health Sciences and Related Employment	21.9	78.1	15	85.4	16.1	83.9	15	84.7
Natural Sciences and Related Industries	89	11	77	23	85.9	14.1	79	21.3
Social Sciences and Services	44.5	55.5	26	74	37.6	62.4	27	73.2
Total	**64.9**	**35.1**	**58**	**42.5**	**62.3**	**37.7**	**56**	**43.6**

[1]These are only a few selected programs within the engineering and applied sciences field of study.

Source: Statistics Canada, *The Daily*, 22 Jan. 1999.

To what extent has the Canadian welfare state championed women's paid employment in the last three decades by enacting progressive labour market policies? Canada's labour market policies in regard to women can be described as *middle range*; they include some progressive legislation that enhance women's employment rights, while other crucial polices are residual or absent entirely. Full employment for adult Canadian women has never been a priority for either federal or provincial governments (and only for a time was it considered a major political goal for adult men). By and large, efforts by successive Canadian governments in the past three decades to improve the employment situation have been weak. The male breadwinner model has shaped most employment policies, and women (along with visible minorities and Aboriginals) have served in varying degrees as a "reserve army of labour." As noted in Chapter 3, a large number of Canadian women employed part-time desire full-time employment, and many women—especially those living on the margins of society—can find no employment at all. This is the case for a substantial minority of Aboriginal women, solo mothers, and visible minority women (Statistics Canada, 1995). For those who do find work, the employment situation is often far from adequate. As Sheila Neysmith and Jane Aronson note:

> The availability of a pool of immigrant women makes it possible for higher income families to hire such persons to do home-based work. Feminist policy analysts have called for expanding services to care for children and elderly persons. The questions not raised are: who is going to do the work, [and] under what conditions ...? The employment patterns of recent immigrants, combined with the demographic characteristics of Canada's aging population, suggest that it will be low-waged women of colour who will do the work. (1997: 481)

At the same time, even educated women who have gained access to the male dominated professions continue to realize lower occupational returns on their education than their male counterparts. The "occupational return index" (see Figure 4–1) scrutinizes female and male university graduates in the three highest categories of occupations—self-employed professionals, employed professionals, and high-level managers—and shows the probability of women degree-holders being in these occupations compared to men. While the gender gap has been narrowing consistently, the probability for women gaining access to these careers remains substantially lower than for men.

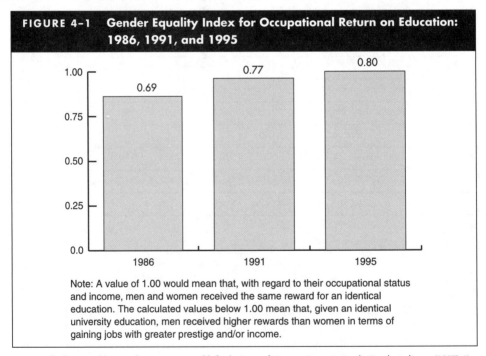

FIGURE 4–1   Gender Equality Index for Occupational Return on Education: 1986, 1991, and 1995

Note: A value of 1.00 would mean that, with regard to their occupational status and income, men and women received the same reward for an identical education. The calculated values below 1.00 mean that, given an identical university education, men received higher rewards than women in terms of gaining jobs with greater prestige and/or income.

Source: Federal-Provincial/Territorial Ministers Responsible for the Status of Women, *Economic Gender Equality Indicators* (1997) 41.

This somewhat positive picture of the occupational return on education for university trained women holds true for only a minority of Canadian women. The growth in paid employment for women in recent decades has been in two areas—relatively secure public sector employment and less attractive service jobs, many of which are located in the more loosely regulated private sector. Women gainfully employed in the private service sector often are involved in "non-standard employment," jobs that belong to pink-collar ghettos that tend to be low paid, non-unionized, and lacking security and sometimes even statutory protection, although not to the extent found among their American counterparts. Lower wages and sporadic employment mean low returns when drawing unemployment insurance benefits (UI), and sometimes too few continuous hours of paid work even to file an unemployment claim.

The data shows that male employees are more likely than females to benefit from unemployment insurance, a finding that has changed little over the past decade. Male employees also more frequently receive UI training benefits (60 per cent), job-creation UI benefits (61 per cent), benefits involved in work-sharing arrangements (68 per cent), and self-employment assistance benefits (Statistics Canada, 1995: 68–69). Compared with women, men's UI benefits over and above regular benefits are tied less to their family role than to their labour market role (or potential). This is evident from the fact that female employees account for virtually all (99 per cent) UI maternity/parental benefits (discussed below), as well as the majority (59 per cent) of those claiming sickness benefits. In both instances these benefits are largely associated with women's additional unpaid caring work in families. Women in paid employment, whether part- or full-time, are much more likely than males to exit temporarily from their jobs because of personal/family duties. The likelihood of women in full-employment doing so over the last decade has in fact doubled, from three days away from paid work per year in 1980 to six days in 1994. In contrast, men have shown only a marginal increase over the decade, taking less than one day off from work due to personal/family duties in 1994 (Statistics Canada, 1995: 68–69).

Canadian governments have made little effort to balance the gendered nature of regular and additional unemployment benefits. The most recent response to curb high persistent unemployment across many of the provinces has been to rename the UI program—now called *Employment Insurance* or EI—and tighten the eligibility requirements, resulting in an overall federal government reduction in the unemployment insurance budget. Although Canada still has a relatively generous (un)employment insurance system compared to the US and the OECD average (Myles, 1996), the recent tightening of eligibility requirements has taken its toll: unemployed workers eligible for EI benefits have dropped in numbers from 89 per cent in 1989 to 50 per cent in 1996. At the same time, as of January 1997, an "hour system" has been established. Unemployed workers are now required to work a minimum of 910 hours over the year (equivalent to 26 weeks at 35 hours per week) prior to establishing a new EI claim, with most claimants receiving 55 per cent of their previous earnings. The minimum earnings of a potential claimant are set at $6.70 per hour. The maximum weekly rate for a claimant until the end of year 2000 is $413. Only low-income persons (with an annual income under $25 921) with children are eligible to receive a Family Supplement. In 1997 it was possible to increase the benefit rate to a maximum of 65 per cent, but it could not exceed the maximum weekly rate noted above (Human Resources Development Canada, 1998). Self-employed persons and those employed part-time and/or part-year—i.e., in non-standard employment, the vast majority of whom are women—are unlikely to meet these new, more stringent EI requirements, especially those who are non-union members.

In key respects, Canadian policy-makers at both the federal and provincial levels have been only moderately successful in creating legislation that promotes women's economic independence and social equality. Policies enacted as national programs in some countries—including wage subsidies, training programs to launch women into higher paying and lifelong careers, and projects that support women's non-traditional employment—have tended to be sporadic in Canada. They frequently are short-term and typically do not provide essential social benefits, including transportation and childcare, without which many unemployed women cannot participate.

Rather than creating women-friendly policies, a number of Canadian provinces recently adopted *workfare* programs that require recipients of social assistance to enrol in government subsidized "training for work" programs. While many Canadians believe that workfare is reformative—everyone should earn his or her own keep—evidence shows that workfare is far from progressive from the point of view of both employed workers and many social welfare recipients. Similar to strategies embraced in the early industrial period that attempted to undermine the power of the craft guilds, corporations in Canada generally have been supportive of the new workfare programs, since they provide an avenue for employers to displace higher-paid unionized employees. Jobs that included security and fringe benefits are eliminated and replaced by those that are lower paid, and with fewer or no benefits, pitting the unionized worker against the vulnerable welfare recipient. As Sharma puts it, it is "a race to the bottom. The only winners are those who own businesses relying on cheap labour. Employers rarely hire workers at the end of the workfare programs, so that the programs operate as a subsidy to business, paid by the tax payer, with no requirement to actually provide stable employment at decent wages for people" (1997: 4).

Workfare is also problematic from the viewpoint of the social assistance recipient, for (at least) two interrelated reasons. First, the majority of jobs found through workfare programs are "dead-end," with minimum wage and without benefits or security. Second, individuals undertaking workfare jobs risk losing special benefits provided under social assistance, including subsidized housing, help with childcare, and health care supplements (e.g., dental care for children), which are of fundamental importance to poor families in general and especially to solo mothers. *Compass*, a Nova Scotia "welfare to work" program, is a case in point. Although successful for a small number of participants, an overall evaluation of the program suggests that it is "a misbegotten and costly government attempt to melt welfare dependency and alter the realities of the market economy by badgering business into creating artificial jobs" (Valpy, 1998: D1).

On a more positive note, low-income women in Canada are able to access health care insurance as a citizen's right. Canada's universal health insurance plan provides physician and hospital services to all citizens and permanent residents independent of both need and labour force participation (Benoit, 1998). As discussed below, this is not the case in the US, where employers and employees are expected to make substantial monthly insurance payments so that workers and their families have access to basic health care coverage. Many workers, including women in low-paying jobs and solo mothers, cannot afford to pay health insurance premiums and have to go without this employment related benefit.

Another area in which the Canadian federal government and some provinces have exerted greater effort in changing the gendered order of things is employment equity. This has involved a series of legislative changes over the past three decades to prevent discrimination against women by employers in regard to pay differentials and unequal access to work. Equal pay legislation dates to 1956, with the *Female Employees Equal Pay Act*, which was rescinded and in 1966 rolled into the *Canada Labour Code*. The phrasing was altered from "identical or substantially identical work" to "same or similar work" within the same workplace. However, as Baker points out, "the law placed a heavy burden on the complainant, which may account for the lack of success of complaints" (1995: 78). Three other pieces of legislation followed. The *Canadian Human Rights Act* was passed in 1978, forbidding discrimination and differential wages for female and male employees in the same workplace executing work of equal value. The 1984 *Employment Equity Act* (EEA) came next, with the aim of achieving "equality in the workplace and to correct conditions of disadvantage experienced by certain groups." Four disadvantaged groups were named by the new legislation: women, Aboriginal peoples, visible minorities, and people with disabilities. The EEA legislation required that employers under federal jurisdiction periodically provide employment statistics for the designated groups, but criticisms have been levelled at the lack of practical enforcement procedures (Baker, 1995: 78–79). In December 1995 Bill C-64 was passed, broadening the scope and tightening the rules of EEA. For the first time the EEA protected private as well as public sector employees under the federal jurisdiction. Women employed in the federal government, communications, mail delivery, national banks, the airlines, and broadcasting are included under Bill C-64 and are eligible to claim employment equity. Parallel legislation also was enacted to protect approximately half of provincial government employees, and some unions were successful over the past decade in negotiating employment equity for their memberships.

Despite these legislative changes, women in full-time, full-year employment in 1996 on average earned only 73.4 per cent of the earnings of male counterparts (see Chapter 3). To a large degree this is because the majority of women in private sector jobs are protected by neither progressive legislation nor union contracts. Moreover, many are employed in female dominated establishments where a male comparison group is absent (Wilson, 1991). To make matters worse, a recent move by the Ontario government to pass a law abolishing its provincial pay equity legislation (the Ontario High Court overruled the law) suggests that an uphill battle lies ahead in regard to retaining, let alone expanding, women's employment rights. On a more positive note, in the summer of 1998 the Canadian Human Rights Tribunal found that federal workers (almost all of whom are female and most holding low-ranking positions) were owed retroactive pay due to wage discrimination, estimated to be in the range of five billion dollars. However, this ruling is being challenged by the federal government and a final resolution is delayed, indicating a divergence between employer support for gender wage equity rather than the reality of equitable wages for female and male employees.

In addition to the dimensions of governmental policy that promote/discourage women's economic independence, access to retirement pensions for women and men is another important consideration. Not much more than a few decades ago, as many as 70 per cent of older women in Canada survived on incomes that fell below Statistics Canada's official Low Income Cut-Offs. Economic independence for older women was the privilege of a small minority; employed women tended to work for low wages and frequently exited from employment altogether in order to carry out crucial non-paid caring work, with a minority of women re-entering the labour force only in later life. Among other things, this meant that after retirement women tended to have very small pensions or savings, and many had neither. In contrast, their male partners were much more likely to spend their retirement years supported by a government pension, often an employer-sponsored pension, and sometimes invested private savings.

Subsequent Canadian federal governments attempted to rectify the gendered nature of social provision for seniors by reforming *Old Age Security* (OAS), the *Guaranteed Income Supplement* (GIS), and *Canada Pension Plan/Quebec Pension Plan* (CPP/QPP). By 1993 the poverty rate among senior women had dropped strikingly by 45 per cent. While Canadian senior women were still twice as likely as men to be poor, the progressive changes made in social benefits went some distance in granting older women economic independence. Among the changes helping senior women was the citizens' right to exclude up to seven years of low income/no income of full-time childcare when initiating their CPP/QPP claims. The reforms also gave wives access to part of their husband's employment-based pension benefits, made it possible to transport pensions from job to job and between full- and part-time employment, provided survivor and orphan benefits on the death of a woman's parenting partner, and indexed these provisions to inflation. These developments were positive for women on two accounts: 1) women on average live longer than men and therefore are more likely to be affected by shifting inflation rates; and 2) more senior women than men are poor, so they are more likely to benefit from a progressive package.

In recent years, however, political parties of different stripes have attacked Canada's universal pension system, arguing that it is too costly for taxpayers and is awarded at the expense of society's younger generations. The outcome has been a gradual move towards the reduction of welfare state funding of social provision for seniors, which challenges older women's goal of economic independence. In 1989 OAS was changed from a universal entitlement; the benefit can no longer be claimed by seniors in higher income brackets. The result of this change is that there no longer is a united voice among seniors in regard to the OAS benefit. State retrenchment is also evident in the government's move to encourage citizens to invest in Registered Retirement Savings Plans (RRSPs). Given women's comparatively lower incomes, greater longevity, more precarious employment histories, and larger familial responsibilities than men, they are less likely to possess the economic means whereby to purchase RRSPs for their retirement years (Statistics Canada, 1995: 89).

A new *Seniors' Benefit* is being proposed for implementation in Canada by 2001, a "reform" that would replace present forms of assistance to elderly women and men. The seniors' benefit would not be universal, but based on the overall "family income." The proposed benefit for seniors living with a partner would be based on their combined retirement incomes. Those without an employment history—almost all cases being older women—would no longer be able to claim social provision independently of their partners as long as both reside in the same dwelling. They would be eligible for the seniors' benefit only if their combined retirement income fell below a certain limit. This means that women without a strong prior attachment to the workforce or with low earnings—but partnered with someone possessing a retirement income over a designated amount ($40 000 in 1997)—would be without an independent income, financially reliant on their companion. If the proposed seniors' benefit is made law, senior women in Canada, especially women with insecure employment histories, will likely find themselves in a situation not unlike that of their foremothers, one that predated the welfare state reforms in pensions of the past two decades.

Family Leaves and Benefits

Leaves from paid employment during childbirth and the early life of infants, as well as childcare services, have also been debated strongly in many industrial capitalist countries, including Canada. Adherents to a notion of family as "functional" for society when based on complementary sex roles—typically understood as males in the role of paid breadwinner and females in the role of unpaid domestic worker and primary carer of dependents—maintain that this gender division of labour follows from biological differences between women and men in their reproductive capacities. According to Parsons (1955: 23), "the fundamental explanation of the allocation of the roles between the biological sexes lies in the fact that the bearing and early nursing of children establish a strong presumptive primacy to the relation of the mother to the small child and this in turn establishes a presumption that the man, who is exempted from these biological functions, should specialize in the alternative instrumental direction." In short, social motherhood and fatherhood are viewed by some writers as distinct due to biological processes associated with childbirth; and children's social development, including their capacity to learn basic trust, is said to be dependent upon full-time care by biological mothers. Without daily maternal attention, children are thought to be in danger of *maternal deprivation*—the psychological impairment of children bereaved of their mother's close physical and emotional contact—and likely to experience defective adulthood adaptation (Erikson, 1965).

Research over the past two decades has produced contradictory evidence regarding the apparent "naturalness" of the male breadwinner/female carer model of family life. Feminist sociologists have been at the forefront of the critique of functionalist analyses of family sex roles. Posing the question as "functional for whom?" feminists have argued that while women's assignment of primary carer of children may be beneficial for capitalist employers wanting to keep employee benefit packages to a minimum, governments interested in trimming their welfare state budgets, and men reluctant to share parenting, full-time motherhood is arguably far less "functional" for women in regard to both their economic independence and social adaptation (Oakley, 1976; Thorne, 1983; Eichler, 1997). Moreover, studies of children in care settings where biological mothers are absent suggest that it is the *quality of the care provided* rather than the presence of mothers that largely determines children's successful psychological and emotional development. In fact, biological mothers unable to carry out adequately their parenting role due, for example, to dire economic circumstances or emotional problems, can have long-lasting negative effects on children. Moreover, the focus on "maternal bonding" renders the economic contribution women make when performing their apparent "labour of love" insignificant (Graham, 1983; James, 1989; Leira, 1992). As Arnlaug Leira (1992: 16) states, "biological motherhood does not necessarily entail a feeling of love and care for a child. Empirical evidence points to highly differentiated reactions to pregnancy, giving birth and nursing. Ambivalent responses, rejection, even hatred are not uncommon."

Tangible growth in mothers' employment in the post-World War II era has brought attention to women's non-paid caring work, and at the same time called into the question the indispensability of mothers as primary caregivers. The welfare state has become a central arena for the creation of mothers' social rights (and those of parents in general) to undertake paid employment and at the same time bear and raise children. Welfare state provisions in the form of temporary family leaves and accompanying benefits have become commonplace in most industrial capitalist countries. Yet the comprehensiveness of the social provision made available, the level of funding, and the flexibility and duration offered differ significantly across national boundaries, and even within national jurisdictions. Canada's social provision in this key dimension of citizens' rights is a step ahead of the United States, but moderate compared to the types and level of social provision provided by Sweden for new families. Before examining the Canadian case, it is worth defining the three main types of family leaves and benefits.

Maternity leave usually refers to a temporary exit from employment granted to a pregnant woman around the time of late pregnancy, childbirth, and early postpartum. The key distinctions about maternity leave are that it is unpaid, for "mothers only," and generally is restricted to the limited period of physical recovery from childbirth. *Paternity leave* is an analogous period for new fathers. The paternity leave includes two kinds of unpaid provision: 1) birth leave or "daddy days" (anywhere from a few days to a few weeks around the birth of a child) made available to biological fathers and, depending on the country or province/state, to adoptive mothers and fathers; and 2) an extra number of weeks for fathers to spend with young infants. *Parental leave* is gender-neutral, where either parent can make a claim (but not both simultaneously) for leave to care for an infant/young child. The parental leave may allow adoptive as well as biological mothers and fathers to decide who will remain employed during their child's early life and who will take "time off" to be with the infant. In some countries the parental leave can be divided between the parents, taken part-time, or spread across time. Virtually all industrial capitalist countries provide at least minimal maternity leave, and many also make available parental leave. It is noteworthy, however, that until recently the United States had no mandatory family leave of any kind (and remains a laggard in this respect). This includes "family-related/childcare leave," a set number of days/weeks per year that natural or adoptive parents can take to spend with their child (or in some cases an elderly family member) in an emergency situation such as illness.

Depending on the country, family leaves are often accompanied by *leave benefits*, whereby the leave taker is paid a certain amount to compensate for lost earnings. Family leave benefits are currently available only in select countries, and even then the level of payment varies widely; typically it is set at a percentage of previous wages, ranging from just over half of income replacement to near full replacement. There are only a few countries in which family leave benefits are accessible to all citizens, regardless of employment status. An example of a universal benefit is the *mother's/maternity allowance* following childbirth—a cash benefit not tied to previous employment status but available to all mothers. *Family/child allowances* are another such benefit, typically a sum based on the number of children and paid directly to mothers.

When viewed cross-nationally, Canada occupies a middling position in regard to family leaves and benefits. Quebec in most respects is far more generous in its social provision than other provinces, approximating European Union family provision systems. As Table 4–3 shows, while all Canadian provinces have provision for maternity and parental leaves, only Quebec makes provision for paternity leave. Outside of Quebec, the family leave benefit level is comparatively low, making it difficult for economically marginalized families to access because of low income-replacement levels. This also serves as a disincentive for new fathers— who tend to be the higher income earners—to become the stay-at-home parent during the duration of parental leave (Baker, 1995).

Maternity leaves in Canada are a relatively recent phenomenon (Mishra, 1996). Under pressure from unions representing large groups of female employees, feminist organizations, and community groups, in 1971 the Canada Labour Code was amended, outlawing dismissal for reason of pregnancy in all workplaces under federal jurisdiction, and at the same time granting women for the first time the right to a maternity leave. According to Alena Heitlinger (1993: 211), "by the end of the decade all of the provinces and the territories had enacted labour laws entitling women employees under their jurisdiction to a maternity leave of 17 weeks or longer, prohibiting their dismissal on the grounds of pregnancy, and in some cases, guaranteeing the same or comparable work on return after childbirth." At the same time, federal and provincial human rights legislation granted women legal protection against discrimination by employers, as well as against employment dismissal, due to pregnancy and childbirth.

TABLE 4-3	Family Leaves and Benefits in Canada: 1997		
Leaves	**Duration**	**% Pay**	**Recipient**
Parental	10 wks*	55% of wage**	either adoptive or natural parents
Mother's/Maternity	17 wks	55% of wage**	reserved for natural mother only
Father's/Paternity	None***		
Sick Child Leave	none		
Child Contact Days	none		

*Quebec proposal: 30 wks combined leaves, plus 26 extra wks for a third child
**Quebec proposal: 75% wage.
***Also under discussion in Quebec.

Sources: Childcare Resource and Research Unit. 1995. Child Care in Canada: Provinces and Territories. Toronto: Childcare Resource and Research Unit; Human Resources Development Canada: 1998. The New Employment Insurance System. Ottawa: Human Resources Centre of Canada; Gouvernment du Québec. 1997. New Elements of the Family Policy: Our Children at the Heart of Our Decisions. Montreal: Bibliotheque nationale du Quebec.

However, a minimum duration of continuous employment is required in order to meet eligibility requirements for job reinstatement following childbirth. The range is 6 months in the federal jurisdiction to 12 months in some provinces, with a norm of 1 year of continuous employment with the same employer to qualify (Heitlinger, 1993: 221). A Canadian woman falling within the qualifying period of her province/territory is entitled to 17 or 18 weeks of unpaid leave, usually starting no earlier than 11 weeks prior to the expected date of birth and ending no later than 17 weeks following the actual date of birth. Yet due to the fact that many women have jobs that are classified as "non-standard employment"—including contingent workers holding short-term contracts, part-time employees with irregular hours, seasonal workers, including students and farm labourers, and domestic workers—the take-up rate for maternity leaves in Canada remains below 50 per cent of all working mothers.

Gender-neutral parental leave rights did not become available in Canada until the beginning of the 1990s. At first extended to adoptive parents, eventually natural fathers were able to avail of parental leaves providing they met minimum requirements. Under federal jurisdiction, this involves six consecutive months of continuous employment with a single employer for one period of unpaid parental leave. The maximum parental leave period is 24 weeks and must be taken within 52 weeks of the date of birth or, for adoptive parents, arrival under their care and custody. A parent's eligibility for parental leave is based on his or her own entitlement at the time the leave is taken. Two parents who qualify for parental leave are neither required to take their share of parental leave at the same time, nor hindered from doing so. In line with its other comparatively generous family provisions, Quebec has adopted a European-style parental leave policy: as of April 1997 the act respecting labour standards regarding parental leave was amended in order to increase the provincial parental leave to up to 30 weeks for parents with 1 or 2 children, and a further 26 weeks for the birth or adoption of a third child (Government du Québec, 1997).

Entitlement to maternity and parental leaves are altogether separate from entitlement to maternity or parental *benefits* in Canada. The former fall under labour standards legislation at the federal/provincial/territorial levels, while the latter fall under the Employment Insurance Act (discussed above), and are thus a federal matter. At present, an EI claim for maternity or parental benefits requires a minimum of 700 hours or 20 weeks of work in the past 52 weeks or since the last claim. After a 2-week waiting period, maternity benefits can be claimed for a maximum of 15 weeks. Maternity benefits can be activated as early as 8 weeks before birth and as late as 17 weeks after giving birth. Parental benefits are also paid from UI/EI contributions, with a limit of 10 weeks, and cannot be drawn at the same time as a maternity benefit.

Examined comparatively, Canadian government maternity and paternal benefits are meagre, in 1999 at the EI rate of 55 per cent of previous earnings, reduced from 57 per cent in 1993, with a minimum earnings set at $6.70 per hour. Once again Quebec shows favourably. The Quebec government hopes to top up the federal EI benefit to a wage replacement of 75 per cent for the proposed 30 weeks of parental leave (and provide an additional $100 per week for the proposed extended 26 weeks of parental leave for a third child). In addition, with regard to eligibility for maternity benefits, Quebec plans to replace the minimum federal earnings hourly rate by a less stringent requirement: an employee would have to earn a minimum of $2 000 over the previous 52 weeks in order to qualify. This new policy would extend the maternity benefit to self-employed workers as well as a large number of those in non-standard employment. However, implementation of these proposals depends on the outcome of ongoing negotiations between the Quebec and federal governments over the redistribution of monies now allocated to the maternity and parental federal employment insurance program. Should these negotiations fail, the Quebec government has proposed that salaried and self-employed workers pay a slightly higher payroll contribution (Government du Québec, 1997).

Employed workers in higher-paid and unionized jobs in the rest of Canada, as well as many federal and provincial government employees, have negotiated through their employment contracts similar additional family benefits. However, a substantial number of workers in other areas of the country are unable at present to avail themselves of these extra provisions that have been shown to ease family/job tensions for working parents. Due to the kinds of jobs many Canadian women find themselves in—contingent work, part-time and part-year employment, and short-term contracts—often they are unable to access even basic family benefits because they are deemed ineligible, not having worked the minimum number of hours and/or received high enough wages to establish an employment insurance claim. This finding, in addition to the fact that to date there is no provision for paternity leaves or benefits, indicates that most Canadian provinces offer only scanty support to parents (especially new mothers) facing the tensions of balancing family and employment. As is shown below, Canada has adopted a similarly reluctant approach when it comes to public provision for childcare.

Childcare Provisions

Non-family services for the care of young children first became an issue in Canada and other countries during the early industrial period. Impoverished children, many of whom were the offspring of solo mothers, abandoned or widowed, were sometimes placed in charity foundling homes and orphanages while their parents searched for employment. In the case of solo mothers, domestic or factory work might eventually be found and the child brought back home. Other times a child might be relinquished permanently to the authorities. (Acton et al., 1974)

Some enlightened thinkers of the period argued that non-family childcare in principal was not a harmful development. Others argued that well-organized "kindergartens" (preschools/nursery schools) could enhance a child's social and intellectual advancement. This perspective was especially prominent in many countries of Continental Europe, where public kindergartens have been in operation for over a century (Baker, 1995: 189).

Non-family childcare was viewed more positively whenever women's economic independence was deemed important for the economy and society. As noted in the previous chapter, the shortage of labour power in virtually all industrial capitalist countries during the Second World War drew mothers of young and school-aged children into paid employment in large numbers, necessitating non-family solutions for the care of children, if only until the war ended and the male "breadwinners" returned home.

Socialist countries that have encouraged women's economic independence also have made extensive social provision for non-family childcare (Heitlinger, 1993). This has been the case for industrial capitalist countries with strong social democratic traditions, especially Sweden and Finland, where a model of public responsibility has led to the development of nationwide institutionalized childcare systems (Leira, 1992; Tyyskä, 1998). Other countries, however, have viewed childcare essentially as a *private responsibility*, based on the viewpoint that the parental (i.e., mother's) role in caring for children is paramount to their successful adaptation to adulthood and to a harmonious family life. In these cases, government involvement in the family is seen as a last resort to rescue children who are deemed at risk. Otherwise the family unit is held as sacred and parents are awarded the primary responsibility of socializing and caring for their children on a daily basis. In almost all cases this means that it is the mother's duty to give essential and continuous care to her children, the mother's ideal place being the private space of the home. Furthermore, there is little need for public policies that support subsidized childcare and related issues, since these concerns apparently are taken care of already in the home by natural mothers (Sainsbury, 1996: 95–96).

Canada in most respects fits the personal responsibility model of childcare (Eichler, 1997). Although public kindergartens first opened in Ontario in 1883, it was not until after the First World War that they became commonplace in the province. Those that were opened catered mainly to the educated middle-classes who wished to "enrich" their children's early development. The nursery school/kindergarten concept remained controversial throughout much of this century, however, due predominantly to the belief among many educators and the general public that children in such settings suffered from maternal deprivation. In addition, "conservatives as well as trade unionists thought that nursery schools would encourage married women to work outside the home and compete with male breadwinners, leading to the dissolution of 'the family'" (Baker, 1995: 199). Very gradually some provinces expanded public primary school education to include a half day of instruction for four- and five-year-olds, although this practice was neither required by federal law nor standardized across the provinces. Today only New Brunswick and Quebec provide full-day kindergarten five days a week through their public school systems.

As paid employment for mothers in the 1960s and 1970s rose dramatically, so did the demand for non-family childcare for preschool children at even younger ages. Despite the call from parents, feminists, and policy-makers for national childcare, Canada has yet to embrace the concept of childcare as an essential public service. Funding, delivery, and management of childcare services are provincial matters, and to date no province has been able to come close to meeting public demand for accessible, affordable, regulated preschool and after-school childcare services. Quebec again stands out as an exception. Throughout 1994/95, the Quebec government consulted the public regarding how to finance childcare services, as well as how the early-childhood education system could be revamped to better serve the province's children. In late 1996 the Quebec government announced a comprehensive public policy plan to meet the needs of children between birth and age 12. Phased in over a four-year period, the plan will mean that children between birth and age four years will be eligible for enrolment in "childhood centres," which will be adapted from existing childcare centres and family daycare centres. The first stage began in September 1997, when new childcare services for four-year-olds in high-risk communities and full-day kindergarten for all five-year-olds were made available. By the year 2001 there will be 73 000 spaces accessible for children from birth to 4 years of age. The new childcare policy requires parents to pay a minimum cost of $5 per day. For solo parents with annual incomes below $20 000, the payment is offset by the new integrated child allowance. Thus a solo-parent family with an annual income of $14 000 will pay an extra $786 for childcare, but will receive an integrated child allowance of $2 845, replacing the former $248 single-parent allowance (Gouvernment du Québec, 1997: 22). Another component of Quebec's childcare policy, available through the provincial school system, will be free after-school care for children up to age 12.[1]

Outside of Quebec, access to regulated childcare is far from satisfactory. In 1995 there were more than 5 million children between birth age and 12 years living in Canada. Of these, 3.25 million had mothers in the paid labour force. Yet the proportion of children in this age range for whom there was a regulated childcare space in 1995 (including Quebec) was a mere 8.4 per cent, while the percentage of subsidized childcare spaces for children 3–5 years of age was 35 per cent (Gornick et al., 1997). The unlucky majority of employed parents are forced to seek help wherever they can, including: paying for unregulated private daycare; depending on partners or other family members and perhaps doing shift work; hiring live-in or daily domestic help; organizing cooperative strategies with friends; and, when all else fails, exiting from paid employment. Moreover, in many provinces a minority—and in some a majority—of regulated spaces are expected to generate profit, which research indicates to be less beneficial for children and more expensive for parents (Johnson and Dineen, 1981; Heitlinger, 1993).

In the early 1980s the likelihood of quality and affordable non-family daycare for all employed parents looked more promising. All provinces had passed childcare regulations to support children's healthy development and well-being, and all offered some funding for at least those families unable to meet costs. The federal government also indicated some willingness to accept childcare as an essential public service by sharing the cost of non-family childcare for low-income families. Yet under the *Canada Assistance Plan* (CAP), provinces had to pay upfront for childcare for families in financial straits and then apply to the federal government for matching funds. Solo mothers especially were affected because while they had no partner to share the responsibility, frequently neither could they find a space for their child even when they were eligible for a childcare subsidy (Baker, 1995: 201). In 1988 the federal government attempted to remove childcare coverage from CAP under a proposed *Child Care Act*. If enacted, the proposed legislation would have removed federal funding for childcare from social welfare assistance, while opening up the possibility of reducing federal contributions to the provinces. The legislation also suggested that federal funding be extended to private/for-profit childcare facilities, and proposed neither national standards for regulation of childcare centres nor minimal formal qualifications for childcare workers.

After vocal opposition from almost every interested party, the federal government abandoned any change in the status quo, so that "by the mid-1990s, the childcare situation was in decline in much of Canada. Universal funding had been eliminated or decreased in a majority of jurisdictions and fee subsidies for low income parents had been reduced, frozen and capped by provincial/territorial governments" (Friendly, 1997: 109).

More positively, the federal government provides tax relief to Canadian parents to help offset childcare expenses. Tax-free payments were made by 85 per cent of Canadian families with children in 1997 (Finance Canada, 1997). Yet the system is less than redistributive, as parents are required to provide receipts of childcare payments in order to receive the deduction. Many employed parents cannot attain receipts for care-providers working in the informal "black market." Nor is the tax deduction any use for families too poor to record a taxable income. In any event, "commodified childcare purchased in the open market tends not to be of high quality. A free market in childcare typically contains a large number of small-scale, under-resourced, fragmented, cottage-industry producers, whose product is relatively invisible to working parents, its frontline customers" (Heitlinger, 1993: 227).

A fairer child-related policy was passed in July 1998. The *National Child Benefit* provides federal funds ($850 million in 1998) over and above the child tax benefit to all families with children, to offset the costs of childcare and related expenses. The actual benefit level is calculated automatically by the income declared on tax returns. In addition, through their social assistance programs the provinces offer means-tested benefits (based on proven need) to families to help them meet some out-of-pocket childcare expenses.

As with its parental leaves and benefits and employment-related policies, Canada's non-family care arrangements for children of employed parents reveal a moderately friendly welfare state from a female perspective. Apart from the creation of kindergartens as part of primary school public education in a number of provincial jurisdictions, support for government-licensed and affordable childcare centres has been and remains limited. This is despite the fact that even cost-benefit analyses indicate that a tightly regulated public childcare system with college-trained, well-paid staff would have numerous long-range gains for society, including higher income and improved job security for employed women, larger tax revenues, enhanced child development, and superior life prospects for Canadian children (Philp, 1998: A8).

Instead, employed parents in Canada have had to rely by and large on *ad hoc* arrangements, sometimes placing their children at risk in unregulated home-based or community programs that tend to be costly and often inadequate. It appears that Canada's political leaders do not view children as a common resource. Nor is child-rearing viewed as the public responsibility of society at large. In short, a "principle of caring," which forms the basis of a gendered welfare state, is only partly present in Canada. As the window below reveals, the American approach to social welfare has been even less substantial than the general Canadian experience.

A THIRD WINDOW ON THE UNITED STATES

Comparative evidence suggests that other Western industrialized nations faced the growing dependence of families and businesses on female labor much earlier in time, and responded to that need with strong state policies .... Given the much weaker role of the United States in this area, coupled with the decline in organized labor over the past 30 years, the business community has had much more influence here on the development of family responsive policies. (Glass and Fujimoto, 1995: 381)

In almost all forms of social provision tagged as crucial for women's achievement of economic independence and capacity to maintain an autonomous household, the US welfare state
lags behind Canada and, indeed, most other industrial capitalist countries. As observed, the
US has yet to move beyond the private responsibility model of citizenship; individual women
and men are required to provide for themselves and their dependents, with the welfare state
provision kept at a minimal level, available to individuals deemed "deserving" only when all
else fails. Both historical and ideological factors shape the minimalist American approach
towards social welfare. American industrial capitalists and industrialists over the past century have met their labour force needs to a large extent by relying on new immigrant labourers, who were unorganized and willing to work for comparatively low wages and few social
benefits. The availability of a cheap immigrant labour force has had contradictory effects for
paid workers, providing employment for new immigrants while at once weakening the
labour power of American citizens, themselves often former immigrants or "second-gen-
eration" Americans.

The contradiction extends to American women's employment opportunities and access
to work-related and broader citizenship benefits. The relatively abundant pool of cheap immigrant labour, in addition to a weak union movement and a small welfare state service
sector, has limited American women's access to relatively attractive public sector jobs, as
well as access to benefits that balance paid and unpaid work. The only exception in the
twentieth century was during wartime. As in Canada, the labour shortage was such that
federal and state governments adopted active employment practices in order to recruit previously unemployed female citizens to work in light and even heavy industry, and even
went so far as to establish 3 012 childcare centres across the country in order to accommodate newly employed women's childcare needs (Sidel, 1986: 119).

Apart from exceptions made to fulfil wartime labour-force shortages (most wartime
childcare centres were subsequently closed), the dominant ideology in the US in regard to
gender equality in employment and family life has been a restricted form of equality limited
to individuals' opportunities to compete on the free market for jobs. Whereas other industrial capitalist countries have focused their attention on actual gender equality outcomes—
and pursued both employment and social welfare policies to this end—state and federal
governments in the US, even more so than Canadian counterparts, have chosen to leave it to
the individual to avail him or herself of opportunities as they are made available. As Barbara
Reskin and Irene Padavic (1994: 161) point out, "whereas European societies place a premium on social welfare, American ideology places individual freedom above all else. The
American tradition of individualism is at odds with the notion that a country has a stake in
raising the next generation."

Below is a brief review of US employment-related policies, parental leaves and benefits,
and childcare policies. The available evidence reveals that only those American women in
better jobs (who tend to be white, educated, and from economically privileged backgrounds)
enjoy relatively high incomes and at the same time have access to employment-related benefits in the form of *corporate welfare*. One result is sharp divisions between American
women along social class and racial/ethnic lines. Women who are dependent wives but located in high-status, male breadwinner families, as well as women with secure careers,
stand in a privileged position above the majority of American women. Insecure and low-paying jobs, accompanied by neither employer-related nor universal state social benefits, mean
that large numbers of women in the US are likely at some point in their lives to fall into
poverty and to stay there much longer than counterparts in Sweden and even Canada, among

other industrial capitalist countries. Given that American divorce rates are the highest in the industrial capitalist world, female homemakers who are economically dependent upon their breadwinner husband are likely to find themselves in similarly dire straits following separation or divorce.

Unemployment benefits in the US are illustrative. To qualify for unemployment benefits, attachment to the labour force alone does not cut it for American women. While federal legislation makes unemployment and social insurance contributions compulsory, each state sets its own rules regarding type of coverage, level of contributions, as well as how its unemployment program is administered. Typically excluded from coverage are farmworkers, personal service workers (including private household workers who clean, cook, garden, and care for dependent family members), part-time employees with wages falling below minimum eligibility requirements,[2] short-term contract contingency workers with too few weeks of continuous employment, as well as employees who quit their jobs voluntarily or are fired with "just cause."

Once these factors are taken into account, at any point in time only about one in four unemployed workers receives unemployment insurance reimbursement, and the usual maximum time that benefits can be drawn is six months (Tausky, 1996). While some union contracts include a supplement to the state UI benefit by increasing the base amount or extending the duration period, low levels of unionization mean that relatively few unemployed workers are so-privileged and that those who are tend to be men. Much more so than men, American women tend to be employed part-time or part-year, often in poorly paid sales or service jobs that do not meet the minimum earnings requirements for collecting unemployment insurance benefits. The same applies to live-in domestic/childcare workers, who are largely new immigrant, Black, and Hispanic women (Hodson and Sullivan, 1995: 135). In fact, many women in the US are forced to make ends meet by taking on two or even three part-time jobs, all of which fall short of meeting the minimum earnings UI requirement. According to Diane Sainsbury (1996: 114–15), "stiffer availability for work tests and disqualification for voluntary quits disadvantage women. Family tasks set limits on the ability to take an available job, and domestic reasons often cause women to leave a job. Among job leavers, women outnumbered men, and domestic quits have not been recognized as involuntary."[3] Even refusal to accept rock-bottom wages and inadequate working conditions is reason enough in many states to disqualify the unemployed from claiming UI benefits (Hodson and Sullivan, 1995: 135).

Old age and survivor social security benefits are also contingent on particular employment characteristics. The US federal *Social Security Act* dates to 1935, a part of President Roosevelt's "New Deal" strategy to aid American families during the Great Depression of the 1930s (Baker, 1995: 110). Initially the Act provided old age and survivor benefits only to employees in commerce and industry. By 1980 about 90 per cent of all jobs were covered officially. Excluded are many occupational categories that are barred as well from access to UI benefits: employed persons of non-profit organizations, the self-employed, farm employees, and in-house workers whose earnings fall below minimum wage specifications (Sainsbury, 1996: 58). In addition, social security benefits are based on the insured employee's length of workforce attachment and average hourly earnings. Given American women's more contingent attachment to the labour force and lower hourly wages, they are less likely than men to be eligible for old age security benefits. In fact, US women in male breadwinner families are better off in regard to old age security benefits than married women with benefits based on their own earnings. US tax laws are such that the combination of breadwinner and non-working spouse together receives a larger retirement benefit than the two-income family, and the more equal a couple's income, the lower their retirement and survivor benefits (Sainsbury, 1996: 58–59). Facing particular discrimination are divorced women without paid employment during their marriage, and those who divorce before the 20-year minimum requirement for entitlement to a spousal benefit at half the employed earner's retirement benefit.

About 4 in 10 marriages in the US end in divorce (Macionis, 1996: 311), and children generally stay with their mothers, who tend not to share custody with their spouse. The US, like Canada, has no advanced child support system; the well-being of dependent children frequently is contingent on non-custodial parents meeting their court-ordered obligation to share continued responsibility for their children. Many "dead-end dads" fail to meet their maintenance obligations altogether or contribute only a portion of the mandated payment. Even though the private enforcement model of child support (based on a private agreement between the divorced couple or drawn up in court) has been bypassed recently by Congressional amendments to the *Social Security Act*—mandating that states be responsible for establishing paternity up to the child's eighteenth birthday, and setting into place an enforcement system that requires employers to withhold child-support contributions from the earnings of non-custodial parents failing to meet their obligations—many continue to avoid economic commitment to their children by changing employers or even states (Baker, 1995: 325–29). There are also many other separated and divorced fathers who, even when they want to, cannot afford to meet their child-support obligations.

In summary, a brief examination of some of the employment-related policies in the US shows that even when pursuing paid work, American women often are left poor, with lower take-home pay, less secure employment, and fewer insured benefits than male counterparts. This is especially the case for mothers—divorced or never married—maintaining solo-parent households. Because of their desperate economic situation, many are forced to turn for help to the only form of social benefit apart from food stamps—*Aid to Families with Dependent Children* (AFDC), routinely referred to as "welfare" (Burtless and Weaver, 1997).

The forerunner of AFDC, "mothers' pensions" (also known as *Mothers' Aid Laws*) were introduced in 1911 and set the tone for following social welfare programs. Individual states had the authority to decide whether or not a solo mother and her children were "deserving." Eventually 40 states had such laws, but they varied greatly. Mothers' pensions in some states were restricted to widows and their children, while in other states deserted and divorced mothers were eligible as well. Only in a few states were unwed mothers deemed deserving (Polakow, 1993: 54). To qualify, solo mothers had to demonstrate that they were able to provide a positive home environment for their child/children. Among other things, this meant that they had to make their homes available to inspection by local officials, provide religious education for their children, refrain from taking in male boarders or other men, and make sure their children succeeded in school (Bomersbach, 1994: 172).

Mothers' pensions were displaced in 1935 with the passing of the *Social Security Act*. The Act included five new programs, including two programs for "able-bodied" predominantly male breadwinners—*Old Age Assistance* (discussed above) and *Workmen's Compensation*—and three welfare programs for dependent persons—*Aid to the Blind, Old Age Assistance*, and *Aid to Dependent Children* (ADC). The first two were designated for those with a suitable work ethic and continued link to employment. The latter three programs were based on the ideology of relief for those in dire straits. ADC transferred cash benefits to the caregiver of children whose fathers were deceased or had reneged on their parental responsibility, thereby substantially increasing the number of solo mothers receiving benefits by the late 1930s (Baker, 1995: 111–12). Nevertheless, "because the 'suitable home' provisions, a left-over from the mothers' pension program, were still enforced, many black children and children of unwed mothers continued to be excluded. Race and moral fitness continued to operate as regulatory mechanisms that perpetuated the stigma suffered by single mothers" (Polakow, 1993: 56).

In 1950 ADC was amended to *Aid to Families with Dependent Children* (AFDC). While funded jointly by the federal and state governments, each state established its own eligibility requirements and benefit levels, and administered its program. Bearing in mind that during this post-war period women's employment was no longer championed, like its forerunners AFDC granted economic support to solo mothers on the basis of proof of domesticity and dedication to parenting. The ideology shaping the AFDC program throughout the 1950s and early 1960s was the primacy of women's mothering role; the earnings of solo mothers in paid employment were subtracted from their welfare benefits, which were reduced dollar for dollar. The "man in the house rule" (which also underscored the Canadian social assistance program) assumed that women were men's dependents—the mere presence of a man meant withdrawal of benefits, whether or not he contributed to the family's upkeep (Baker, 1995: 112–18).

In an attempt to battle the growing poverty and ill-health among the nation's children and elders (under the banner "War on Poverty"), two new health care programs were developed: *Medicaid* for the "deserving poor" and *Medicare* for seniors. In addition, the food stamps program was expanded and housing aid was made available. Although benefits varied from state to state and were generally below the official US poverty line, which was less generous than that set by Canada (Kamerman and Kahn, 1981), more and more American solo mothers applied for AFDC. It offered their families a standard of living that full-time employment in the lower-tiered jobs available to them could not realize, because AFDC provided solo mothers a "social wage" in the form of health care, housing, and other relief benefits that, ironically, they could not afford when employed (Sainsbury, 1996: 81–83). Black, Aboriginal, Hispanic, and other minority solo mothers, doubly discriminated against in employment by virtue of both their sex and race/ethnicity, were especially likely to seek AFDC benefits. Thus, "between 1967 to 1971 the proportion of eligible female-headed families who received benefits increased from approximately 50 to 90 percent" (Polakow, 1993: 57).

Critics of AFDC maintained that the program created dependency of solo mothers and their children on state handouts, rather than promoting economic independence and individual responsibility. Beginning in the early 1970s, the ideology of welfare in the US shifted and AFDC established new "incentives" for solo mothers in regard to gainful employment, changing from relief for full-time mothering to "working for relief." Solo mothers were expected to enrol in training and employment schemes; those with no children under age six were required to seek employment; and the "thirty-one-third rule" was enacted, permitting recipients to keep the first $30 they earned per month, as well as one-third of the rest of their monthly wage. The new regulations once again left solo mothers trapped in the poverty cycle:

> The *Work Incentive Program* not only proved ineffective in moving women off welfare but served as a source of continuing harassment for single mothers. Since a minimal allowance was given for child care, since child care itself was frequently unavailable or unaffordable, and since most women had access only to low-wage jobs, with no support system when children were ill nor not in school, poor mothers found themselves in a no win situation. (Polakow, 1993: 57)

New legislation also required that solo mothers reveal their child's paternity or otherwise be denied welfare benefits. Any child support collected by employers or the state from non-custodial fathers was subtracted from the solo mother's welfare benefit, encouraging no improvement in the economic standing of solo mothers and their children (Kahn and Kamerman, 1988). Moreover, since many non-custodial fathers of poor children are poor themselves, the policing system of child support had little direct benefit to needy children.

From the mid 1970s to the late 1980s, especially under the Reagan administration, government attempted to undermine the nation's "welfare culture" by tightening eligibility requirements and drastically reducing social benefits. Childcare, Medicaid, food stamps, housing, and school lunch programs were among those axed entirely or diminished radically. Large numbers of solo mothers and their children were suspended from receiving AFDC, leaving them without means to attain health care and housing, or even to feed their families. The elimination of these safeguards, combined with high divorce rates and persistent racial inequality, has worsened the *feminization of poverty*, as well as the *infantilization of poverty* among US women and their children. By 1986 solo-parent families, the vast majority of which are headed by women, were the poorest of all family categories in the US (Baker, 1995). Government efforts to enforce child maintenance also remain contradictory, especially for children of unmarried mothers, whose paternity is often difficult to secure, but without which they are denied welfare benefits.

Social programs for the poor were reduced further in 1991, with the most drastic cuts in AFDC since the program's inception in 1950: benefits remained below the national poverty line in every state; federal funding made it impossible for state governments to adequately administer their programs; and the states were given too much leeway in determining eligibility requirements (Baker, 1995: 114–15).

The present US administration has devised the latest version of welfare reform, with Bill Clinton pledging (during his 1992 presidential campaign) "to end welfare as you know it." The newest welfare reform passed by Congress in 1996—*Personal Responsibility and Work Opportunity Act*—poses serious risk to the nation's poorest women and children, who will no longer be eligible under the new legislation. AFDC is now replaced with a federal block grant, *Temporary Assistance for Needy Families* (TANF). It is similar in some respects to the new block funding approach recently adopted in Canada, the CHST (see above), with the important difference being that Canada's federal contribution is more comprehensive, including health care, as well as more generous.

The new American law eliminates individual entitlement to welfare benefits; the states can now decide outright if a solo mother or child is eligible for cash aid. In order to qualify for a TANF grant, which is determined by the level of their AFDC in preceding years, states have to demonstrate that adult recipients have been gainfully employed within a set time. The family head must take up employment within two years from the onset of welfare benefits, and states cannot grant TANF for more than five years in total to a given family. Although there is no evidence that illegitimacy rates will fall, the new law continues to give states the option to deny benefits to unmarried teenaged mothers and to dictate *family caps* that disallow higher monthly benefits to mothers who conceive a child while on welfare. If the states can meet this new federal restriction, their level of TANF will be reduced accordingly. Many critics believe that the new welfare reform law is a categorical change from the past, abolishing a mainstay of government support of more than six decades. While reflecting the public's strong belief that all healthy adults should make their own way, "the new law has serious shortcomings. By abolishing the entitlement of needy children to cash assistance, it places a large and extremely vulnerable population at risk. By allowing states to cut spending on welfare, it tempts them to divert resources to other uses, including tax reductions or benefits for more affluent citizens" (Burtless and Weaver, 1997: 29).

Despite pressure by feminist groups, unions, and other organizations calling for the enactment of mandatory maternity and parental leaves and benefits for all workers, a strong business lobby has prevented Congress from moving in this direction. To date, as shown in Table 4–4, there are no required paid benefits available; the only requirement of the 1993 federal legislation, the *Family and Medical Leave Act*, is that medium and large firms have to grant unpaid parental leave to female and male employees. Businesses with fewer than 50 employees are exempt even from the parental leave law, despite the fact that these firms employ over three-quarters of the US labour force. Moreover, as Reskin and Padavic (1994: 163) note, "the law is of no value to parents who cannot afford parental leave."

TABLE 4–4	Family Leaves and Benefits in United States: 1997		
Leaves	**Duration**	**% Pay**	**Recipient**
Parental	12 wks	zero	either adoptive or natural parents
Mother's/Maternity	none		
Father's/Paternity	none		
Sick Child Leave	none		
Child Contact Days	none		

Source: US Department of Labor's Employment Standards Administration, Wage and Hour Division. 1993. The Family and Medical Leave Act of 1993. Fact Sheet No. 028.

Inaccessibility to parental leaves and benefits means that many American women, especially those in non-standard employment, are forced to *exit* from their jobs at the birth of their child, thereby losing both an income and any job seniority acquired prior to pregnancy. Another consequence is the entrenchment of gender inequality within families and society as a whole. Women are forced both to shoulder the burden of loss of income and employment opportunities and to bear the charge of reproducing the next generation.

Childcare arrangements in the US are another example of minimal welfare state provision. As with parental leave and other family policies, childcare falls under the mandate of state governments. The result is both tremendous variation in regulated childcare services across and within states—demand outstripping supply—and high out-of-pocket costs. According to the US Census Bureau, families with mothers in the workforce most often rely on *informal care* for their preschool children, most of which is free (provided by friends or family members) or paid by working parents. In fact, 4.5 million (43 per cent) of America's preschool children in 1994 received their primary care from relatives other than their mothers. Just over one-quarter were in daycare centres (21 per cent) or nursery schools (8 per cent) in 1994 (Casper, 1994).

While these figures represent a near doubling of childcare spaces available a decade earlier, much of the growth (over half in the mid 1990s) has been in profit-making childcare facilities; children aged 3–5 years in subsidized care accounted for only 15 per cent (Gornick et al., 1997). In fact, the US records the highest percentage of for-profit childcare centres of all countries (Adams and Johnson, 1991).

Federally funded childcare programs, including the early-intervention *Start Program*, have also expanded over the decade, but are targeted mainly towards those on social assistance or living below the poverty line, and even these restricted services meet only a small segment of eligible children, anywhere between 10 and 20 per cent (Hayes et al., 1990: 214–18). Lack of adequate childcare spaces in non-profit public facilities means that families with higher incomes are far more likely than poor families to have their children in organized programs. According to Lynne Casper (1994: 4), "among children living in families with incomes of at least $4 500 per month, one-third of preschoolers were primarily cared for by organized child care facilities compared with about 1 in 5 children in families with lower monthly family incomes." Social class plays an even larger role in the case of older children due to the paucity of subsidized (affordable) after-school programs. The phrase "latchkey kids" describes those children who are left without adult supervision. Approximately 7.6 per cent of the children of employed US women in 1991 were said to be providing "self care" (Casper, 1994: 3). Research also shows that finding appropriate childcare in the US is the chief source of stress for employed mothers (Ross and Mirowsky, 1988). It also eats up a substantial portion of the family income; in fact, "it constitutes one of the largest work-related costs" (Reskin and Padavic, 1994: 153). In 1993 the out-of-pocket costs varied from 7 per cent (of total income) for families above the poverty line to 21 per cent for those families falling below (Casper, 1994).

Rather than moving to develop a national system of childcare as a way to improve quality of services and at the same time expand entry to parents excluded from accessing existing arrangements, the US has followed, as with other forms of social provision, a minimalist approach. It leaves the market to sort out the question of childcare demand and supply, and expects parents themselves (or, for the lucky ones, their employers) to pay for this "consumer item." It is true, as in Canada, that the US federal government has helped to ease the economic burden of childcare on families by making available tax credits or deductions for childcare expenses, and by adding new funding in its 1999 budget.[4] Yet because such deductions are not refundable, they are of little use to low-income families too poor to pay taxes. Moreover, the childcare tax credit can be claimed only for *licensed* daycare arrangements. This means, among other things, that the majority of American families whose children are either in family daycares, or taken care of by relatives or neighbours, cannot claim the tax credit. Only 39.9 million people (13.3 million families) in the US received an "earned income tax credit" (childcare tax credit) in 1992 (Congressional Research Services, 1992). Some scholars argue that American feminists, with their near-singular focus on equal rights in the eyes of the law, are partly to blame for the paltry state of the *actual* social rights of American women in everyday life:

> Equal rights does not challenge the structure of the economy or the role of government. Asking to be treated as men are treated is a fundamentally conservative position that asks for no special support from government or special consideration from employers for working mothers …. [American] women have trapped themselves in a competitive model that leaves no room for the special needs of women who are the primary child-rearers. (Mason, 1988: 19, 45)

As the next section reveals, Swedish women are far less likely than their American counterparts to face this two-tiered system of social provision, and thus are less likely as a whole either to experience stress balancing family and working life, or to live in poverty.

A THIRD WINDOW ON SWEDEN

> As is well-known, the Swedish public welfare sector is the largest one in Scandinavia and, indeed, in Europe .... The distinctively Swedish element, however, is not so much the social insurance—transfer payments—as the social services; in particular personal social services to the elderly, disabled and children are much more of a public (municipal) provision than in other European countries, using mainly female employees: doctors, nurses, schoolteachers, preschool personnel, home helpers, etc. (Olsson, 1993: 375)

Compared with Canada and the United States, women's social rights in Sweden are both more numerous and more generous, and this remains the case even in the decade marked by the so-called "crisis in the welfare state" (Esping-Andersen, 1996). Reasons for this emanate from a variety of factors, including historical traditions discussed in previous chapters; cultural values; the consensual nature of Swedish labour relations since the mid-century; a strong social democratic political heritage; and a positive view of the state held by a wide spectrum of citizens.

While elimination of class inequality was the initial impetus behind Swedish welfare state policies in the post-World War II period, the gendered face of poverty soon became apparent. Policies encouraging women's economic independence and enhancing the well-being of families date back to the 1930s, and continue to shape welfare state policy at the national level. While Swedish women have yet to enjoy genuine equality with male counterparts, their degree of economic security and quality of life, as well as that of their children, is among the highest in the world (Haavio-Mannila and Kauppinen, 1992). How can this be the case?

As noted in Chapter 3, Swedish women's achievement cannot be explained adequately by the organization of paid and unpaid work alone. In respect to the kinds of tasks Swedish women perform, they are not qualitatively different from their North American sisters. Nor is the explanation linked to lesser occupational sex segregation for Swedish women (Charles, 1992). Rather, the explanation for tangible advantages in social rights for Swedish women involves investigation of the extensive role of the nation's welfare state in promoting gender equality, ranging from active economic policies to comprehensive family and childcare policies.

In contrast to the increasingly lethargic laissez-faire stance on full and secure employment characteristic of both Canada and the US, where demand for workers is dependent on market needs, Sweden continues to adopt, even during the recent recession period, an *active* welfare state economic policy. Initially, working-class male breadwinners gained strong state support to enhance their full employment, with substantial state investment in employment training, geographic relocation for purposes of employment, and retraining programs for the unemployed. Responsibility for administering state labour market programs rests with the National Labour Market Board, county labour boards, and local employment offices.

With the rapid growth of the service sector beginning in the late 1960s and early 1970s, Swedish women became the chief recipients of government sponsored training programs for future employment. Women at the lower end of the economic scale received top priority, since their need for economic independence was deemed the greatest. Helen Ginsburg (1983: 142–43) discusses the potential help received by a newly divorced, middle-aged woman with only seven years of education, seeking employment. After taking a "working-life and education" course, the local Employment Service might deem her eligible for public support to complete her schooling: "afterwards, still receiving the grants, she might be placed in an upper-secondary-school vocational course for about the same amount of time. With such a long-range training plan, a job-placement officer would be in close contact with her during the entire period to make sure her schooling was going well; and the grant would be made one step at a time."

Deep economic recession in the early 1990s led to a rapid increase in unemployment in Sweden (reaching 8–9 per cent by mid-decade, but showing a gradual decline since then to 8.1 per cent in 1998), that initially impacted male employees but eventually led to job losses for women, particularly solo mothers located in lower-paying service jobs.[5] As in North America, Swedish employers attempted to restructure their economic activities to meet the demands of an increasingly global marketplace characterized by ever-bigger multinational firms in fierce competition to increase market shares. However, the Swedish government's response to economic restructuring was different than those of Canadian and US governments, who sought to reduce their expenditures on security for the unemployed, as well as state investment in programs aimed at activating the labour market. The response of the Swedish government was to *increase* its role in labour market policy. In short, the main approach of the Swedish labour market policy is the *activation principle*: "this strategy implies that placement of individuals in the regular labour market should always be the top priority" (The Swedish Institute, 1995: 1). Alternatively, those without work are required to enrol in an available active labour market program. Cash payments such as unemployment benefits are used only as a last resort. No doubt the Swedish government's active role in placing its citizens in regular employment (strongly supported by labour unions) has hindered widespread implementation of efficiency strategies of employers in the direction of "non-standard" employment without benefits—contingent employment, temporary contracts, piecework, and the like (Björnberg and Gardberg, 1996: 274).

The welfare state policies easing Swedish women's non-paid caring work has been likewise substantial and increasingly more women-friendly in the second half of the twentieth century. The first *maternity policy-oriented* legislation in Sweden was passed under the *Labour Safety Act* (LSA), banning women employed in an industrial occupation from returning to their job in the first four weeks after childbirth (Ohlander, 1994: 29). While it was passed with the health of employed mothers and newborns in mind, the LSA had other, less desirable consequences. The crux of the problem was that no cash benefits were guaranteed under the compulsory leave, thereby worsening the economic situation of new mothers and their children. As with similar North American legislation, ASA assumed that women were dependents of a male breadwinner, even though many women were solo mothers forced into gainful employment to support themselves and their children.

The tide began to change in Sweden in regard to women's access to family-related benefits during the Great Depression of the 1930s. While governments in most other industrial capitalist countries (including Canada and the US) enacted discriminatory legislation to restrict married women's employment so to reserve jobs for male breadwinners (the so-called *marriage bars*), Sweden passed no such laws proscribing married women's paid work. Instead, with the support of the unions, the social democratic government of the time followed an alternative legislative path that help women to combine employment and family life (Hobson, 1993; Jonung and Persson, 1994: 47). Reasons for doing so appear to be twofold: a concern for the future of the Swedish population and a desire to improve the equality of Swedish women. Social engineers Alva and Gunnar Myrdal were influential at the time through their work on the nation's impending "population crisis" (Myrdal, 1941). They pointed out that economic straits brought on by the severe depression were among the main factors behind Swedish women's decision to reduce the size of their families. Many remained unmarried for fear of losing their job, and others who did marry were reluctant to have a family. Low fertility was in effect their chief strategy to avoid poverty (Hoem, 1993).

In 1939 Sweden passed statutory legislation that made it unlawful for an employer to dismiss a woman because of pregnancy, childbirth, or marriage. At the same time, female employees with low incomes were granted a minor cash benefit during the maternity leave. Equally significant was the economic support awarded to all solo mothers in the form of a government-run *advanced maintenance system for child support*, a welfare state provision that continues to this day and is instrumental in keeping solo mothers from dropping into poverty after separation, divorce, or desertion. Practical assistance was provided also in the form of *housing/rent subsidies* (although means-tested, even today about 80 per cent of solo mothers receive these subsidies). In 1946 the (1913) *old age insurance* scheme was revised, changing its main coverage, which previously insured wage earners, to entitlement based on citizenship. This meant that married and solo mothers caring for children in the home were able to claim basic old age provision (Sainsbury, 1996: 63–64). The means-test requirement was also removed from disability pensions, making way for equal access to all citizens regardless of gender or economic standing. In the early 1960s means-tested requirements were similarly dislodged from widows' pensions, and the eligibility age dropped to 60 years. Nevertheless, patriarchal traditions remain to the extent that widows' or survivors' benefits have to relinquished upon remarriage, while cohabiting widows may retain their benefits (Sainsbury, 1996: 65).

Other family-related benefits based on citizenship that proved important to Swedish women include the *universal child (family) allowance*, instituted in 1948. This general allowance, which has been eliminated in Canada (with the exception of Quebec and its new integrated child allowance) and never existed in the United States, endures in Sweden. The child allowance is paid to all children up to age 16 years, regardless of parental income or employment status. The universal allowance continues for children beyond this cut-off as long as they remain in secondary school. In addition, school lunches, primary health care provided by nurses and midwives in child-health and youth clinics, dental care, and an assortment of recreational activities have been awarded gratis to all Swedish children (Jonung and Persson, 1994: 50).

The maternity leave/parental insurance system that evolved in Sweden is another cornerstone of the Swedish welfare state pivotal to women's relative equality in paid employment and family life. As early as 1955 a universal maternity leave was institutionalized, with benefits awarded to all new mothers for a three-month period. In 1963 the maternity leave was extended to six months. At that time the leave was accompanied by either a flat-rate benefit paid by the state to non-employed women or a maternity allowance based on the previous earnings of employed mothers.

The *Parental Insurance Act* of 1974 marked a major change in attitude by the Swedish welfare state towards the responsibility of caring work during infancy and the first few years of a child's life. The new act was gender-neutral to the extent that it gave both men and women an opportunity to combine paid work and parenting, whereas previously it had been assumed that only mothers should stay home with a newborn and receive the accompanying cash benefits. The act enlarged the principle of care to fathers by granting them the right to absent themselves from paid work for six or fewer months (and receive a cash benefit) while their partner returned to employment. To qualify for the earnings-related provision, the parent taking leave had to be employed for at least 6 months during the year of birth, or 12 months during the prior 2 years. The 1974 act also raised the benefit level to 90 per cent of earnings. Solo parents were eligible for the full parental leave and benefits. In 1975 the parental leave was extended to 7 months, and in 1978 to 9 months, still at 90 per cent of earnings, with 1 extra month at a per diem grant. In 1979 parents earned the right to avail themselves of the parental leave and benefits on a part-time basis, spread over and up to eight years, ending on a child's eighth birthday. In 1980 the act was reformed to include coverage for 9 months at 90 per cent of wages, a 3-month flat-rate benefit, and a statutory "speed premium" on the next child if conceived with 24 months. In addition, either parent was eligible for an extra 4 months of paid leave (at 90 per cent of earnings) when a child was sick, and fathers were entitled to 10 extra "daddy days" with full parental benefits when their child was born. In 1981 extra child allowances were awarded for parents with 3 or more children, and the speed premium was extended to 30 months. In 1989 the parental leave was extended further to 12 months and the sick children's benefit was extended to 3 months (then to 4 months in 1990).

TABLE 4–5	Family Leaves and Benefits in Sweden: 1997		
Leaves	**Duration**	**% Pay**	**Recipient**
Parental	12 months total	80% of wage for 10 months	either adoptive or natural parents
Mother's/Maternity	1 month	90% of wage	reserved for natural mother only
Father's/Paternity	1 month	90% of wage	either natural or adoptive father
Sick Child Leave	4 months	80% of wage	either natural or adoptive parent
Child (age 4–12) Contact Days	2 days/year	80% of wage	either parent to take child to and from daycare or school

Source: The Swedish Institute. 1997. "Equality Between Men and Women." Fact Sheets on Sweden. Stockholm.

Sweden's economic recession in the early to mid 1990s placed pressure on the welfare state to scale back previous social policy reforms that consumed a substantial portion of annual state spending. Yet as Table 4–5 shows, family leaves and benefits in Sweden have remained in place, although the reimbursement levels have been lowered.

On the other hand, during this same period of economic recession and pressure on the welfare state to curb spending, Sweden's government developed other policies to encourage greater participation of fathers in family life. Despite the possibilities created under the Parental Leave Act to help parents combine employment with family life, the vast majority of those taking parental leave and collecting benefits were Swedish women. In 1995 the government passed legislation that set aside 1 of the 12 months of parental leave as a paternity or "father's leave," with accompanying benefits in the form of 90 per cent of previous earnings, which all employers are obliged to grant fathers. At the same time a parallel "mother's leave" and benefit was taken from the parental leave, with similar obligation for employers and the same 90 per cent reimbursement level (The Swedish Institute, 1997). The result of both earlier and this more recent family-related policy change is that Swedish men have increased substantially their non-paid caring work in the family, beginning in the 1970s and increasing after 1995. At the same time, Swedish women in the past two decades have decreased their non-paid caring work and increased their paid work (Jonung and Persson, 1994: 59).

As discussed above, maternity and parental benefits in Canada are based exclusively on labour market status. In the United States, mothers must have the "right" employer or live in the "right" state to receive even minimum health care insurance. By contrast, public health care service is available to all Swedish residents, regardless of employment status (Sainsbury, 1996: 94–95). The *Swedish Parental Insurance Act* also grants parents access to a benefit that is not attached to their employment status, but rather on the basis of their citizenship. The parental leave and benefits and other social provisions have created a situation whereby nearly all Swedish women continue to be employed until their first child is born, and subsequently re-enter the workforce after their child's first birthday.

A second closely related social provision underlying women's dual status of employee and parent has been childcare services. Whereas childcare policies in Canada and the US parallel each other in accentuating private family responsibility, a *public responsibility model* has been the earmark of the Swedish welfare state in the past few decades (Leira, 1992). Public childcare in Sweden is the responsibility of the municipalities, and since the beginning of the 1970s, spaces available for local children have expanded rapidly. In direct contrast to both Canada and the US, the most common form of childcare for preschoolers, as well as for older children after school, is *public provision*. Because of the parental leave provision, virtually all Swedish children spend their first year with their mother or father; in 1991, for example, 95 per cent of infants were cared for solely by their parents. To take 1989 as a sample year: 24 per cent of children were being cared for by parent(s) receiving parental benefits; 34 per cent were in subsidized regulated municipal childcare centres; 17 per cent were cared for by subsidized regulated municipal family daycare givers; 10 per cent were in private (paid and unpaid) arrangements; and the rest were being cared for by full-time homemakers or by parents alternating between caring for their child and studying. The proportion of Swedish children in regulated subsidized childcare arrangements has increased steadily. By 1994 the figure was 54 per cent in regulated municipal childcare centres, and the figure was 61 per cent by 1996 (Björnberg and Gardberg, 1996: 273). Just under 80 per cent of children aged 3–5 years were in regulated subsidized childcare (Gornick, 1997).

The National Board of Health and Welfare, which sets nation-wide standards for all social welfare provisions, early on established strict childcare standards to be enforced rigorously by municipalities. The outcome has been a substantial investment in the training of childcare workers and "day mothers" caring for children in private homes. In addition, public funding has been set aside to build and maintain municipal childcare centres. Municipalities receive a grant covering roughly 50 per cent of costs from the National Board of Health and Welfare; all employers (but not employees) contribute 2.2 per cent of their total salary budget towards childcare services; and most parents pay a 10 per cent user fee (Baker, 1995: 321–23), although some pay a higher percentage, depending on their earnings, the number of hours that their children spend in daycare, and the number of children in their family (Björnberg and Gardberg, 1996: 273). Solo parents are given preferential treatment in accessing places for their children in the municipal centres, and tend to pay lower fees, as is the case for new immigrant families and parents of disabled children.

Despite the occasional lack of childcare spaces—and some questionable policies that attempt to deal with this problem (such as restricting municipal childcare when one or both parents are unemployed or when a sibling is born)—and criticism of the government's investment in the establishment of a universal childcare program rather than offering grants to stay-at-home parents in the form of allowances or child tax credits, Sweden's policies in the area of childcare are noteworthy in aiding Swedish women's economic independence and capacity to maintain an autonomous household. The same holds true for social assistance, the final social policy that will be examined here.

In direct contrast to both Canada and the US, where social assistance benefits have been a *major* mechanism whereby poor women, especially solo mothers, have met their subsistence means (although typically below official poverty lines), the number of Swedes on social assistance, including solo mothers, is small and of relatively short duration, albeit with some increase during the recent recession. Swedish women's—including solo mothers—sturdy attachment to the labour force and comparatively high hourly wages result in far fewer solo-mother households experiencing poverty prior to state benefit transfers. For example, in the early 1980s approximately one-third of Swedish solo mothers experienced pre-transfer poverty. The comparable US figure was over 50 per cent (Sainsbury, 1996: 84). At the same time, social benefits, both those discussed in detail and others such as subsidized housing, have been important in lifting a substantial minority of Swedish women from poverty, and for raising low-income others above the poverty cut-off level. In 1983, for example, social transfers diminished poverty from 30 per cent (pre-transfers) to 5 per cent (post-transfers) for solo Swedish mothers. As Sainsbury (1996: 84) notes: "if these transfers had been means-tested, it is unlikely that they would have had this effect since most of these mothers had earnings."

Some women in Sweden nevertheless are dependent upon social assistance, and solo mothers are more prone to draw on these means-tested benefits than married or cohabiting women. As with regard to other state welfare benefits, the standards governing social assistance are set by the National Board of Health and Welfare and administered by municipal governments (Baker, 1995: 104). In 1980 roughly 18 per cent of solo mothers received social assistance for an average of 4.2 months, and only 4 per cent of these were drawing social assistance benefits for 1 year. In the 1990s, with the rise of unemployment and negative economic growth, more solo mothers have had difficulty maintaining households on their own earnings plus social benefits, and thus there has been an increase in solo mothers on social assistance. Data indicates that the costs of social assistance have doubled over the last 5 years, and that couples with children comprise about 15 per cent of recipients and

TABLE 4-6	Childcare Policies—Public Support and Supply: Canada, the United States, and Sweden					
	Guaranteed Childcare Coverage	National Child Benefit	Public Funds Committed Over Next 5 Years	Child Tax Relief* *US dollars	% of Children (age 3–5) Receiving Subsidized Childcare	% of Children (age 5) in Pre-primary or School
Canada	No	Yes	Yes	$851	35	98
United States	No	No	Yes	$685	14	87
Sweden	Yes > 18 mo.	Yes	Yes	No	79	79

Source: Adapted from Gornick et al. (1997) and updated by author.

solo mothers around 25 per cent. The average length of time spent drawing social assistance also has increased marginally. Nevertheless, compared to North America, social assistance in Sweden continues to serve as a temporary economic buffer rather than a major source of income over the long term (Sainsbury, 1996). Among other things, this means that far fewer mother-headed families in Sweden suffer the social stigma of "welfare"; nor do they live below the poverty line for long periods of time as "wards of the state." The vast majority of Swedish women are privileged in that they are economically independent of both male breadwinners and means-tested welfare state social assistance; and when they do find themselves dependent, they tend to be so for a much shorter duration than their counterparts in Canada and especially the US.

SUMMARY AND CONCLUSION

This chapter has discerned both similarities and differences among Canada, the United States, and Sweden in reference to social policies that impact women regarding their paid and unpaid work. Furthermore, even in the recent decade marked by recession and increasing marketplace globalization, there exists significant variation among the three welfare states in regard to the type and range of social policies employed to help women achieve equality as paid and unpaid workers. Such variation, as has been argued in earlier chapters, is not a recent phenomenon but rather is congruous with the historical circumstances faced by women in their respective countries, and will likely remain intact with the present major restructuring of the global economy.

Chapter 5 draws on the author's own primary and secondary comparative research on midwives' work and social rights in Canada, the US, and Sweden in order to present the reader with a specific case example of the main thesis of both this chapter and the book in general: the significant variation of gender equality across the three countries.

ENDNOTES

[1]While attractive when compared to existing arrangements in the other provinces, also included in the proposed Quebec childcare system is a request to relax standards that control the number of children a childcare employee can attend, as well as the number of children a childcare centre can enrol. Given that Quebec currently has the most relaxed standards in the country in this regard, critics argue that quality will be sacrificed for increased equity of access to services. Nevertheless, the Quebec developments in regard to public daycare can be seen as a definite step in the right direction (The Childcare Resource and Research Unit, 1995).

[2]In 1994 the national median minimum wage was $3.80 per hour. A person employed full-time and full-year earning minimum wages had an annual income of (US) $7 600. This is only 60 per cent of what the federal government declared a family of four needed to maintain a household above the poverty line.

[3]Involuntary unemployment typically means leaving a job for reasons beyond one's control, including layoffs and sickness.

[4]US President Bill Clinton has recently announced additional funding (US $20 billion) for childcare over the next five years, which involves: larger block-funding grants to the states for childcare facilities; augmentation of the earned-income tax credit program in order to reach more working parents; tax credits for stay-at-home parents; provision for a new tax credit for businesses to provide on-site childcare to employees; and funds to establish an additional *Early Head Start* program (ACF Office of Public Affairs, 1998).

[5]It is worth noting that, in contrast to Canada and the US, Sweden includes among its unemployed all persons performing non-paid domestic labour in the home as well as women seeking part-time and full-time employment. The same applies for male and female youth who are seeking employment but have no previous attachment to the labour force. This means that a wide range of Swedish women have access to government-supported training and employment programs, including those who in North America would not fit the policy's definition of being "ready and available for work."

MIDWIVES' WORK AND SOCIAL RIGHTS

"God dealt well with the midwives and the people multiplied and waxed very mighty." (Exodus, 1.20)

"The name 'midwife' for me carries a certain odium, because I never heard it when it doesn't call to my mind a picture of Sairey Gamp and Betsy Prig, untrained, unkempt, gin soaked harridans unfit for the work they were supposed to do, and a menace to the health of any woman whom they might attend." (William B. Hendry, MD, Obstetrician, Chairman of the Maternal Mortality Committee of the Canadian Medical Association, 1931)

INTRODUCTION

Drawing on primary and secondary research on midwives' work and social rights in Canada, the United States, and Sweden, this chapter offers the reader a specific case example of the book's overall theme: the significant variation in women's work situation and social status across the three countries.

Sweden has long valued midwives as legitimate health workers central to achieving the goal of equitable, quality care for birthing women. In the modern period Sweden also has made extensive social rights accessible to midwives to help them balance their paid and unpaid work. Conversely, Canadian midwives historically have been subordinate to a male physician elite, and even today in the two provinces where they receive legal status and public funding, an entrepreneurial model of professional work has been implemented, with scant attention given to midwives' non-paid caring. The historical as well as current situation of US midwives is in many respects even more precarious than its Canadian counterpart, due to a legacy of male medical dominance, little public provision for health services and, most recently, the corporate takeover of health, including maternity care by large private insurance companies oriented towards making a profit out of health care. The latter has resulted in even greater insecure employment for American midwives, while at the same time the bulk of their unpaid caring work remains hidden from public view.

The overview of midwifery that follows examines the tensions that arise between three interconnected domains: 1) the political commitment of welfare states to provide health *equity* to citizens; 2) service professionals' *worker rights*; and 3) the expressed wishes of individual clients for *consumer choice* in their health services. It is argued here that the problems associated with midwifery as a service occupation are neither idiosyncratic nor a recent phenomenon. The dilemmas that midwives face due to conflicting expectations regarding equity for all clients and consumer choice for individual birthing women, on the one hand, and midwives' own issues as workers on the other, are found in earlier historical periods and are common today among other health service professionals, including physicians. The dilemmas are, however, especially vexing for female caregivers such as midwives, who also tend to shoulder responsibility for a second shift of unpaid work activities after their paid workday has ended (Benoit and Heitlinger, 1998).

Yet national differences, especially regarding the organization of the welfare state, also affect the interplay of forces found in midwives' daily practice. Though health care services are being restructured in all three countries under examination, analysis of the primary and secondary data on midwifery in Canada, the US, and Sweden indicates that principles of equity for birthing women and worker rights for Swedish midwives continue to figure largely in the organization of maternity care services. On the other hand, health care restructuring in Canada and the US has mainly been about enhancing system efficiency and expanding individual consumer choice of health provider and place of birth, with concerns about equity of health services for all birthing women and worker rights for midwives receiving much less attention.

The data analyzed for this chapter is collected from both secondary and primary sources. The secondary sources comprise published and unpublished reports and monographs, including government documents and academic writings of a general sort in the area of health care and, more specifically, on maternity care providers and services in Canada, the US, and Sweden collected over the last decade and a half. The primary sources include empirical materials collected through a series of projects dealing with women's mothering/family role, comparison of health organizations and professions, gender and the health division of labour, and family/employment tensions. Only the two more recent studies are mentioned below.

"Envisioning Quality Maternity Care in Canada and Sweden" (1993–96)

The Canadian portion of this project was taken up with primary data collection of two types: 1) site observations of the offices of midwives, family physicians, obstetricians, and public health nurses; 2) 35 personal interviews with a cross-selection of these health professionals. Also as part of this project are interviews conducted with Canadian and US midwifery students studying at the Seattle School of Midwifery, as well as a round-table discussion with their US midwifery instructors.

The primary data sources for Sweden are of two types: 1) observations during site visits at selected midwife clinics, a birthing centre, hospital maternity wards, and youth clinics; 2) 40 personal interviews with Swedish midwives, and a small number of additional interviews with other health providers and authorities.

The interviews conducted in both countries ranged between one and two hours. The interview guide included: 1) standard demographic questions; 2) questions about education and employment history and personal family situations, especially regarding the organization of non-paid work in the home; 3) questions concerning the present organization of midwifery practice, midwives' relationship to neighbouring health occupations (particularly medicine and nursing), perspectives on their professional association and unionization, and the overall picture of the health division of labour. All respondents had an opportunity to contribute additional data at the end of their interview.

"Restructuring of Maternity Care Services in Canada, Sweden, and Finland" (1997–ongoing)

The project initially began in the province of British Columbia and has involved interviews with officials in the Ministry of Children and Families, the Ministry of Health, including its Women's Health Bureau branch, regional health authorities, and a selection of midwives who have passed their registration exams and are now established in private practices and reimbursed by public funds. Respondents also included representatives of women's community groups and a sample of women clients from around the province who were asked their views about the restructuring of maternity care services in their province. Parallel research was begun in Finland in the fall of 1998, and further research is planned in Finland, Sweden, and select Canadian provinces in 1999–2000.

All tape-recorded interviews from the two projects have been transcribed verbatim, and content analysis has been used to code the data and identify overarching themes. Three themes identified by the content analysis of the primary data sets mentioned above, and also recurrent in the analysis of the secondary data, are: 1) *equity* of maternity care services for the population; 2) consumer *choice* in service providers and place of birth for individual clients; and 3) *worker rights* for midwives. As we shall see below, on all three counts the role played by the state is of crucial importance in regard to which of these themes emerges as the central organizing principle(s) of a country's health care system.

The outline for this chapter closely follows the format of the rest of the book. Initially midwives' work and social rights are examined in historical perspective, followed by a sustained focus on midwifery in present-day Canada, with windows opening on the United States and Sweden.

MIDWIVES' WORK AND SOCIAL RIGHTS IN HISTORICAL PERSPECTIVE

> There are two ancient professions for women: prostitution and midwifery. The names of the great courtesans thread through history; of midwives we know considerably less. (Sorel, 1984: 157)

The Premodern Period

The practice of attending pregnant women during childbirth was, in virtually all pre-industrial societies, the domain of female midwives or *wisewomen*. Midwifery is one of the oldest specialized social services, demonstrating the willingness of a particular group of female care-givers to respond to calls for help from those in need (Böhme, 1984). The midwife's care of birthing families was recognized in the earliest books of the Old Testament and was an established occupation in ancient Greece and Rome. Concerning the Roman midwife:

> She will have a quiet disposition, for she will have to share many secrets of life. She must not be greedy for money, lest she give an abortive wickedly for payment; she will be free from superstition so as not to overlook salutary measures on account of a dream or omen or some customary rite or vulgar superstition. She must also keep her hands soft, abstaining from such wool-working as may make them hard …. Such persons will be the best midwives. (Lefkowitz and Fant, 1982: 163)

During the European mediaeval period the age-old practice of midwifery became tainted with witchcraft, apparently because "midwives had access to fetal tissue, which—while forbidden by the Church—was in great demand as a magical charm by healers and practitioners of the magical arts" (Achterberg, 1990: 122). Nonetheless, birthing families of aristocratic standing and otherwise continued to call on midwives for help when facing the inevitable uncertainties of childbirth. According to Ann Oakley and Susanne Houd, "*old wife* is one term for a traditional woman healer and midwife. Others are *good woman, cunning woman* (*cunning* meaning "knowledge more than others"), or *wisewoman* (the French term for midwife is still sage-femme). Such women were the main providers of health and midwifery care in pre-industrial Europe and Colonial North America" (1990: 18–19).[1]

Except for the fact that they had accumulated a body of wisdom gained from observation and mutual aid, traditional midwives in most early societies were merely one among the community of inhabitants they served. Successful midwives were referred to other kin and neighbours; some were elected informally as "experts of the life-world" (Böhme, 1984).

In addition to practical skill and a trustworthy character, traditional midwives were expected to be available continuously for those in need of maternity care. Such "continuity of care" was based on an assumption underlying other preliterate healing occupations. In contrast to the situation of modern professionals who, as Everett Hughes (1971: 424) puts it, "do not merely serve, [but] define the very wants they serve," poor as well as wealthy patrons in the premodern era diagnosed their own health concerns and advised those whom they called to their bedside about how best to treat them (Jewson, 1974). The traditional midwife was placed accordingly in a dependent caregiver role vis-à-vis village women. An unwritten community code of midwifery practice was that, regardless of her own familial circumstances and schedule, the midwife was never to refuse a call for help, but to be always available for local birthing women. It was at least partly on the basis of *being there* (Driedger,

1993) for others that the traditional midwife became publicly venerated, even if not viewed as such by learned physicians of the period. The result was a style of caring that, while having limited capacity to handle medical emergencies or cure acute illness, nevertheless granted local inhabitants a philosophy of care that was familiar to their world.

Yet for all its benefits, traditional midwifery was organized within a peculiar set of social and economic circumstances that were not easily transferred to urban industrial capitalist societies. First, the style of continuity of care practised by traditional midwives was confined largely to the sequence beginning with the onset of labour, the birth itself, and the 10-day "lying-in" that followed. Prenatal care as we know it today was virtually nonexistent in the premodern era. Second, while occupying a key position, the traditional midwife seldom worked alone, outside a division of labour; the continuity of care she granted local birthing women was most often performed with an apprentice at hand. Both midwife and apprentice were able—in fact, expected—to assemble a network of female kin and neighbours to assist with domestic chores and to help the birthing woman "pass the time" before she returned full-time to her role of wife and mother. Finally, it should be pointed out that continuity of midwifery care, in the traditional sense, frequently was suspended by a yet largely untamed "nature" (Shorter, 1982). As Jane Lewis reminds us: "motherhood was undoubtedly a dangerous business. As late as the 1930s mothers ran a greater risk of mortality than coalminers .... Women feared the pain of childbirth and they feared death" (1990: 11–12).

The fact remains that the midwife, much like the academically trained physician, during this long stretch of history was very limited in her capacity to provide a safe birthing experience. Even if parturient women had the means whereby to secure and pay for the services of a local midwife, there was no guarantee that the birthing process would unfold in a straightforward manner. The advantage of labour and delivery in her own home, surrounded by those she called together—of being "brought to bed" (Leavitt, 1986)—was all too frequently accompanied by anxiety, fear, and even death. As Katharine Park (1992: 62) notes: "the dangers of pregnancy and childbirth seem to have accounted for the shorter life expectancy of medieval women." At risk too were infants; 15 to 30 per cent—even more in some centuries and particular regions of pre-industrial Europe—are reported to have died before reaching their first birthday (Stone, 1977).

Historical accounts of freelance professionals, including midwives, have shown that their rights as workers were few (Marland and Rafferty, 1997). Fee-paying clients in most instances determined the terms and conditions of the two-party contract (Jewson, 1974). Demands could be made on the midwife's time above and beyond what might be considered a "normal" working day; the midwife served the client as the latter saw fit (Benoit, 1989). Terry Johnson (1972) terms this professional-client relationship a form of "patronage control" in his reference to the medical profession, but the concept could apply easily to premodern midwifery as well. It was the better-off birthing women who were paying for the *choice* of a particular midwife. However, the midwife of earlier times was not likely to know much about the obstetrical history of her privileged clientele: "even if she was the local midwife and knew the mother socially, she would have no knowledge whatsoever, prior to the labour, of what exactly presented itself beneath the mother's voluminous skirts" (Towler and Bramall, 1986: 44).

Nevertheless, to employ Albert O. Hirshman's terms (1970), patronage control rendered privileged clients a strong "voice" regarding when and how the midwife was to serve them. While midwives could always "exit" from a relationship should it become too exploitative and instead devote themselves to caring for poor women (who might be able to give some reward in kind or nothing at all), freelance midwives were unlikely to reject a moneyed client.

The Modernization of Midwifery

Continental Europe

The late eighteenth century marked the beginning of a new era for both birthing women and midwives in Western Europe. European governments, many of them imperial powers, initiated an assortment of *pronatalist policies* based on the notion that a healthy mother will likely give birth to a healthy infant who will grow into a healthy worker and/or solider.[2] In pursuance of this plan, steps were taken to improve the health of birthing women and at the same time to upgrade the standards of midwifery practice. In Denmark, for example, a national midwifery school was founded in 1787 and legislation was passed to regulate the occupation. Similar schools and state operated systems for the examination and registration of midwives appeared around this time in Moscow, St. Petersburg, and Austria (Donnison, 1981). In many German states a local *Hebammenmeister* was selected to organize midwifery training and to regulate the practice of graduates. In France, following an official inquiry into midwifery practice in 1728, lying-in hospitals were built in strategic locations across the country and staffed by salaried midwives who received formal training in newly established state midwifery schools (Ackernecht, 1967). In brief, as Deborah Sullivan and Anne Weitz note:

> The history of midwifery on the European continent reveals that independent midwifery can flourish under physician supervision and legal limitation as long as it does not compete directly with medicine. While licensure restricted independent European midwives to normal childbirth and prohibited them from using instruments, it left them with considerable functional autonomy. (1988: 206)

These assessments of government initiated activities in Europe are correct in part. Although initially concerned more with producing healthy soldiers and thus strong armies than with improving the health of birthing women and their infants, they were in fact forerunners of the modern-day public health (and maternity) care systems found across Europe, as well as state provision of formal training, legal status, and public employment for midwives. However, midwives' subordination to physicians in the modern health care systems, and the prohibition of midwives' use of sharp—including obstetrical—instruments, were not universal across Europe, as the case of Swedish (and Finnish) midwives demonstrates.

Sweden and Finland

Formal education and regulation for midwives in Sweden has a long history (Marland and Rafferty, 1997). In fact, the first official instruction for midwives was given in the Church ordinance of 1539 which, among other things, laid down that midwives should assist both poor and rich women without discrimination. A subsequent ordinance of 1685 declared that midwives should receive what was fair for their services *and* help the poor.

The modernization of education for Swedish midwives began in the later eighteenth century. It was financed by an imperial state, supported in part by an influential merchant class aimed at expanding Sweden's economic might and military power, a system referred to in Chapter 3 as *mercantilism*. Mercantilism was built around a strong national state that involved itself in conquering other areas of the globe, setting up colonies and international trading routes, and enhancing the wealth of the national treasury. Large, strong armies were fundamental to achieving these goals, and large, strong armies were dependent upon (male) health. In Sweden, trained and licensed midwives were singled out by the mercantile state as vital to reducing the infant mortality rate and helping more babies grow into manhood, ready to serve the nation (Romlid, 1997).

The original training school for midwives and obstetricians, which also served the function of a maternity hospital—the first in the country—opened its doors in the capital city in 1775 (Vallgarda, 1996). It was the *Collegium Medicum*, a professional association founded in 1663 with Crown support and comprised of prominent Stockholm physicians,[3] that was assigned the task of ensuring that midwives received adequate training, were properly examined, and were located strategically across the empire's cities, towns, and rural parishes (Romlid, 1997: 39–40). Some midwifery recruits were permitted to study free of charge and others were supported by their home municipality. While the theoretical education was given mainly by obstetricians, much of the training remained practical. Trained midwives in Sweden had the duty to attend all deliveries, even during prolonged labour when a physician was also present (Vallgarda, 1996).

However, in contrast to her Continental counterparts (and in Britain and its North American colonies), the Swedish midwife was actively encouraged to seek training in the use of sharp instruments as well as obstetrical forceps. Provided she passed a special examination, the Swedish midwife was entitled to use these devices if facing a difficult labour and unable to help the woman by other means. This "maverick" resolution of the Swedish authorities did not sit well with physicians abroad. At a time when women were still barred from entering the medical profession in most European countries, it was deemed outrageous that Sweden was permitting *midwives* to enjoy the same rights and privileges as obstetricians and other physicians. Despite vocal opposition,

> Swedish policy remained intact. It was only in 1919 that the midwives' privileges to use sharp instruments and the blunt hook were withdrawn. Henceforth midwives' right to use obstetrical instruments would be restricted to forceps. The midwives' use of forceps has remained a skill and a right considered necessary to her ability to perform her work efficiently; the midwife needs to know at what point to call in an obstetrician, and midwives are still able to apply forceps in emergencies. (Romlid, 1997: 45)

As a province of the Kingdom of Sweden, in Finland too, midwives were trained to use obstetrical instruments during this period. In the middle of the eighteenth century a modest number of trained and licensed midwives from Stockholm began to practise in the small towns of northwest Finland. Even after Finland separated from Sweden, and formal training for midwives was established on Finnish soil—taught in the Finnish language, midwives' salaries paid by the Finnish state, and midwifery services organized by municipalities—Finnish midwives continued to be trained in the use of sharp instruments. The broader competence as well as the new employment opportunities of the Finnish midwife gradually led to the professionalization of midwifery in Finland by the late nineteenth and early twentieth centuries.

In brief, as Sweden entered the modern period, two important developments were in place: 1) extensive state support for maternity health services for birthing women; and 2) formal education and integration of midwives in the emerging public health care system. This was also the case, albeit to a lesser extent, in other Nordic countries and Continental Europe. But for reasons that are discussed below, these developments were far more difficult to achieve in both the United States and Canada. In order to understand why this might be so, we will take a brief glance back at early developments in the mother county.

Britain

As with Continental European and Nordic countries, premodern Britain depended on the ancient but informal institution of midwifery to carry birthing families through the reproductive process. As early as the Tudor period the English monarchy began to take a more active role in the regulation of health services, beginning with the incorporation of the Royal College of Physicians in 1512. An initial attempt by the English Crown to certify midwives was started around the mid-sixteenth century, at which time the local parish bishop and a trustworthy "doctor of physicke" were appointed to examine hopeful midwives. But due to internal conflicts and strong resistance from an increasingly powerful medical profession, the British state avoided the path subsequently taken by Continental governments, choosing instead to establish neither national midwifery training nor licensure for British midwives.

Throughout the next century, men in Britain slowly began to specialize in midwifery, initially calling themselves "male-midwife," "midman," "man midwife," "endroboethogynist" or "accoucheur" and, finally, the present-day term, "obstetrician." Their position was established when the British surgeon, Peter Chamberlen the Elder, modified the levers used by mediaeval barber-surgeons and invented the obstetrical forceps. British midwives were denied access to this "secret instrument" of the new male obstetrics at about the same time that their Swedish counterparts were being trained officially to use it. Exclusive right to handle the obstetrical forceps made it possible for the British male physician to gain a foothold in what was hitherto "women's business" alone. This development was a direct challenge to the role of the female midwife, traditionally the senior attendant at all normal deliveries.

It was not until the dawn of the twentieth century that the tide began to turn slowly in favour of the female midwife. The concerted efforts of social reformers calling for improved maternity care for birthing women, aristocratic women's expressed desire to help their "lower-class sisters," and support from influential obstetricians ultimately resulted in the *Midwives' Act* of 1902, which "ensured a future for the female midwife" in Britain (Oakley, 1976: 51). Jean Donnison (1977: 174–75) concurs, noting that without the *Midwives' Act* the British midwife "would probably have vanished from the scene within the next fifty years, squeezed out by her medical competitors." As we will see, the reluctant role of the British state in matters concerning midwives' education and professional status had a major influence on the success of midwifery in its North American colonies.

United States

The earliest style of midwifery practice in colonial America was in many ways analogous to that of Britain (Wertz and Wertz, 1977). Historical records make mention of one Ann Hutchinson, who was "very helpful in the times of childbirth, and other occasions of bodily infirmities and well furnished with means for those purposes" (Litoff, 1978: 4). Epitaphs of colonial women indicate the important role they played as midwives. Elizabeth Phillips was a New England midwife whose career spanned 40 years, ending only with her death in 1761; her grave maker proclaimed that "by ye blessing of God, she ... brought into this world above three thousand children" (Litoff, 1978: 4). Perhaps her prodigiousness reflects how the American midwife was required to "be diligent and ready to help any woman in labour, whether poor or rich." Still, this tended to be the extent of the restrictions placed on her. As Sullivan and Weitz (1988: 2) explain, "colonial American midwives worked under an incomplete system of municipal licensure. Where licensure existed, and unlike on the European continent, it was not accompanied by training programs. As in Britain, American midwives were considered moral guardians rather than health care providers."

By the end of the nineteenth century, notable differences in the situation of midwives had developed between Britain and the United States. In the US—where democratic ideology discouraged state legislatures from passing statutory requirements for medical training (Starr, 1982); where there existed no landed aristocracy; and where there emerged significant numbers of "male midwives" without the protection of anything similar to Britain's Royal College to win for them an exclusive mandate over abnormal childbirth—the call to upgrade midwifery from traditional to professional standing found little fertile ground (Arney, 1982: 39–40). On the contrary, gaining access to the traditional midwife's home-birth clientele emerged as a high priority for the fledgling profession of obstetrics seeking a foothold in the childbirth market. These new medical specialists of "women's diseases" fought vigorously to secure an ever firmer foothold in the midwife's traditional domain of practice. Ultimately they succeeded in placing most aspects of female reproduction under a medical umbrella, to a degree unknown in other Western countries. The occupation of midwifery increasingly was discarded in the US in favour of a "single standard of obstetrics." As Donnison (1981: 8) explains, "professional uncertainty among American obstetricians led many to argue that as long as pregnancy and parturition [childbirth] were regarded as normal events, and the midwife in consequence was allowed to continue practising, their specialty would never receive the recognition they considered it deserved as an integral part of scientific medicine."

US midwives likewise were excluded from the educational reforms aiding the cause of the new male obstetrics. The influential *Flexner Report* of 1910 highlighted the abysmal situation of American (and Canadian) medical education, reporting that 90 per cent of all physicians received their training from profit-making schools that offered few or no resources for authentic clinical training. Abraham Flexner recommended the elimination of all "diploma mills," and the tightening of education and licensure standards for North American physicians. The female midwife, as with other traditional healers (and black and female physicians), became an easy target for the reformed medical profession, although even by the early century the high maternal and infant death rates among midwife-attended cases were matched closely by those attended by physicians (Arney, 1982).

As late as 1910 approximately 50 per cent of all births in New England were attended by traditional midwives in women's homes (Kobrin, 1966). Despite this, the vast majority of these midwives were poor immigrant women and "black grannies" who lacked the formal education, credentials, organizational base, and aristocratic patronage of their British counterparts that might have helped them gain access to the political machinery taking shape in industrial America. At the same time, the emerging US middle classes increasingly were alarmed by high maternal and infant mortality rates. Obstetricians were quick to point to the "hopelessly dirty, ignorant, and incompetent" midwives as the cause (Kobrin, 1966: 351), although statistical data from this period clearly indicates that general practitioners and even obstetricians themselves were at least as negligent and unhygienic in their practices as were midwives (Wertz and Wertz, 1977).

Despite their lack of objective warrant, US obstetricians continued their call for the elimination of the "double standard" of maternity care practice that they alleged was "ruining the nation." The result was a drawn-out midwifery debate between 1900 and 1920, during which each side accused the other of incompetence and lack of genuine commitment to clients. Eventually the obstetricians won the day, not least because of strong backing from the powerful American Medical Association. Midwifery frequently was portrayed as an antiquated "folk occupation" that had no place in modern America (Starr, 1982). In the words of J.L. Huntington, a then prominent Boston obstetrician active in the dispute: "as soon as the immigrant is assimilated ... then the midwife is no longer a factor in his home" (quoted in Kobrin, 1966: 257). Ultimately, however, state governments and even obstetricians themselves came to realize that midwives might provide a useful service for poor birthing women. The Great Depression of the 1930s proved a turning point in US obstetricians' out-right resistance to midwives. A small number of midwives were granted legal permission to receive formal training and subsequently to serve those urban and rural women without the means to pay for obstetrical care (Campbell, 1946).

In 1925 Mary Breckinridge, an American graduate nurse and British Central Midwives' Board-certified midwife, established a nurse-midwifery program in the Kentucky Mountains. Joined in 1929 by other American midwives schooled in England and by immigrant mid-wives from the British Isles, Breckinridge formed the American Association of Nurse-Midwives. Social reformers lobbied state legislatures to finance a "frontier nursing service"; by 1934 a num-ber of small maternity hospitals had been established in the states of Georgia, North Carolina, and Florida, staffed by midwifery graduates from local training programs (Litoff, 1978).

Unlike her European counterpart, however, the emerging American nurse-midwife was no match for her competitor, the obstetrician, who enjoyed both the authority of legal office and also nationwide monopoly over maternity care delivery, sanctioned by both state and federal legislatures (Starr, 1982). Not until 1971, in fact, did the powerful US College of Obstetricians and Gynecologists acquiesce to the nurse-midwives' role of primary birthing attendant, which meant that US midwives were finally permitted to "catch the baby" without physician supervision.

Canada

Much like their US neighbours, families in frontier Canada had little contact with "learned physicians," depending instead on their own or their kin's healing cures. In times of particular concern they would call on one of many specialized healers—bone setters, homeopaths, eclectics, and apothecaries among them. Parturient women, regardless of economic standing or cultural background, would call upon the local midwife.

Although little is known about the midwives who attended Aboriginal women prior to settler contact, we do know that Aboriginal midwives from eastern Canada employed an unofficial communication link—the "moccasin telegraph"—sending whispers of an imminent birth (Barrington, 1985: 31). Research in British Columbia suggests that Aboriginal peoples in the pre-contact period, and perhaps for some time afterwards, viewed childbirth as part of a natural and creative life process. The midwife upheld the fundamental moral and ethical value systems that reflected the holistic philosophy of contemporary Aboriginal life. Laws typically passed from generation to generation, and it was often women elders, with their rich personal experience of childbirth and other female life events, who were considered "keep-ers of the culture." In fact, the label "midwife" is not a recognizable term among the different linguistic groups scattered along the Pacific northwest coast, where language tends to reflect the various roles that midwives played. Among the Nuu-chah-nulth, the term midwife translates as "she can do everything"; among the Coast Salish it means "to watch/to care"; and the Chilcotin interpret it as "women's helper" (Benoit and Carroll, 1995).

One of the first references to midwifery among non-Aboriginal birthing attendants appears in a deed published by a Mr. Massicotte, "which reveals that the women of Ville-Marie [Montreal], in solemn concave assembled, on February 12th, 1713, elected a midwife Catherine Guertin for the community" (Abbott, 1931: 28). Mention is made in government documents of Madame Bouchette, a midwife trained in France, who was sent to the French colony of Quebec in 1722 on an annual salary from the King of 400 livres; and also of Mlle. Bery, who travelled from France in 1730 to serve the women of St. Foye. Due to frail health, eventually she was replaced by a younger colleague, whose government wage was raised from 400 to 600 livres (Abbott, 1931: 28). In 1775 Colonel Sutherland, the commander of the British settlement of Lunenburg, Nova Scotia, requested four pounds per annum from the Crown for the salaries of two practising midwives. And as late as the 1930s, traditional indigenous midwives and formally trained "foreign" midwives (recruited, as in outlying areas of the US, mainly from Britain) could also be found practising in the 5 000 coastal communities dotting the Newfoundland and Labrador coastlines (Benoit, 1989).

Pressure to transform the original maternity care system in the young country began in the late eighteenth century. The first *Medical Act* attempted to regulate the practices of "physic and surgery" in Upper Canada in 1795 by making it illegal to practise midwifery without a license, exempting only those holding a university degree. The impracticality of such a ruling soon became apparent, and the small degree-holding segment of the medical profession was left vulnerable to public criticism (Canniff, 1894: 22). The original *Medical Act* was repealed in 1806 and traditional midwifery remained immune from the licensing laws of the Ontario Medical Board for the next half century. In 1866, however, the permission awarded by the provincial government to unlicensed female midwives to practise was withdrawn; thereafter midwifery was exclusively the legal mandate of those holding medical degrees. Given that no female physicians were licensed in Ontario until the 1880s—and few women worked in this capacity for many decades to come—the province's men enjoyed a legal monopoly over the birthing chamber by the time of Confederation in 1867. The growing number of physicians trying to make a living in Toronto and other provincial urban areas could now look to *accouchement* as a feasible entry to family practice. Although some physicians (known as the "traditionalists") opposed this turn of events embraced by their colleagues (the "radicals"), and called instead for formal training and legalization of midwifery, their efforts proved unsuccessful (Biggs, 1983). The medical majority won the day by convincing government authorities that "women don't want midwives about them [for] as a rule they have no confidence in them" (*Canada Lancet*, 1875: 60).

Yet midwives continued to practise in outlying regions of Ontario, where physicians were in short supply, well into the twentieth century. Even in urban areas, competition between physicians and midwives persisted on the home-birth front for several decades after Confederation (Benoit, 1991). But "doctor births" were eventually to become the norm. In fact, only one-sixth of recorded births in Ontario were not attended by physicians by 1897, and only a few of those "medically unattended" births were recorded to have been attended by midwives (Oppenheimer, 1983: 40–44).

Midwives in other parts the country remained active long after their Ontario counterparts had lost their place in the birthing room. Although as early as 1788 the colonial government enacted licensing requirements on health practitioners in Quebec, certified female midwives (examined by a health board to determine their proficiency), were granted the right to practise alongside male physicians operating in Montreal and its surrounding environs. Meanwhile, in the countryside, *sage-femmes* continued to remain unregulated, controlled by local clergy and by birthing women themselves. In 1879, however, the Quebec College of Physicians and Surgeons, following events in Ontario, extended control over female midwifery (Laforce, 1990). For the next half century, Quebec midwives in rural areas were permitted to practise, provided that their competence was physician-certified. Such was the case as well in New Brunswick and Saskatchewan, where as late as 1924 at least 50 per cent of births were not attended by medics (Biggs, 1983). Traditional "granny midwives" continued to practise in Newfoundland and Labrador well after the Second World War. Granny midwives (also affectionately referred to as "aunties") were considered by local inhabitants as "the salt of the earth" because of the steadfast and continuous care they gave to birthing women and newborns, not merely sporadically, but typically many times over, until a woman's childbearing period had drawn to a close or maternal death had cut the cycle short (Benoit, 1991). In the words of one of them:

> I first learned to doctor the women by going about with my mother who was also a midwife …. My mother was still smart at the end, but getting blind when she gave up and I took her place in the village. People after that used to come to me with their problems and, of course, I always went to visit the sick, and when a woman would be nearing her time, I'd be there at hand. The people I nursed were really close together; they trusted a woman like me over a stranger from some foreign part. (Benoit, 1990: 184–85)

Nevertheless, in the long-run midwifery in most areas of the country was undermined, and childbirth attendance emerged as the mandate of the medical profession (Benoit, 1998).

Increasing medical dominance over birthing arrangements in Canada did not result in more appropriate care than that previously provided by midwives. This was especially the case for poor and destitute pregnant women, who frequently were left with neither physician nor midwife during their confinement. Some of these forsaken women were given physical assistance by philanthropic institutions, including the *Society for the Relief of Women During Their Confinement*, established in 1820 in Ontario (Oppenheimer, 1983). Yet voluntary organizations did not provide accommodation, which placed the onus of supplying shelter to homeless parturient women with a few hospitals. The result was that as late the 1920s (when the first national statistics became available) the Canadian infant mortality rate was 92 per 1 000 live births, and the maternal mortality rate was 5.6 deaths per 1 000 birthing women (Buckley, 1979: 134–35). As one commentator pointed out at the time: "more babies die in Canada yearly, under one year old, from preventive causes than soldiers have been killed during the war" (quoted in Buckley, 1979: 133).

Although "health teams" comprising midwives, physicians, and public health nurses working out of community clinics were advocated by some prominent Canadian health reformers, the opposing medical and nursing lobby eventually prevailed. By 1930 the modern structure of the Canadian maternity care system was all but in place. As a substitute caregiver, the obstetrical nurse was awarded the less than prestigious position of "doctor's hand-maiden" and expected to show "wifely obedience to the doctor, motherly self-devotion to the patient and a form of mistress/servant discipline to those below" (Buckley, 1979: 134). The medical profession's perspective on human reproduction as a potentially abnormal event needing close monitoring and frequent obstetrical intervention was endorsed by all care-givers on the maternity ward, including the new obstetrical nurse. Provinces both west and east of Ontario and Quebec eventually followed the same path, suppressing midwifery and promoting the medically-dependent obstetrical nursing specialty. The only exception was in the more isolated northern areas—i.e., northern Newfoundland and Labrador (discussed

Midwifery in Newfoundland and Labrador: Survival at the Margins[4]

The first consequential step in the transition of Newfoundland and Labrador's traditional home-birth system occurred in the late 1920s when an enlightened government administration, following the lead taken by socially-minded governments elsewhere in the British Commonwealth, began to lay the cornerstones of what was to become known as the *Cottage Hospital System*. This novel health care scheme resulted in the construction of a number of strategically-located small public hospitals staffed by a team of midwives, general duty nurses, and physicians, who provided medical care as well as back-up during obstetrical complications.

Meanwhile, in most metropolitan areas of industrialized North America, midwifery in all its guises was facing "professional death" due both to the successful encroachment into childbirth of (male dominated) obstetrics and to the speedy bureaucratization of maternity care. The alternative occupational avenue for Newfoundland and Labrador midwives was in fact quite comparable to contemporaneous developments in Western Europe. Without qualification, birthing clients assisted by the cottage hospital midwives held their midwifery attendants in very high admiration, granting them professional status in the area of maternity care. Although many "granny midwives" also enjoyed high community status, their numbers were small compared to their cottage hospital counterparts. In other ways, too, the two generations—traditional home-birth attendants and cottage hospital midwives—differed widely. Granny midwives received little or no formal education, garnering their practical skills via informal apprenticeship and home-birth attendance.

Cottage hospital midwives, by contrast, have always been trained midwives, believing that specialized formal knowledge of the reproductive passage, acquired through vocational schooling, is essential for qualified birth attendance. In addition, cottage hospital midwives stress that they felt fortunate to work within a maternity division of labour. Granny women's "independent practice" in clients' homes, cut off from contact with colleagues and with little or no access to doctors, support staff, and life-saving apparatus, enticed none of them.

Cottage hospital midwives pursued formal schooling "in order to learn all there was to know about nursing and midwifery." Most eventually received dual certification, typically seeking midwifery credentials after attaining a nursing diploma. The vocational midwifery training of the cottage hospital midwives involved ample delivery instruction and conveyed the current obstetric techniques essential to expert attendance. Many midwifery recruits—both locals and those "come from away"—settled in the town where the cottage hospital was situated, eventually accumulating a substantial stock of "local knowledge" of the customs and traditions of townspeople and those who lived in surrounding districts. It is noteworthy that nearly all cottage hospital midwives expressed an "inner calling" for a full-time midwifery career; early on they experienced a deep commitment to serving pregnant women, whatever their family circumstances and geographical location, but especially a desire to help "those mothers who were not so fortunate."

Cottage hospital midwives enjoyed a high level of occupational freedom in contrast to both granny midwives—who were forced to endure the close monitoring of kin and neighbours—and employees of large, bureaucratic hospitals, who were answerable to their "gatekeepers"—staff physicians and administrators. In cottage hospitals, it was the attending midwife, working in consultation with her colleagues, who was the primary caregiver; the doctor was called only when the midwife judged that obstetrical intervention would improve the care of mother and newborn. Such a low but sufficient level of medical involvement on cottage hospital maternity wards meant that the midwife-client relationship was neither scientistic nor impersonal. "It was such a nice and safe atmosphere," says one client about the cottage hospital maternity ward. "It was always everybody knew everybody else—the patients, the midwives and even the doctor on call in case something went wrong."

This unique system of maternity care located on the margins of Canada slowly declined with the centralization of provincial health and maternity services in a small number of bureaucratic hospitals located in larger, urban areas. Although often strongly opposed by the staff and local community, one cottage hospital after another was closed down or transformed into a health care centre without maternity facilities. Physicians and midwives moved to find work in urban centres or left the province altogether. Only in the province's northern areas, still deemed marginal by central authorities, has cottage hospital midwifery in its original form endured.

above) and northern Manitoba—where nurse-midwives were recruited from abroad to serve the local inhabitants (Kaufert and O'Neil, 1993). The common view was expressed by a physician: "the art of midwifery belongs to prehistoric times; the science of obstetrics is the latest recognition of all ancient sciences" (Biggs, 1983: 32). The question of "lady nurses or midwives" was decided in favour of the former. However, this maternity care arrangement proved detrimental not only to midwifery as a viable career choice for Canadian women. As Buckley (1979: 149) notes, pregnant women, too, were disadvantaged since "the exclusion of trained midwives ensured that future generations of women would be denied an alternative to the gynecological and obstetrical monopoly held by the predominantly male profession."

In summary, it is obvious from the historical overview that the path of modernization was neither straightforward nor necessarily positive in regard to either midwives or birthing women. A comparative perspective on midwifery has revealed amazing *diversity* in regard to midwives' working conditions, access to formal education, and social status. Furthermore, in countries such as Sweden, all birthing women gained the citizen's right to access midwifery services free of charge, while the availability and public coverage of midwifery services in Canada and the US has been comparatively meagre.

Much depends, it seems, on the role taken by the state in negotiating midwives' mandate vis-à-vis medicine and the market. In the examples of early Britain, the US, and Canada, the state acted as a virtual "silent partner" of patriarchy and capitalism, providing little by way of legal protection or public funding for a viable midwifery vocation. Yet, as outlined above, a very different historical process shaped midwives' position in Sweden. In the early-modern period it was the pronatalist and later the democratic state that gave strong support to midwives. Similarly, by the twentieth century the Swedish state—no longer mainly concerned with saving babies and creating healthy workers and soldiers—continued to support a strong midwifery occupation in order to provide equitable and high-quality maternity care to Swedish women.

In brief, different types of states and health professions, including medicine and midwifery, often "intermingle and interpenetrate each other" (Coburn, 1993: 129). As Elliott Krause (1988: 49) puts it: "the rise or fall of professional group political/economic or guild power is a complex topic, demanding respect for historical and political processes, profession by profession and nation by nation."

The remainder of this chapter examines the present situation of midwives in the three national examples. Due to a complexity of demands bought on by both external and internal factors, Canada, the United States, and Sweden are all in the process of restructuring their welfare states, including public health and maternity care services. Not surprisingly, the working conditions and general social rights of midwives in all three countries are affected by this process. As revealed below, midwives' comparative situations continue, in broad strokes, to reflect the historical record presented above.

MIDWIVES' WORK AND SOCIAL RIGHTS TODAY

> Midwives have had a chequered career at the hands of historians, those who competed with them to provide midwifery care, legislators, organizers of maternity services, and women with whom they laboured. There is a sense in which midwifery has come to represent a metaphor for the broader struggles and debates about race, class and gender. (Marland and Rafferty, 1997: 3)

The Canadian Case

Although in the process of change, Canada throughout the twentieth century has been exceptional among other industrial countries for having no legal provision for midwives. The *Canadian Health Act* (Canada House of Commons, 1984) states that "the primary objective of Canadian health care policy is to protect, promote and restore the physical and mental well-being of residents of Canada and to facilitate reasonable access to health services without financial or other barriers." Equity of health services has not been a distinct goal. Rather, "the *Act* states under the accessibility principle that *reasonable access* must not be impeded or precluded by the uniformly applied terms and conditions of service provision" (Birch and Abelson, 1993: 631–32). Another section advises that reasonable access is meant to apply only to what have been deemed by the medical profession to be required hospital and physician services (Evans, 1992).

The Canadian welfare state, in short, has compromised equity by enshrining *medical dominance* over health care services. What this means in practice is that provincial health ministries (which oversee health service provision and negotiate physicians' reimbursement), have allowed physicians to work as private entrepreneurs who, through their provincial medical associations, bill the government for medical services that physicians alone deem essential to adequate maternity care. Each province has a *Medical Practitioners Act* that has, until this

TABLE 5-1 Statistics on Certified Midwives and Infant Mortality in Canada, the United States, and Sweden			
	Canada	**US**	**Sweden**
Number of Midwives	230*	8 700**	6 800***
Number of Midwives per 10 000 People	0.08	3.2	75.6
Midwife-assisted Births (%)	< 2	6	8.5
Infant Morality Rate****	6	8	4

* Based on 1998–99 data gathered by the author on fully registered midwives in Ontario (154 as of March 1999), Alberta (23 as of fall 1998), and British Columbia (53 as of March 1999). No figures are given for Quebec, where legislation regarding midwives' registration is pending the provincial government's response to the evaluation of a pilot project of eight birth centres staffed by midwives from a variety of backgrounds. No data are available for Saskatchewan either, which passed legislation to legalize and regulate midwifery in May 1999.

** 1998 figures

*** 1997 figures

**** 1995–96 figures

Sources: OECD, 1998d; Shroff, 1997; Rooks, 1997; David-Floyd, 1998; Benoit, 1998.

decade, restricted the performance of "midwifery services" exclusively to licensed members of the College of Physicians and Surgeons. An "exceptions" clause was put in place in rural and northern areas that allows trained midwives to "catch babies" and not be held liable for doing so. Public funds for maternity care services have been available almost exclusively for specific activities performed by licensed physicians.

As a result of physicians' exclusionary strategies—what Gerald Larkin (1983) has called *occupational imperialism*—unless they have money to seek such services on the private market, Canadian women have not had access to midwives as primary attendants. Private-practice midwives in Canada have had to work outside of the official health care system and formal health care settings. Typically a client seeking midwifery services has received her prenatal and postnatal visits at the midwife's home, and given birth—assisted by the midwife—in her own home. When a home-birth was not practicable, the midwife has worked as a "labour coach" in the hospital. For these varied services, the client would have paid the midwife out of pocket. Fees have varied greatly across midwifery practices, ranging from $800–$2 500, but sometimes higher for a reputable midwife in an urban setting. While these fees have not been fixed and some private-practice midwives have used a sliding scale determined by the client's ability to pay, Canadian women who have accessed private-practice midwives have tended to be drawn from a small pool of educated, middle-class women with some measure of discretionary income.

Faced with offering their services outside of formal institutions, until recently the situation for midwives themselves has been less than ideal. While some have had adequate economic resources at hand so as to undertake midwifery as a sideline, many other private-practice midwives have been forced to support their "midwifery habit" with a second or even third part-time job. These private-practice midwives, some of whom have been living near or below the poverty line, have had to contend as well with an absence of employment benefits of any kind; the persistent threat of being charged with criminal negligence; and a lack of control over their work and personal schedules. "The midwife's personal and professional lives are more intertwined than most, with no time of day reserved for herself or her family. Clients' personal crises and unpredictable timed labours intrude on a 24-hour basis. Each woman [midwife] either copes with this or retires according to the limits of her stamina and her support systems" (Barrington, 1985: 50).

Recent developments in Ontario and British Columbia have gone some way to extend access to midwifery services to clients from less privileged backgrounds, as well as to improve midwives' working conditions and overall social status. Today, in both provinces, certified midwives have gained the legal right to practise their profession, and their services are paid by public funds, thereby securing for them a viable income. At the same time, the number and types of women accessing midwifery services have expanded, to the extent that around three per cent of Ontario birthing women have a midwife as their primary attendant (Shroff, 1997), and a smaller number in BC, as legalization and public funding occurred there more recently (see Table 5–1). The overall Canadian figure is still less than two per cent, and the demand for midwifery services continues to outpace availability in many regions of both provinces. Although an in-depth discussion is beyond the scope of this book, it is worth noting that the likelihood of publicly funded midwifery services in other Canadian provinces remains uncertain. Alberta, for example, recently legalized midwifery, but provides no public provision for services (James, 1997). Birthing women still have to pay for a private-practice midwife, whose fees since legalization have increased to $2 000–$3 000 due to provincial government requirements that certified midwives purchase malpractice insurance. A similar development seems likely in at least some of the other provinces. Quebec may prove an exception, as it is with regard to parental insurance and childcare services. Eight pilot projects of strategically located birthing centres, staffed by certified government-salaried midwives, are now being evaluated as a potential model of midwifery practice for Quebec midwives (Hatem-Asmar and Blais, 1997). Such a model, if implemented, would differ substantially from that endorsed by Ontario and BC midwives, and it would reflect more closely the Swedish midwifery model described below.

How is this "woman-centred" model of midwifery care in Ontario and BC seen from the perspective of midwives as *workers*, most of whom are mothers themselves? Despite frequent representations of it as the "new midwifery" (Bourgeault and Fynes, 1997; Shroff, 1997), it can be argued that it is but a modified version of the private-practice model. As with its private-practice counterpart, the new woman-centred model is founded on the principle of *continuity of care*. In private-practice midwifery, continuity of care literally means continuity of *carer*, a single midwife caring for her client from the onset of the client's pregnancy, throughout her labour and delivery, and into postpartum. Ontario and BC midwives who spearheaded the integration processes in their respective provinces have broadened the notion of continuity of care underlying their woman-centred model to include *teams* of midwives. While less demanding on the individual midwife's schedule than the private-practice concept of continuity of carer, team midwifery nonetheless is not very "women-friendly" for individual midwives as *workers*, particularly if they are mothers themselves or have substantial caring responsibilities beyond their paid employment. Certified Ontario and BC midwives are still required to work on a 24-hour/7-day (weekly) schedule, although they can arrange to share on-call duties with another midwife in their team, or work over-time to compensate for a colleague taking leave for sickness or vacation, etc. Thus, much like Canadian physicians' model of group practice, woman-centred midwifery in Ontario and BC is very demanding of the caregiver's time and energy, requiring that she be ready and willing to serve a client day or night. Female physicians in group practices with a large maternity case-load are caused particular stress by their on-call duties when they have children of their own; the same is likely to be the case for midwives under the woman-centred model.

In short, in many ways woman-centred midwifery is a "new female professional project" (Witz, 1992) that favours one group of workers—those without inordinate non-paid caring responsibilities—over another. As one BC midwife states: "two of my close colleagues have had to consider the choice 'midwifery or motherhood' …. These women are strong advocates of women's issues, and excellent midwives, but because of various inflexibilities within our profession we have lost them! I have even heard such comments from other midwives as 'women should get their child-rearing done before midwifery'!" (College of Midwives of BC, 1996). Jane Sandall (1995: 205) makes a similar observation about woman-centred midwifery in Britain, where "whilst some women and midwives may be building a paradigm of 'woman-centred' practice based on an equal partnership, the result may be an elite core and casualised periphery based on ability to give a full-time flexible commitment to work." To put it another way, one result of the "new midwifery" underway in parts of Canada may be increased stress for some midwives both "at work," while attending to the needs of birthing women, and "at home," while carrying out their largely unrecognized second shift (Hochschild, 1989).

A FOURTH WINDOW ON THE UNITED STATES

One of the most striking features of US midwifery at present is that it is divided by two distinct groups of midwives: nurse-midwives, who first qualify as nurses and then complete a state recognized nurse-midwifery program (increasingly at the Masters degree level); and independent (lay) midwives, who train through a variety of routes, sometimes receiving little or no formal education and other times attending (non-nurse) midwifery schools such as the Seattle Midwifery School. There is no federal law that establishes the status—legal or illegal—of independent midwives across the country. Individual states have either legalized midwifery, made it illegal, or else passed no legislation one way or other (Sullivan and Weitz, 1988). Thus in 1993 midwifery was illegal in 18 states and legal in 25, having an ambivalent status in the remainder. "In states where [independent] midwifery is illegal, midwives run the risk of prosecution for practicing medicine without a license and for child abuse, manslaughter, or homicide if a mother or baby suffers injury or death" (Weitz, 1996: 288). Independent midwives are marginalized further by their lack of access to government program funding, as well as most forms of private insurance health care.

Nurse-midwives are integrated far more into the US health care system than their independent colleagues (Rooks, 1997; Davis-Floyd, 1998). Given that, in most respects, the work situation of independent midwives in the US parallels that of counterparts in Canada (outside of Ontario, BC, and Quebec), the following pages will focus primarily on the work situation and general social status of US nurse-midwives.

As noted, nurse-midwives in the US have been important providers of maternity care for disadvantaged and low-income women for decades. Research shows that nurse-midwives provide care that is safe and more efficient than the physician alternative (Bullough, 1975). After some struggle, nurse-midwives in a number of states gained third-party reimbursement from the government sponsored Medicaid program and through some private insurance plans. Nevertheless, the kinds of services reimbursed to nurse-midwives, and the rate of coverage, remain highly controversial issues across the US even today. Although many nurse-midwifery services—including prenatal care, patient counseling, and teaching—have proven cost-effective through related reductions in hospitalization and reduced dependency on expensive medical technology and personnel, nurse-midwives are not always reimbursed for such services. Alternatively, when they are reimbursed, it is at a lower rate compared to more invasive medical procedures performed by physicians. Nurse-midwives caring for Medicaid clients especially are disadvantaged, because they typically receive a lower rate of reimbursement for prenatal and postnatal care services than nurse-midwives caring for privately insured birthing women.

The result of this lack of uniformity regarding third-party reimbursement includes underutilization of the specialized skills of these workers and lower quality of client care than could be realized (Rooks, 1997). This is the case particularly, it seems, in profit-run Health Maintenance Organizations (HMOs) and other privately managed care organizations. Due to the organizational mandate to rationalize and streamline client care, in many cases nurse-midwives employed by organizations working under a strict capitation reimbursement scheme have little or no control over the services they offer. For example, prenatal appointments may be scheduled every 15 minutes; obstetrical routines dominate the organization of care; and the nurse-midwife has little opportunity to give personal care to clients. A similar situation is often the case for nurse-midwives employed in private physician-owned maternity clinics where obstetricians control the midwives' workday. On the other hand, some nurse-midwives in the US have joined together as a team and offer woman-centred care to birthing clients, who typically are reimbursed by private insurance. However, as discussed in reference to certified midwives in Ontario and BC, woman-centred care has its own set of problems.

While midwives have a presence in the US, with some new opportunities arising, full recognition and freedom to practise their specialized skills have not materialized under many of the for-profit models of practice developed in the recent decade, thereby limiting the full potential of midwifery as a profession. Recent statistics gathered by the *American College of Nurse-Midwives* clearly demonstrate the present marginality of its members: obstetricians and family physicians in the US are still the primary attendants in about 94 per cent of births, leaving the remaining 6 per cent attended either by nurse- or independent midwives (Davis-Floyd, 1998). Moreover, virtually all US midwives are at risk from managed care cutbacks and the drastic escalation in malpractice insurance costs. Rose Weitz summarizes the precarious situation of US nurse-midwives:

> Despite the attempts to keep nurse-midwives under medical control, during the 1970s and 1980s growing numbers of nurse-midwives began opening private practices with only loose connections to the doctors who provided their back-up support …. In the last few years, however, the rising cost of malpractice insurance—$35 in 1983 and $10 000 a decade later—has limited independent practice as an option … and led many nurse-midwives to abandon independent practice and return to working for hospitals or medically run clinics. (1996: 285)

It can be argued that the failure of efforts by US midwives—nurse- and independent—to gain solid occupational turf has resulted in part from the structure of national maternity care delivery. The American form of health care delivery—*corporate medicine* (Starr, 1982)—not only leaves dissatisfied a large segment of its workforce, but is also comparatively costly in terms of human life. The US spends more on health care services than all other capitalist countries—14.3 per cent of its GDP in 1995; while the comparable figure for Canada was 9.8 per cent, and 7.7 per cent for Sweden (World Bank, 1997).

Health care services in the US, notwithstanding some laudable government programs for the very poor and the elderly,[5] are for the majority "consumer goods," items purchased on the market for a comparatively high price (Macionis, Benoit, and Jansson, 1999). While, on average, Europeans look to government for about 80 per cent of health care costs (in Canada and Sweden the figures are about 70 and 85 per cent respectively), the US government funds only 42 per cent of health care services (US Bureau of the Census, 1996). People with comfortable incomes can purchase outstanding health care, including maternity care: the US has some of the world's top obstetricians with access to the latest medical technology. Yet lower-income people fare worse than their counterparts in either Canada or northern Europe. While a little less than three-quarters of the population has access to some kind of private insurance, health care coverage is inadequate in all but the most expensive plans. Even more telling is that some 40 million people (about 15 per cent of the population) have no health insurance or government coverage at all. Almost as many lose their coverage temporarily each year, generally because of layoffs or job changes.

Such inequity in regard to basic health and maternity care services results in health statistics that include the following: 1) over 25 per cent of US women have no access to any prenatal care; 2) the US has relatively high infant mortality rates compared to Canada and most European countries; 3) maternal morbidity is also comparatively high, due among other things to the overuse of obstetrical technologies and drugs during labour and delivery (United Nations Development Programme, 1995); and 4) the US shows comparatively high rates of episiotomies, inductions of labour, fetal monitoring, use of obstetrical forceps, and Cesarean sections (Rooks, 1997).

In 1994 President Clinton attempted to overcome these problematic features of the health care system by proposing a far-reaching reform termed *managed competition*. Under the "competitive" element of this proposal, employees would bargain collectively with various health care providers and health organizations to provide the public with the best care for the greatest value. The "management" dimension proposed that government would oversee the entire process, ensuring that no one was left uninsured and outside of the program, as well as arbitrating among the various health provider groups (including physicians and midwives) so that fair and viable work practices could be maintained. The "Clinton Plan," as it came to be called, was hardly radical in its conception. But, after lengthy debate the Clinton reforms became a "road to nowhere," with Congress rejecting the plan and agreeing on nothing to replace it (Hacker, 1997).

At this time, anything close to a national health care service remains elusive in the US, with both midwives and birthing women counting among the losers. Yet public concern about health care runs high, as privately organized managed care is seen more and more by many US citizens to be "mismanaged care." A proposed patients' rights bill now under debate in Congress is but the latest of attempts to move forward the health agenda in a country that has an historical resistance to social welfare reform in general.

As the following window on Sweden reveals, it is not inevitable that midwifery as a profession be so marginalized and midwives' social status so precarious.

A FOURTH WINDOW ON SWEDEN

Sound health and equal access to services for all citizens are the key goals of the modern Swedish health care system. Nearly all hospitals and other care facilities today are owned and administered by elected county councils or local authorities (Sweden has 23 county councils and 3 local authorities), and most health professionals, including physicians, are salaried. The end result is a health and maternity care system based on two characteristic features: democratic ethics and decentralization (Twaddle and Hessler, 1987; Benoit, 1994). Midwives serve as a linchpin to the entire system.

Maternity care services in Sweden are dispensed at the local level through a network of publicly funded *Barnmorske Mottagnings* (Midwives' Clinics), sometimes referred to as Type 1 facilities or Maternal-Child Health Clinics (McKay, 1993). Virtually all Swedish women (99 per cent) receive care via this route, without any out-of-pocket payment. Typically a pregnant woman is attended by a clinic midwife assigned by district. The midwife arranges for the woman to be seen by the clinic's maternal health physician during early stages of pregnancy. Three examinations by the attending physician was typical two decades ago, but according to respondents, there is now greater flexibility, resulting in fewer physician examinations for healthy pregnant women (Taped interviews, Stockholm County, 1995). My research also indicates slight variation within counties regarding the average number of physician examinations. Discussions are underway whether, in fact, even a single medical examination is necessary for a woman undergoing her second or subsequent pregnancy where no complications occurred with the first child. If all appears normal, the midwife attends to the pregnant woman's varied needs (and, if such be the case, those of her partner) until the birth is imminent.

Those women with complicated medical histories or special health concerns are referred by antenatal midwives working out of a Midwives' Clinic to one of the 80 central/district county hospitals (Type 2 facilities), where other midwives specialize in areas of labour and delivery, postpartum, breastfeeding, and gynecology. Childbearing women with serious obstetric concerns that cannot be handled at the primary- and secondary-care levels are referred to one of the 10 regional/teaching hospitals (Type 3 facilities) for care by an interdisciplinary team of midwives, obstetricians, gynecologists, and pediatricians.

Great care is taken to collect complete health histories of birthing women; the resulting data is available for analysis so that comparisons can be made across hospitals and Midwives' Clinics. Swedish women carry their own health records, and midwives are required to keep women fully informed of the progress of their pregnancy: what kinds of medication are available, the conditions under which they are not advisable, and any potential side effects. In the final analysis, pregnant women make the decisions concerning what kind, if any, medication they will take to ease the pain of labour. They also decide who, apart the attending midwife, should be included in their birth team. As much as possible, women's wishes for privacy and choice are honoured (McKay, 1993; Benoit, 1997).

Midwifery practice in clients' homes is rare in present-day Sweden (Vallgarda, 1996). Kajsa Sundstrom-Feigenberg explains the transition to hospital births:

> The shift away from giving birth at home gathered speed in the 1930s. By 1940 hospitals and maternity homes were handling 65% of all births in Sweden and the proportion rose to 94% in 1950 and 99% in 1960. This meant that district midwives, whose principal task previously had been to assist at births in the home, now had to choose between maternity work at a hospital and exclusively antenatal care in a district. (1988: 36)

The remaining one per cent of births occur in one of the country's two birth clinics providing comprehensive (prenatal to postpartum) midwifery services or, for a very small number of births, at home. While home-births are legal, they generally are not encouraged and are attended mainly by formally trained midwives. One example is the home-birth services offered by midwives located at the Midwives' Clinic attached to the alternative *antroposofisk* (anthroposophical) hospital in Järna, located just south of Stockholm. The general philosophy adopted by midwives and their colleagues in this unique health setting follows that of the radical thinker Rudolf Steiner. The Steiner philosophy maintains that the capacity for conscious spiritual understanding can be found deep within every person, and can be awakened through sustained concentration and meditation. It is a principle of the Steiner movement that all its practitioners should hold orthodox/formal qualifications as well as learning the anthroposophical approach to health maintenance and healing. The comparatively small number of home-birth midwifery advocates in Sweden significantly differ from many of the independent Canadian and US midwives, who tend to embrace instead an informal style of training that involves practical know-how and everyday experience.

In many areas of Sweden, Midwives' Clinics also operate "hot lines"; women enrolled at the clinic are encouraged to call their midwife (when the clinic is closed to the public) should they seek answers to questions arising outside of planned visits. In addition, a parallel group of psychologists (200 in 1993) are located in the Midwives' Clinics, coming to the aid of midwives (and child or pediatric nurses) and patients needing special help in handling the psycho-social and emotional aspects of reproduction. As Susan McKay (1993: 115) reports: "there is a great interest in Sweden in social obstetrics—that is, social factors that affect obstetric outcomes—and interdisciplinary teamwork for better maternity outcomes—is highly valued."

After six weeks at home with their new baby, mothers return to their local Midwives' Clinic for a check-up and contraceptive advice, often from the midwife who helped them prenatally. Swedish midwives are legally permitted to prescribe birth control pills and the "morning after pill," insert IUDs, distribute condoms, and indeed, to perform primary gynecological care for women from teenage years into old age. According to one of my Swedish midwife informants, 70–80 per cent of contraceptive/family planning advice and prescriptions in 1995 fell within the mandate of Swedish midwives. Another respondent describes her role in this way:

> Many people think that the midwife is standing there assisting deliveries. But she is not; she is promoting health … health, individual health promotion regarding sexual issues. And these are influenced by culture, and lack of it. So that's why the midwife must try to understand what it is that makes a woman not breastfeed, not use contraceptives …. [We] look then at the whole reproductive issue, the whole health of women. I feel very strongly that I am this type of midwife. (Taped interview: Upsalla, Sweden, 1995)

In brief, Swedish midwives working in Midwives' Clinics and other public health institutions are able to provide care for healthy women across their reproductive lives. Although during the narrow time-frame of pregnancy-to-postpartum the average Swedish woman does not receive care from one particular midwife (short-term continuity), she receives continuity of a philosophy of midwifery care from the same occupational group. Furthermore, Swedish midwives as an occupational group of primary care workers go a long way in providing the nation's women with general "well-woman" care *across their reproductive lifecycle*, comparable (some would argue superior) to that offered by family physicians in Canada and the US.

Sweden, like Canada and the US, is under pressure to restructure its welfare state. A small number of experiments were initiated in the early–mid 1990s, including a form of private practice wherein a midwife manager heads and operates on a daily basis an independent clinic, hiring midwives (and other providers) on salary, whose services are reimbursed in part or in full by the local health authorities—thus creating a privately managed but publicly funded midwifery service. Although only a few such private midwifery practices have been permitted to open, and the experiment has now been placed on hold, it is interesting to note that the Swedish debate about "private midwifery" highlights some of the points made in this chapter.

In the mid 1990s I interviewed the midwives managing Sweden's two main private midwifery practices. They claimed that their new team-midwifery model was attractive because it gave birthing women greater short-term continuity of care (the promise of a single or small team of midwives available to women across their pregnancy and during hours when public midwives' clinics are closed), and thus the potential for a closer partnership with their midwife/midwives. However, these midwife managers had little to say about the impact of the new style of private practice on the equity of midwifery care or on midwives' rights as workers, concerns that are paramount on the minds of midwives working in public employment.

Perhaps it is not surprising that Swedish midwives in the public sector express less positive views about the team midwifery experiment. Many of those interviewed acknowledged that while "public competition" between the private midwifery practices and the public midwives' clinics may encourage their respective workers to become more dedicated to their clients, respondents in public employment also noted that the private practices tend to select a certain class of client (educated; middle-class) and of midwife (those without family responsibilities; those willing to work flexible schedules, including evenings and longer hours). The first concern contradicts one of the main principles of the Swedish health care system—equitable health care for all. The latter concern, as noted in Chapter 3, suggests the creation of a two-track career system such as has been advocated by some writers as the way forward for women in Canada and the US seeking managerial careers (Schwartz, 1989). This type of system, however, has been highly criticized by some feminists, who fear that creating "mommy tracks" and "male tracks" will reinforce stereotypes suggesting that women have lesser career attachments, thereby undermining women's gains in the workplace (Ehrenreich and English, 1989). Swedish midwives in public employment likewise fear that the private practices, if allowed to increase, may create an internal hierarchy among midwives similar to what has been observed in parts of Canada as well as Britain. As already noted, the Social Democratic government elected in Sweden in 1995 has placed a ban on further team midwifery practices for the conceivable future.

It is too early to state conclusively whether this alternative midwifery model has enhanced efficiency and increased client satisfaction. According to the majority of Swedish midwives interviewed, most Swedish women are content with their maternity services and, likewise, most midwives are pleased with their working conditions, social security, and benefits. Of course, as discussed above, most Swedish midwives fall short of rendering short-term continuity of care to birthing women. However, it should be kept in mind that Sweden's welfare state in the modern era has attempted to validate women's contribution as workers in the public and private spheres, while at the same time has built a maternity care service that offers high-quality care by midwives to all women. Consumer demand for short-term continuity of care has not, in fact, been a focal point of the feminist health movement in Sweden. As one midwife respondent notes, "perhaps some people think it is very important to meet the same midwife all through[out], but I haven't heard that most people think that [lack of short-term continuity of care] is a problem" (Taped interview, Stockholm, 1995).

More important, it seems, is that Swedish midwives show a caring attitude combined with expertise in primary reproductive concerns. Sara Goodman (1995) maintains that this largely has been realized by Swedish midwives, who are able to blend "hands, heart, and mind" in their daily activities and, I would note, still have energy and time for non-paid caring work in the home.

SUMMARY AND CONCLUSION

Drawing on primary and secondary comparative research on midwives' work and social rights, this chapter has presented evidence that indicates significant historical variation in their work situation. The data shows that midwives in some historical instances have had access to legal status, publicly funded education, and secure mandates to practise. In other instances these important elements of midwives' occupational status were denied.

As shown in Figure 5–1, such variation continues to exist today in regard to midwives' social rights and control over their work in Canada, the United States, and Sweden. Swedish midwives in public employment, followed by their counterparts in publicly funded private practice, enjoy the most extensive social rights and control over their work. Canadian midwives in publicly funded private practice have comparatively fewer social rights and less control. US midwives in publicly funded private practice, and even more so their colleagues in corporate employment, score comparatively low on both social rights and control over their work. Canadian freelance midwives and especially their US counterparts receive the lowest marks of all.

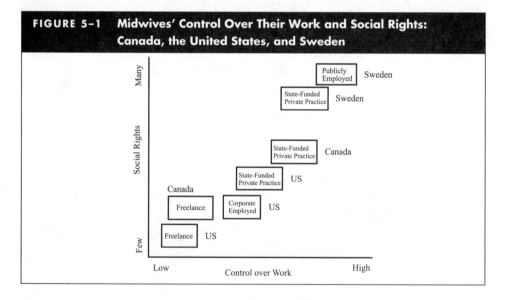

FIGURE 5-1   Midwives' Control Over Their Work and Social Rights: Canada, the United States, and Sweden

*This figure does not include Quebec midwives working in the experimental birth-centre pilot projects. However, if this project eventually becomes institutionalized in Quebec, it will create an alternative model of midwifery practice in Canada that may be similar in some respects to the model found among publically-employed midwives in Sweden.

Source: Compiled by the author using data from various sources.

The final chapter summarizes those preceding it, and discusses the main conclusions that emerge from the overall study of women's work and social rights in the three countries examined.

ENDNOTES

[1]Still other terms are found in the literature on the history of maternity care. In Danish, the term for midwife is *jordmor* or "earth mother." Danish women traditionally delivered their babies on the ground, and the midwife lifted the newborn from the earth, from which it was believed that the child gained life-giving strength. The term incorporates the word "mother" because it was assumed that the midwife should herself be a mother, with her own birth experiences to draw upon when helping other women. In Swedish, the term for midwife is *barnmorska*, meaning "baby's mother attendant."

[2]The shortcomings of traditional midwifery were not solely the responsibility of midwives. Additional factors included the frequency of pregnancies; women's arduous work roles during and after the reproductive period; and, perhaps most important, diet, which in average households was deficient in both quality and quantity, and worsened by periodic famine.

[3]The *Collegium Medicum* was transformed into the Swedish National Board of Health in 1813.

[4]Based on author's research on midwifery in Newfoundland and Labrador in 1986–88.

[5]In 1965 Congress created Medicare and Medicaid. Medicare pays some of the medical costs for people over age 65; in 1994 it insured 34 million men and women, 13 per cent of the population. Medicaid, a medical insurance program for the poor, provided benefits to 32 million people, about 12 per cent of the population. An additional 26 million veterans (10 per cent) can obtain free care in government operated hospitals.

WOMEN'S WORK AND SOCIAL RIGHTS: LOOKING TO THE TWENTY-FIRST CENTURY

"The patriarchal dichotomy between women and independence/work/citizenship is under political challenge, and the social basis for the ideal of full (male) employment is crumbling .... An opportunity has become visible to create a genuine democracy, to move the welfare state to a welfare society without involuntary social exiles, in which women as well as men enjoy full social membership." (Pateman, 1989: 204)

INTRODUCTION

In a relatively short period of history—less than two centuries—the work activities of women in Canada, the United States, and Sweden have changed dramatically from those predating capitalism. History reveals a wide variety of societal forms included under the umbrella of "pre-capitalist society." In the earliest societies work was not envisioned as a separate human activity, but rather understood as akin to living itself, and interwoven into a larger cosmic order. Yet even in hunter-gatherer societies essential tasks were assigned along gender lines. Men undertook activities associated mainly with hunting away from camp; women tended to pursue activities located within or near the camp, activities that spanned gathering, food preparation, and the biological and social reproduction of the next generation.

At the same time, as illustrated in Chapter 2, these gender roles were fluid rather than rigid. Depending on such factors as season, climate, and the availability of game and wild food-stuffs, as well as family circumstance, men also could be found taking part in many of the activities normally assigned to women. Nor was it unusual for women to hunt for small game while gathering wild roots and berries. Women gatherers were expected as well to take note of any fresh tracks or other signs of big game animals, taking such knowledge back to the camp for the hunters to use in planning expeditions.

A second point made in Chapter 2 was that these early societies had no surplus wealth to be stockpiled by one or another social group or gender. Any accumulated resources were distributed based on a principle of sharing or generalized reciprocity, a principle founded on pragmatism rather than any particular "nobility" of hunter-gatherers. The survival of the individual as well as the group depended on this practice. In short, while gendered work roles were present in hunter-gatherer societies, women were awarded recognition for their work activities and resources were shared equitably between the sexes. The concept of "patriarchy" thus cannot be applied to this original form of society.

These positive aspects of women's situation in hunter-gatherer societies began slowly to erode in small-scale agricultural (gardening) societies. An increasingly sedentary way of life combined with the necessity of protecting accumulated wealth (economic surplus) led to rigid and less equitable work patterns. Women emerged as the main gardeners, expending comparatively more energy and time than men in primary production. At the same time, women gardeners carried out most of the domestic caring tasks necessary for men's maintenance and the social reproduction of the next generation. Yet it is important to note also that the majority of small-scale agricultural societies were based on matrilineal descent and matrilocal residence. These features ensured women recognition for their labours within the extended household as well as protection by their clan. Moreover, although the principle of sharing desisted across clans, generalized reciprocity continued to operate within individual matrilineal clans.

On the other hand, women in small-scale agricultural societies were bound more closely to the vicinity of the village than women gatherers had been. The land beyond became male territory, where men performed gender-specific activities including trading, political negotiation, and warfare. Women and children located within the village compound were left unarmed and vulnerable during wartime. Sometimes large numbers were captured by enemy clans and subsequently sacrificed or enslaved, creating an underclass of slaves.

In resource-wealthier fishing societies, such as those that developed along Canada's northwest coast during the pre-contact period, the social and gender inequalities found in small-scale agricultural societies became more pronounced. This was the case especially in those fishing societies that were organized around patrilocal residence patterns and along patrilineal descent lines. In these societies (which accounted for the majority of fishing societies) women's multidimensional work roles—gathering, fish preservation, domestic activities, and child-rearing—typically were viewed as secondary to men's boat-building and fishing activities. Furthermore, compared with other pre-capitalist forms of society, warfare and slavery were far more common. A substantial minority of women and children in the pre-contact fishing societies of Canada's northwest coast were slaves taken as trophies of war (Donald, 1997). They remained isolated from their kin and marginalized within their owner's family. Hard labour was demanded of slave women, who received little by way of economic reward or social status.

Thus when Europeans arrived in the New World beginning in the sixteenth century, there existed a diversity of Aboriginal peoples living in intact societies with varied gender systems for organizing productive and caring work, assigning social status, and distributing societal resources. The Europeans, however, were not interested in creating open dialogue with Aboriginal peoples or developing cooperative relationships. French and British colonists instead sought to impose their own cultural norms and traditions, including notions of gender, on the original inhabitants of the New World. European attitudes towards Aboriginal people included elitism and outright racism. At the same time, "white man's" contagious diseases decimated some tribal groups to the point of extinction. The legal transcontinental market in slaves from areas of Africa to plantations in the southern United States and the continuing interchange of slavery on both sides of the US-Canadian border until well into the nineteenth century are reminders of the dark side of European contact.

The situation of women in the large-scale agricultural (farming) societies that eventually took shape across Canada and the US was not an improvement on their pre-contact counterparts. Colonial settlements enacted patriarchal laws and customs that in many ways severely limited women's prospects at every stage of their lifecycle. Colonial women were expected to perform extensive work activities, typically beginning when they were young girls. These included helping men in the planting, weeding, and harvesting of crops; attending to farm animals and domestic work; and caring for husbands, children, and elders. Yet this work burden seldom resulted in an equal share of resources. Land ownership was almost exclusively a male preserve. Marriage rendered the colonial wife subordinate to her husband. A deserted wife or widow had neither rights to her children nor equal share of family property or wealth, and daughters were seldom mentioned in their father's will. Colonial women were silenced further by an almost exclusively male religious and political elite.

Colonial Canada and the United States eventually were transformed by a new economic system called capitalism. As described in Chapter 3, capitalism prizes individual competition and profit-making, characteristics that came to be seen as more rational, modern, and superior to earlier economic systems. While at first marginal to colonial life, the emerging market economy led by merchant-capitalists ultimately came to dominate the work lives of more and more inhabitants, settlers and Aboriginal peoples alike. When the US and later Canada entered the modern age during the nineteenth century, distinct divisions became evident in class, race, and gender.

Capitalism was also a masculine project. The new gender ideology known as the doctrine of separate spheres challenged women's role in production, which had been taken for granted (if not always valued highly) in all previous historical periods. Notions of women's "proper" place within the private sphere of the home, protected from the outside world of competitive markets and harsh politics, were embraced by the ruling elites, middle-class social reformers, many male labour unions, and even many women themselves. This ideology was promoted even though the majority of women could ill-afford to live the kind of life it prescribed. Working-class women were forced by necessity to seek work for pay, engaging themselves in a wide range of paid and unpaid activities in order to sustain themselves and their families.

In the early stages of capitalism, women's paid work activities were largely organized within the putting-out system controlled by merchant-capitalists. This new system of production pitted poor women—compelled to make a living by engaging in piecework in their own homes—against craftsmen, whose economic situation was under serious challenge by new modes of production. Other women found employment as domestics in the homes of wealthier women, thus pitting women against women. Still other women made a living by engaging in the sex trade.

By the last decades of the nineteenth century, industrialization had transformed employment in urban areas of Canada and, to an even greater extent, the US. Factory production had arrived. The ideology driving entrepreneurial activity was based on the notion of "free enterprise" or "laissez-faire" relations between business and government, seen as fundamental to the efficient movement of products to markets.

The state also served to promote the interests of men over women. Legislation passed in Canada in the late nineteenth and early twentieth centuries was based on the belief that women factory workers needed "special" protection by the state. The outcome was that working-class women were barred from most manufacturing jobs apart from light industry. At the same time, the enactment of minimum-wage laws *for women only* reduced their attraction to employers. The combined effect was fewer jobs for women and occupational segregation in more marginal industries. Little consideration was given to how working-class women would make a living outside of factory employment, and, for many, domestic service and prostitution were their only options. A small number of women who had access to formal education found work as teachers and nurses.

First in the US and later in Canada, capitalism moved into a new stage in the early decades of the twentieth century. Markets were expanded in the search for fresh sources of profit. Small independent factories were either absorbed into a few oligopolistic or monopolistic firms, or eliminated completely. Industries increasingly became subjected to the fluctuations of national and international markets. New techniques such as scientific management and the moving assembly line, discovered by the US automobile industrialist, Henry Ford, create efficiency in the workplace and enhanced profits on an ever-larger scale.

Large-scale manufacturing (Fordism) was also accompanied by the growth of work bureaucracies, the so-called "administrative revolution." As firms and plants merged into large-scale enterprises and governmental tasks became more complex and multifaceted, earlier administrative methods proved inadequate. Both private industry and government administration became bureaucratized. Vertically-arranged administrative systems, based on rational rules and regulations and impersonal criteria for the selection of workers and managers, replaced the simpler, more personal and idiosyncratic administrative arrangements of early stages of capitalism.

On a more positive note, large-scale manufacturing and bureaucratic employment were accompanied by important social rights for male workers. Industrial unions became not only legal but also popular. By mid-century, unionized workers had emerged as a "labour aristocracy," offering privileges to their members not available to non-unionized counterparts. Unionized (male) breadwinners were concerned especially with winning from their employers a decent "family wage" to help support wives and children. For some time their efforts proved successful, then stalled during the Great Depression of the 1930s, but improved once again after the Second World War. Virtually absent from the ranks of the emerging labour aristocracy, however, were women wage earners. Even in the light industries, where women were employed in large numbers, men were unwilling to see their female colleagues as equal members of the unions' "brotherhood."

Chapter 3 depicted a similar sex bias tipped in men's direction that also characterized the administrative organizations of this period. The only cracks in this dominant gender ideology pervading economic life occurred during wartime. With men away at the front, women workers were recruited in large numbers to keep factories producing and government bureaucracies functioning smoothly. The feminization of the workforce during the two world wars indicated that women in Canada and the US were quite capable and more than willing to work for pay. This applied equally to married women and even those with small children, providing subsidized daycare facilities were available. However, the apparent shortcomings of the female sex regarding career commitment and their "natural" inclination to stay at home and provide (unpaid) domestic labour and childcare duties resurfaced as soon as the war ended. With able-bodied men in need of jobs, women once again were expected to take their place as a reserve army of labour.

The second half of the twentieth century is differentiated from earlier periods of capitalism by the immense growth of service jobs. The emerging post-industrial society involved a decline of male blue-collar employment in primary and secondary industries and the demand for a new kind of worker, with a different skill set that involved "giving service" to consumers and clients. For centuries socialized in this direction, women were in high demand. Male employment declined as women's employment expanded on both sides of the Canadian-US border. Eventually married women and those with small children joined the labour force of the new "service society."

Other positive developments for women soon followed. Access to higher education and the elimination of age-old barriers to women's entry into management and the professions are cases in point. As discussed in Chapter 5, a more recent development for women in Canada has been the legalization and, in two provinces, public funding of midwifery. In some provincial jurisdictions midwives—the vast majority of whom are women—can finally enjoy the opportunity to work without fear of persecution for practising medicine without a licence, and at the same time are able make a decent living from their work.

On a more sobering note, women's increased economic presence in both Canada and the US has been accompanied by a decline in real wages for families over the last two decades. Paralleling the situation of women in earlier generations, many women today are working for wages because their contribution is crucial to family survival. Chapter 3 noted that women continue to face significant problems while pursuing economic activities, including occupational gender segregation and wage disparity. Gender inequality in employment has eroded very slowly in recent decades. As well, women in both Canada and the US continue to put in more hours per week in combined paid and unpaid work than do men.

Despite similarities observed between the two North American countries, Chapter 4 provided evidence that women's social rights in Canada are more advanced than those of women workers south of the border. In Canada the welfare state has in general adopted a stronger mediating role between capital and labour. The result has been that Canadian women have access to certain social rights (e.g., health care insurance), in addition to employment rights (e.g., maternity and parental benefits), that are not available in the US at the national level. The plural nature of the US political system results in significant variation in women's access to occupational/corporate welfare in the form of workplace benefits. The more privileged employees, who possess specialized skills and education, tend to receive benefits to which many others have no access. This is especially the case for working-class, African-American, and visible minority women. As shown in Figure 6–1, American solo mothers and their children confront poverty to a far greater extent than their counterparts in the 10 other countries surveyed, including Canada. Sweden, the country that has informed the other main comparison to Canada in this book, has very low levels of poverty for children in both two-parent and solo-mother families.

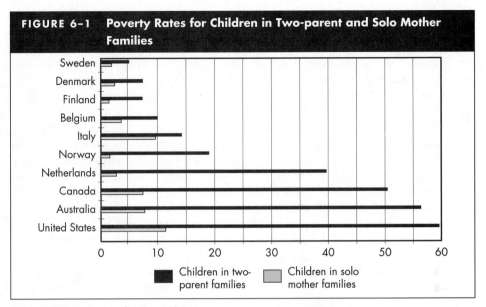

FIGURE 6-1   Poverty Rates for Children in Two-parent and Solo Mother Families

Source: UNICEF, *The Progress of Nations*, (1996) 44.

As shown in Chapter 2, Swedish women's work arrangements across the centuries parallel in many ways developments noted in Canada and the United States. Yet there are important differences between Sweden and the two North American nations that go some way in explaining the comparative advantage Swedish women enjoy today.

Sweden belonged to the Old World, with an historical legacy more closely reflecting that of aristocratic England or France. By the sixteenth century, Sweden had emerged as an imperial power, with territories that stretched across the Baltic and near monopolies on highly prized iron, tar, and copper sources, the "poor man's gold" (Wallerstein, 1974). Nevertheless, Sweden's northern location and lack of wealth compared to Britain and Continental Europe hindered industrial development in Sweden until well into the nineteenth century. By this time the Swedish high nobility had been defeated and the empire had lost virtually all of its territories. Reduced to its present size (apart from a loose union with Norway until the early years of the twentieth century), Sweden began a path of gradual democratization without recourse to exploitation of other territories.

The Swedish peasantry was historically advantaged in that peasant farmers were able to purchase land and thus were not subject to leasehold duties, but only to paying public taxes (Alestalo and Kuhnle, 1987: 9). This fundamental right was won without revolution. Wealthier peasant farmers gradually adopted capitalist labour-saving techniques, thereby reducing the numbers of independent peasants. This resulted, among other things, in an oversupply of labour in rural areas, which was eased in two main ways: 1) a movement to semi-urban and urban industrializing regions where a growing class of merchants and industrialists had established small- and large-scale industrial enterprises; and 2) migration overseas, especially to the US. The transformation of Swedish peasants into members of the working class was a gradual process, and Swedish cities were spared the destitution faced by propertyless peasant migrants found in most urban areas in early-industrial Europe (Esping-Andersen, 1989).

When social democracy took hold in Sweden in the late nineteenth and early twentieth centuries, capitalist farmers as well as wage earners had gained a relatively strong political voice. Both groups are represented in the Swedish parliament by two of the five parties that continue today to vie with middle- and upper-class parties for political power. The comparative strength of the workers' party, the Social Democrats, is indicated by the fact that they have been in power for most of the past half century, and remain so at the time of this publication.

On the other hand, until well into this century progress on the gender front in Sweden has been much more incremental. Patriarchal laws and traditional customs assigned women an array of work tasks but denied them equal right to inherit property or keep their children when marriages dissolved. Much like their North American counterparts during this stage of capitalism, Swedish women were expected to organize their work and family lives within the doctrine of separate spheres. This effected protective legislation that banned women from certain kinds of industrial work, justifying lower wages than men received, rendering their unpaid domestic and caring activities invisible, and ultimately leaving them dependent on heterosexual marriage for economic security.

Only with the development of a comprehensive welfare state beginning in the 1930s did Swedish women start to access opportunities in employment that approximated those previously available exclusively to men. This achievement can be only approximate because Swedish women still face barriers that hinder true equality with men. These barriers, including occupational gender segregation and gender wage inequities, are also found in Canada and the US. Nevertheless, Swedish women enjoy substantial economic independence and also have access to extensive women-friendly social rights found in neither Canada nor the US—nor, indeed, in many other high-income countries. As Pekka Kosonen (1994: 98) notes about Nordic/Scandinavian welfare states in general—among which Sweden's remains the most comprehensive—"the Scandinavian welfare state model is based on universal participation in employment and on universal social policy where the position of the state is central."

The early 1990s were marked by a deep economic recession in Sweden. More recently, Sweden, along with a number of other European countries, joined the European Union (EU). However, to date, the central principles underlying Sweden's social-democratic welfare state, including those that have been instrumental in promoting women's economic independence, remain largely in place. No doubt the comparatively strong role that Swedish women enjoy in the political arena, as well as through unions and women's groups, aids them in their struggle against welfare state retrenchment (Stephens, 1996). Swedish women, including feminists, tend to hold a more friendly view of the state than North American counterparts. From a Swedish perspective, the welfare state "de-emphasises the marginalisation of women and instead concentrates on the political space open to women" (Karvonen and Selle, 1995: 11). Swedish women have made amazing inroads into the hitherto male dominated domain of national politics. In 1997 40.4 per cent of members of Sweden's national parliament were women, the highest in the world. Canadian women in 1997 came in 21st place, at 18 per cent, while US women were number 41 on the list, with 11.7 per cent female representation (Inter-Parliamentary Union, 1997). By 1998, as shown in Table 6–1, the Swedish percentage had risen to 42.7 and Swedish women were still at the top of the ranking system. The Canadian figure had risen incrementally to 20.1 per cent, increasing their ranking very slightly. The US percentage in 1998 was 12.9 and US women remained in the same relative position they occupied the previous year. This means that more so than

Canadian and especially US counterparts, Swedish women have been actively involved in shaping welfare state social policy. They have been instrumental in the struggle to promote women's employment opportunities, retain social programs during the recession of the early 1990s, and involve men in family life. As discussed in Chapter 5, the comparatively advantaged position of Swedish midwives provides further evidence of women's advancement in this country.

TABLE 6-1	Women in National Parliaments, Lower or Single House, as of 5 Dec. 1998: Selected Countries			
Order	**Country**	**Seats**	**Women**	**Percentage of Women**
1	Sweden	349	149	42.7
2	Denmark	179	67	37.4
3	Norway	165	60	36.4
4	Netherlands	150	54	36
5	Finland	200	67	33.5
6	Germany	669	207	30.9
7	South Africa	400	118	29.6
8	New Zealand	120	35	29.2
10	Austria	183	48	26.2
10 (tie)	Vietnam	450	118	26.2
13	Spain	348	86	24.7
16	Monaco	18	4	22.2
19	Eritrea	105	22	21
19 (tie)	Switzerland	200	42	21
20	Canada	301	62	20.1
22	Grenada	15	3	20
24	United Kingdom	659	120	18.2
27	Lithuania	137	24	17.5
29	Rwanda	70	12	17.1
31	El Salvador	84	14	16.7
34	Angola	220	34	15.5
36	Zimbabwe	150	22	14.7
41	USA	435	56	12.9
44	Philippines	217	27	12.4
49	Indonesia	500	57	11.4

(continued on p. 156)

TABLE 6-1	Women in National Parliaments, Lower or Single House, as of 5 Dec. 1998: Selected Countries			
Order	Country	Seats	Women	Percentage of Women
51	Estonia	101	11	10.9
51 (tie)	France	577	63	10.9
57	Panama	72	7	9.7
62	Ghana	20018	9	—
72	Tunisia	163	12	7.4
76	Belize	29	2	6.9
82	Cyprus	56	3	5.4
86	Japan	500	24	4.8
86 (tie)	Singapore	84	4	4.8
96	Chad	125	3	2.4
102	Yemen	301	2	0.7
103	Morocco	325	2	0.6

Source: Inter-Parliamentary Union, 1998.

In summary, at least in regard to the three countries under examination here, there has been no linear progress across historical time, nor across different nation-states in the modern era regarding gender equality in work and social life. The very fact that national governments in the United States, Canada, and Sweden make available social rights for women that range from minimal to comprehensive, illustrates the impartial fit between the rhetoric and the reality of women's lives.

Capitalism as an economic system has changed in profound ways over the past two centuries, and some critics argue that capitalism is now undergoing another transformation, in part due to the "globalization" of production. Sociologists and other social scientists argue that major economic shifts are now underway across the globe, undermining the influence of all welfare states, regardless of their particular geographical location. According to James Laxer (1996: 22), the concept has a strong ideological underside: "gobalization is not merely a description, it is a prescription as well. What can be called the globalization agenda has become the conventional wisdom of the English-speaking world's business elite."

Also embracing this viewpoint is Robert Reich (1991), who argues that transnational corporations increasingly are less concerned with providing for a limited domestic market; now customers with purchasing power anywhere on the globe are the market focus. Reich notes that extraction and secondary manufacturing industries were the first affected by massive layoffs. Blue-collar workers were replaced in large numbers by robots, and many industrial plants completely shut down. Frequently plants were reopened in places where workers are typically non-unionized, providing labour cheaper. The same downsizing of secure employment is said to be now occurring in the private and public service sectors.

New information technologies, including personal computers and the Internet, have undermined the job security of many service workers (Rifkin, 1995).

Scholars writing on "post-Fordism" make a parallel case. They predict a decline in the role of national governments as a negotiating power between employers and workers, as well as the erosion of social policies that have been hammered out over the past three decades. The Fordist welfare state allegedly is being transformed into a post-Fordist "entrepreneurial state" (Harvey, 1989). Feminist scholars have gendered these predictions and pointed out that post-Fordism threatens to undermine women's hard-won achievements of the post-World War II period (Jenson et al., 1988). Especially worrisome, they note, is the threatened demise of social policies on which women depend for income redistribution, public employment, education, health and social services, and social assistance (Armstrong, 1993; Oakley and Williams, 1994). Some feminist scholars argue that a "marketization" of the welfare state is occuring, including the creation of quasi-markets and/or the privatization of core health and social services. Also predicted is the increasing "individualization" of welfare state provision, which involves a gradual movement away from universalism, based on welfare state principles of equality and equity, towards provision in the form of targeted services based on selectivity and prioritization (Lewis, 1993).

This book has presented evidence that calls into question the utility of concepts of globalization and post-Fordism in capturing the complicated trends in the organization of women's work and their access to social rights in Canada, the US, and Sweden. Despite reduction in overall social welfare spending in Sweden in the present decade (which can be seen as one measure of welfare state decline), some developments, including increased subsidized childcare spaces and paternity leaves and benefits, suggest actual growth in women-friendly welfare state provision (Sainsbury, 1996). At the same time, significant differences remain between the Swedish process of social welfare reform and developments in Canada and the US. And the Canadian welfare state continues to be more "caring" of working-class populations generally as well as women specifically when compared to the US system (Myles, 1996). Even when employed, US women wage earners, especially those who belong to minority groups or are solo mothers, face poverty to an extent found in neither Sweden nor Canada.

A question remains as to why Canada and the US, so similar in some ways, tend to diverge in regard to public support for the welfare state. As argued in earlier chapters, the decentralized character of the US federal/state political system goes some way towards explaining the contrast. As others have argued, major cleavages along lines of class and race also play a role (Skocpol, 1988; Polakow, 1993; Quadagno, 1994). Further, Antonia Maioni (1998) contends that the presence of a third party has been pivotal in advancing the Canadian welfare state compared to the two-party US system. Seymore Martin Lispet (1990: 136) makes an additional distinction between the two countries on the basis of *communitarianism*, maintaining that Canadians are much more supportive of "the public mobilization of resources to fulfill group objectives." Of course, Canada too has fundamental divisions— of region (the provinces) and ethnicity (two founding nations, in addition to its Aboriginal peoples). Yet Canadians look to their welfare state as the glue that holds the country together, not an easy feat given its comparatively large territory and small population, two dominant linguistic groups (French and English), mosaic of new immigrants, and powerful neighbour just south of the border (Myles, 1996). As Keith Banting (1992) explains, Canadian "federal welfare programmes, whether delivered directly to individuals or through provincial governments are powerful tools of inter-regional redistribution. They represent one of the few ways in which the federal government can fashion appeals that cut across linguistic and regional divisions."

In short, while there is little doubt that recent changes in the nature of capitalism will further impact the economies and societies of both countries, the historical evidence compels us to keep our eyes open for continuing differences between women's situation in Canada and the US. This point is even more relevant when Sweden is included in the comparison.

A final word about the nature of caring work: this book has presented evidence that calls for a different conception of work than that in common usage in scholarship by statisticians, economists, and even sociologists themselves. This revised conception of work necessitates the inclusion of *caring for dependent others* as a fundamental aspect of work in all human societies. Caring for others, often involving physical, mental, and emotional types of labour, is worthy of sociological investigation on par with the productive activities that have long held the place of privilege in intellectual conceptualizations of work. Research on non-paid and paid work in the twenty-first century must first and foremost be about *time* and its management (Parcel, 1999).

Yet it would be short-sighted to view caring work as a concept that is universal in form and content. Such a limited understanding tends to associate caring activities as a "natural" outcome of female socialization or something inextricably bound to women's biological processes. This perspective overlooks the remarkable variability in the assignment of caring tasks and their societal value over time and across place. Caring work has no singular historical definition. Nor has it been an exclusive female activity everywhere. The burden of caring work in Sweden, for example, has changed substantially over time. Although Swedish women still perform a greater share of this burden than do men, caring work is also shouldered by the Swedish welfare state. Moreover, much of the caring work that Swedish women perform has been moved to the public sector and thereby is accompanied by economic reward. However, these developments in a more balanced division of caring work have been seen much less in Canada, and even less in the United States. Women's inequality in paid and unpaid work is not tied up in their genes, but is a product of societal institutions that, while difficult to disassemble, have sometimes been transformed to women's advantage.

References

Abbott, Andrew. 1988. *The System of Professions*. Chicago: The University of Chicago Press.

Abbott, Maude E. 1931. *History of Medicine in the Province of Québec*. Montreal: McGill University Press.

Abbott, Pamela and Clare Wallace. 1990. *The Sociology of the Caring Professions*. London: The Falmer Press.

Acker, Joan. 1989. "The Problem with Patriarchy." *Sociology* 23: 235–40.

———. 1994. "Women, Families, and Public Policy in Sweden." In *Women, the Family, and Policy: A Global Perspective*, ed. Ester Ngan-ling Chow and Catherine White Berheide, 33–50. New York: State University of New York Press.

Achterberg, Jeanne. 1990. *Woman as Healer*. Boston: Shambhala.

Ackerknecht, E. and E. Fischer-Homberger. 1977. "Five Made It—One Not: The Rise of Medical Craftsmen to Academic Status during the 19th Century." *Clio Medico* 12 (4): 255–67.

Ackerman, E. et al. 1984. *The Prehistoric Occupation of Heceta Island, Southeastern Alaska*. Seattle: Washington State University Press.

Acton, Jane, Penny Goldsmith, and Bonnie Shepard, eds. 1974. *Women at Work: Ontario, 1885–1930*. Toronto: Canadian Women's Educational Press.

Adams, G.C. and C.M. Johnson. 1991. "Child Care and the Family Support Act." *Public Welfare* 49 (2): 9–12.

Adilman, Tamara. 1992. "A Preliminary Sketch of Chinese Women and Work in British Columbia, 1858–1950." In *British Columbia Reconsidered: Essays on Women*, ed. Gillian Greese and Veronica Strong-Boag, 30–339. Vancouver: Press Gang Publishers.

Administration for Children and Families (ACF) Office of Public Affairs. 1998. "President Clinton Announces Child Care Initiative." *White House Fact Sheet*, 7 Jan. http://www.acf.dhhs.gov/news/press/980107.htm.

Akyeampong, Ernest B. 1998. "The Rise of Unionization Among Women: Special 1998 Labour Day Release." Ottawa: Statistics Canada. Catalogue no. 75-001-XPE.

Alestalo, Matti and Stein Kuhnle. 1987. "The Scandinavian Route: Economic, Social, and Political Developments in Denmark, Finland, Norway, and Sweden." In *The Scandinavian Model: Welfare States and Welfare Research*, ed. Robert Erikson et al., 3–38. Armonk, NY: M.E. Sharpe.

Anderson, Karen L. 1991. *Chain Her by One Foot: The Subjugation of Women in Seventeenth-Century New France*. London: Routledge.

Applebaum, Herbert. 1992. *The Concept of Work: Ancient, Medieval, and Modern*. New York: State University of New York Press.

Apter, Terri. 1993 (1985). *Professional Progress: Why Women Still Don't Have Wives*. 2nd ed. London: Macmillan Press.

Arat-Koc, Sadaf. 1993. "The Politics of Family and Immigration in the Subordination of Domestic Workers in Canada." In *Family Patterns, Gender Relations*, ed. B. Fox, 278–96. Toronto: Oxford University Press.

Armstrong, Pat. 1993. "Women's Health Care Work: Nursing in Context." In *Vital Signs, Nursing in Transition*, ed. Pat Armstrong, Jacqueline Choiniere, and Elaine Day, 17–58. Toronto: Garamond Press.

———. 1994. "Caring and Women's Work." *Health and Canadian Society* 2 (1): 109–18.

Armstrong, Pat et al., eds. 1994. *Take Care: Warning Signs for Canada's Health System*. Toronto: Garamond Press.

Armstrong, Pat and Hugh Armstrong. 1988. "Taking Women into Account: Redefining and Intensifying Employment in Canada." In *Feminisation of the Labour Force: Paradoxes and Promises*, ed. Jane Jenson, Elizabeth Hagan, and Ceallaigh Reddy, 65–84. London: Polity Press.

Arney, William. 1982. *Power and the Profession of Obstetrics*. Chicago: University of Chicago Press.

Auster, Ellen R. 1993. "Demystifying the Glass Ceiling: Organizational and Interpersonal Dynamics of Gender Bias." *Business and the Contemporary World* 5 (Summer): 47–68.

Badinter, Elisabeth. 1981. *Mother Love: Myth and Reality*. Translated by Roger DeGaris. New York: Macmillan.

Baker Miller, Jean. 1976. *Toward a New Psychology of Women*. Harmondsworth, UK: Penguin Books.

Baker, Maureen. 1995. *Canadian Family Policies: Cross-National Comparisons*. Toronto: University of Toronto Press.

———. 1996. "Social Assistance and the Employability of Mothers: Two Models from Cross-National Research." *Canadian Journal of Sociology* 21 (4): 483–503.

Banting, Keith. 1992. "Neoconservatism in an Open Economy: The Social Role of the Canadian State." *International Political Science Review* 13: 149–70.

Barley, Stephen R. 1996. *The New World of Work*. London: British-North American Committee.

Barrington, Eleanor. 1985. *Midwifery is Catching*. Toronto: NC Press Ltd.

Baxandall, Rosalyn, Linda Gordon, and Susan Reverby, eds. 1976. *America's Working Women: A Documentary History–1600 to the Present*. New York: Vintage Books.

Becker, Gary. 1975. *Human Capital: A Theoretical Analysis, with Special Reference to Education*. 2nd ed. Chicago: University of Chicago Press.

Bell, Daniel. 1975. *The Coming of Post-Industrial Society*. New York: Basic Books.

Bengtsson, Tommy, ed. 1994. *Population, Economy, and Welfare in Sweden*. Berlin: Springer-Verlag.

Benoit, Cecilia. 1989. "Traditional Midwifery Practice: The Limits of Occupational Autonomy." *The Canadian Review of Sociology and Anthropology* 26 (4): 633–49.

———. 1991. *Midwives in Passage: The Modernization of Maternity Care*. St. John's, NF: Memorial University of Newfoundland ISER Press.

———. 1990. "Mothering in a Newfoundland Community: 1900–1940." In *Delivering Motherhood*, ed. K. Arnup, A. Levesque, and R. Roach Person, 173–89. London: Routledge.

———. 1994. "Paradigm Conflict in the Sociology of the Professions." *Canadian Journal of Sociology* 19 (3): 303–29.

———. 1997. "Professionalising Canadian Midwifery: Sociological Perspectives." In *The New Midwifery: Reflections on Renaissance and Regulation*, ed. Farah Shroff, 93–114. Toronto: The Women's Press.

———. 1998. "Rediscovering Appropriate Care: Maternity Traditions and Contemporary Issues in Canada." In *Health and Canadian Society: Sociological Perspectives* (3rd ed.), ed. David Coburn, Carol D'Arcy, and George M. Torrance, 359–78. Toronto: University of Toronto Press.

———. 1999. "Midwifery and Health Policy: Equity, Workers' Rights and Consumer Choice in Canada and Sweden." Forthcoming in *Professional Identities in Transition: Cross-Cultural Dimensions*, ed. Inga Hellberg, Mike Saks, and Cecilia Benoit. Gothenburg: University of Gothenburg Press.

Benoit, Cecilia and Dena Carroll. 1995. "Aboriginal Midwifery in British Columbia: A Narrative Still Untold." *Western Geographic Series* (30): 221–46.

Benoit, Cecilia and Alena Heitlinger. 1998. "Women's Health Caring Work in Comparative Perspective: Canada, Sweden and Czechoslovakia/Czech Republic as Case Examples." *Social Science and Medicine* 47 (8): 1101–11.

Berheide, Catherine. 1992. "Women Still 'Stuck' in Low-Level Jobs." *Women in Public Services: A Bulletin for the Center for Women in Government* 3 (Fall).

Bernhard, Virgina, David Burner, and Stanley I. Kutler. 1992. *Firsthand America*. Vol. 1. New York: Brandywine Press.

Biggs, Lesley. 1983. "The Case of the Missing Midwives: A History of Midwifery in Ontario from 1795–1900." *Ontario History* 65(1): 21–35.

Birch, Stephen and Juila Ableson. 1993. "Is Reasonable Access What We Want? Implications of, and Challenges to, Current Canadian Policy on Equity in Health Care." *International Journal of Health Services* 23 (4): 629–53.

Björnberg, Ulla and Claudia Gardberg. 1998. "Issues Concerning the Family in Sweden in 1996." In *Developments in National Family Policies in 1996*, ed. John Ditch, Helen Barnes, and Jonathan Bradshaw, 267–83. York, UK: University of York Press.

Blauner, Robert. 1964. *Alienation and Freedom: The Factory Worker and His Industry*. Chicago: University of Chicago Press.

Blishen, Bernard. 1991. *Doctors in Canada*. Toronto: University of Toronto Press.

Bluestone, Barry and Bennett Harrison. 1982. *The Deindustrialisation of America*. New York: Basic Books.

Böhme, Gernot. 1984. "Midwifery as Science: An Essay on the Relationship Between Scientific and Everyday Knowledge." In *Society and Knowledge*, ed. Nico Stehr and Volker Meja, 365–85. New Brunswick, NJ: Transaction Books.

Bomersbach, Robert D. 1994. "New Jersey's Byrant Amendment: Is the Welfare Reform?" *Women's Rights Law Reporter* 15 (2/3): 169–81.

Borchorst, Annette and Birte Siim. 1987. "Women and the Advanced Welfare State: A New Kind of Patriarchal Power." In *Women and the State*, ed. Anne Showstack Sassoon, 128–57. London: Hutchinson.

Boulding, Elise. 1976. *The Underside of History*. Boulder, CO: Westview Press.

Bourgeault, Ivy Lynn and Mary Fynes. 1997. "The Integration of Nurse- and Lay Midwives in the US and Canada." *Social Science and Medicine* 44 (70): 1051–63.

Bradley, Harriet. 1989. *Men's Work, Women's Work*. Cambridge, UK: Polity Press.

Braverman, Harry. 1974. *Labor and Monopoly Capital: The Degradation of Work in the Twentieth Century*. New York: Monthly Review Press.

Brody, Hugh. 1975. *The People's Land: Eskimos and Whites in the Eastern Arctic*. London: Penguin Books.

Buckley, Suzanne. 1979. "Ladies or Midwives? Efforts to Reduce Infant and Maternal Mortality." In *A Not Unreasonable Claim: Women and Reform in Canada 1880s–1920s*, ed. Linda Kealey, 131–49. Toronto: Women's Press.

Bullough, Bonnie. 1975. "Barriers to the Nurse Practitioner Movement: Problems of Women in a Woman's Field." *International Journal of Health Services* 5 (2): 225–33.

Burtless, Gary and Kent Weaver. 1997. "Reinventing Welfare—Again: The Latest Version of Reform Needs a Tune-up." *The Brookling Review* 15 (1): 26–29.

Butter, Irene et al. 1987. "Gender Hierarchies in the Health Labour Force." *International Journal of Health Services* 17 (1): 133–49.

Cameron, Anne. 1981. *Daughters of Copper Woman*. Vancouver: Press Gang Publishers.

Campbell, Marie. 1946. *Folks Do Get Born*. New York: Rinehart.

Canadian Lancet. 1875. Editorial 8: 60.

Canada House of Commons. 1984. *Canada Health Act*. Ottawa: Queen's Printer.

Canadian Policy Research Network. 1998. *Values and Preferences for Canadian Children*. Ottawa: Reneuf Canada.

Canniff, William. 1894. *History of the Medical Profession in Upper Canada, 1783–1850.* Toronto: W. Biggs.

Casper, Lynne. 1994. "Who is Minding Our Preschoolers? Fall 1994." US Department of Commerce: Census Bureau.

Chang, Clara and Constance Sorrentino. 1991. "Union Membership Statistics in 12 Countries." *Monthly Labor Review* 114 (12/Dec.).

Charles, Maria. 1992. "Cross-National Variation in Occupational Sex Segregation." *American Sociological Review* 57 (Aug.): 483–502.

Che-Alford, Janet, Catherine Allan, and George Butlin. 1994. *Focus on Canada: Families in Canada.* Ottawa: Statistics Canada. Catalogue No. 96-307E.

Childcare Resource and Research Unit. 1995. *Child Care in Canada: Provinces and Territories.* Toronto: Childcare Resource and Research Unit.

Chodorow, Nancy. 1978. *The Reproduction of Mothering.* Berkeley: University of California Press.

Clarke, Juanne Nancarrow. 1996. *Health, Illness, and Medicine in Canada.* 2nd ed. Toronto: Oxford University Press.

Coburn, David. 1993. "State Authority, Medical Dominance, and Trends in the Regulation of Health Professions: The Ontario Case." *Social Science and Medicine* 37 (2): 129–38.

Coburn, Judi. 1974. "'I See and am Silent': A Short History of Nursing in Ontario." In *Women at Work: Ontario, 1850–1930,* ed. Jane Acton, Penny Goldsmith, and Bonnie Shepard, 127–64. Toronto: Canadian Women's Educational Press.

Cohen, Marjorie Griffen. 1988. *Women's Work, Markets and Economic Development in Nineteenth Century Ontario.* Toronto: University of Toronto Press.

Cohen, Mark Nathan. 1989. *Health and the Rise of Civilization.* New Haven: Yale University Press.

College of Midwives of BC. 1996. "Letter to the Editor." *BC Midwife* 2 (1): 3.

Collier, Ken. 1997. *After the Welfare State.* Vancouver: New Star Books.

Congressional Research Services. 1992. "Cash and Non-cash Benefits for Persons with Limited Income: Eligibility Rules, Recipients and Expenditure Data, FY 1990–92." Washington, DC: Congressional Research Services.

Cooper, Carol. 1996. "Native Women of the Northwest Pacific Coast: An Historical Perspective, 1830–1900." In *Canadian Women: A Reader,* ed. Wendy Mitchinson et al., 89–118. Toronto: Harcourt Brace and Company.

Creese, Gillian. 1992. "The Politics of Dependence: Women, Work, and Unemployment in the Vancouver Labour Movement Before World War II." In *British Columbia Reconsidered: Essays on Women,* ed. Gillian Creese and Veronica Strong-Boag, 364–90. Vancouver: Press Gang Publishers.

Dalerup, Drude. 1994. "Learning to Live With The States: State, Market, and Civil Society: Women's Need for State Intervention in East and West." *Women's Studies International Forum* 17 (2/3): 117–27.

Das Gupta, Tania. 1996. *Racism and Paid Work.* Toronto: Garamond Press.

Davies, Celia. 1996. "The Sociology of Professions and the Profession of Gender." *Sociology* 30 (4): 661–78.

Davis-Floyd, Robbie. 1994. "The Technocratic Body: American Childbirth as Cultural Experience." *Social Science & Medicine* 38 (8): 1125–40.

Davis-Floyd, Robbie. 1998. "The Ups, Downs, and Interlinkages of Nurse- and Direct-Entry Midwifery: Status, Practice, and Education." In *Getting an Education: Paths to Becoming a Midwife,* ed. Jan Tritten and Joel Southern, 67–119. Eugene, OR: Midwifery Today.

Deckard, Barbara Sinclair. 1979. *The Women's Movement.* 2nd ed. New York: Harper and Row.

Demos, John. 1977. "The American Family of the Past." In *Family in Transition* (2nd ed.), ed. Arlene Skolnick and Jerome Skolnick, 59–77. Boston: Little, Brown.

Deshpande, S. and A. Kurtz. 1994. "Trade Tales." *Mediations* 18 (1): 33–52.

Dickason, Olive Patricia. 1992. *Canada's First Nations: A History of Founding Peoples from Earliest Times*. Toronto: McClelland and Stewart.

Donald, Leland. 1997. *Aboriginal Slavery on the Northwest Coast of North America*. Berkeley: University of California Press.

Donnison, Jean. 1977. *Midwives and Medical Men*. London: Heinemann.

———. 1981. "The Development of the Occupation of Midwife: A Comparative View." In *Midwifery as a Labour of Love*, ed. Interdisciplinary Task Force Association and the BC Association of Midwives, 38–53. Vancouver: Maternal Health Society.

Driedger, Mary. 1993. "Being There: The Key Factor in Satisfaction with Childbirth." In *Midwives: Hear the Heartbeat of the Future*, 606–19. Vancouver: International Confederation of Midwives.

Duffy, Ann and Norene Pupo. 1992. *Part-Time Paradox: Connecting Gender, Work and Family*. Toronto: McClelland and Stewart.

Ehrenreich, Barbara and Dei English. 1989. "Blowing the Whistle on the 'Mommy Track'." *MS* 18 (1/2).

Eichler, Margrit. 1997. *Family Shifts: Families, Policies, and Gender Equality*. Toronto: Oxford University Press.

Ellingsaeter, Anne Lise. 1998. "Dual Breadwinner Societies: Provider Models in the Scandinavian Welfare States." *Acta Sociologica* 41 (1): 59–73.

Elston, Mary Ann. 1977. "Women in the Medical Profession: Whose Problem?" In *Health and the Division of Labour*, ed. Margaret Stacey et al., 115–40. London: Croom Helm.

Elzinga, Aant. 1990. "The Knowledge Aspect of Professionalization: The Case of Science-Based Nursing Education in Sweden." In *The Formation of Professions*, ed. Rolf Torstendahl and Michael Burrage, 151–73. London: Sage Publications.

Erikson, Erik. 1965. *Childhood and Society*. Harmondsworth, UK: Penguin Books.

Errington, Elizabeth Jane. 1995. *Wives and Mothers, School Mistresses and Scullery Maids: Working Women in Upper Canada, 1790–1840*. Montreal and Kingston: McGill-Queen's University Press.

Esping-Andersen, Gøsta. 1989. "The Three Political Economies of the Welfare State." *Canadian Review of Sociology and Anthropology* 26: 10–36.

———. 1990. *The Three Worlds of Welfare Capitalism*. Princeton, NJ: Princeton University Press.

———, ed. 1996. *Welfare States in Transition: National Global Economies*. London: Sage Publications.

Esping-Andersen, Gøsta and Walter Korpi. 1987. "From Poor Relief to Institutional Welfare States: The Development of Scandinavian Social Policy." In *The Scandinavian Model: Welfare States and Welfare Research*, ed. Robert Erikson et al., 39–74. New York: M.E. Sharpe.

Etzioni, Amitai, ed. 1969. *The Semi-Professions and Their Organization*. New York: The Free Press.

European Commission Network on Childcare and Other Measures to Reconcile Employment and Family Responsibilities. 1996. *A Review of Services for Young Children in the European Community*. Brussels: European Commission.

Evans, Robert. 1992. The Canadian Health Care Financing and Delivery System: Its Experiences and Lessons from Other Nations. *Yale Law Policy Review* 10: 362–96.

Falk, R. 1970. *The Business of Management*. Harmondsworth, UK: Penguin Books.

Farb, Peter. 1979. *Man's Rise to Civilization*. London: Secker and Warburg.

Federal-Provincial/Territorial Ministries Responsible for the Status of Women. 1997. *Economic Gender Indicators*. Catalogue No. SW21-171997E.

Finance Canada. 1997. Budget 1997. "Working Together Towards a National Child Benefit System." Ottawa: Government of Canada. .org/fedbis/bis/1453.html.

Finch, Janet. 1989. "Social Policy, Social Engineering and the Family in the 1990s." In *The Goals of Social Policy*, ed. Martin Bulmer, Jane Lewis, and David Piachaud, 160–69. London: Unwin Hyman.

Forestell, Nancy. 1995. "Times Were Hard: The Pattern of Women's Paid Labour in St. John's Between the Two World Wars." In *Their Lives and Times: Women in Newfoundland and Labrador: A Collage*, ed. Carmelita McGrath, Barbara Neis, and Marilyn Porter, 76–92. St. John's, NF: Killick Press.

Fox, Bonnie. 1981. "The Female Reserve Army of Labour: The Argument and Some Findings." *Atlantis* 7 (Fall): 45–56.

Fox, Matthew. 1994. *The Reinvention of Work: A New Vision of Livelihood for Our Time*. San Francisco: Harper-Collins.

Frager, Ruth A. 1992. *Sweatshop Strife: Class, Ethnicity, and Gender in the Jewish Labour Movement of Toronto 1990–1939*. Toronto: University of Toronto Press.

Freidson, Elliott. 1970a. *Profession of Medicine: A Study in the Sociology of Applied Knowledge*. New York: Dodd, Mead and Company.

———. 1970b. *Professional Dominance*. New York: Atherton.

———. 1986. *Professional Powers: A Study of the Institutionalisation of Formal Knowledge*. Chicago: University of Chicago Press.

Friendly, Martha. 1997. "Childcare Policy." In *The National Action Committee on the Status of Women's Voters' Guide: A Women's Agenda for Social Justice*, ed. Nandita Sharma, 107–13. Toronto: James Lorimer and Company.

Gadd, Jane. 1997. "The Drift to the Bottom." *Globe and Mail* (Toronto), 21 June: D1, 3.

Gardner, Arthur. 1995. "Their Own Boss: The Self-Employed in Canada." *Canadian Social Trends* 37 (Summer): 26–29.

Giddens, Anthony. 1975. *The Class Structure of Advanced Societies*. New York: Harper Torchbooks.

Gilligan, Carol. 1979. "Woman's Place in Man's Life Cycle." *Harvard Educational Review* 49 (Nov.): 431–46.

———. 1982. *In a Different Voice*. Cambridge, MA: Harvard University Press.

Ginsburg, Helen. 1983. *Full Employment and Public Policy: The United States and Sweden*. Lexington, MA: Lexington Books.

Glass, Jennifer and Tetsushi Fujimoto. 1995. "Employer Characteristics and the Provision of Family Responsive Policies." *Work and Occupations* 22 (4): 380–411.

Glazer, Nona. 1993. *Women's Paid and Unpaid Labour: The Work Transfer in Health Care and Retailing*. Philadelphia: Temple University Press.

Goode, William. 1969. "The Theoretical Limitations of Professionalization." In *The Semi-Professions and Their Organization*, ed. Amitai Etzioni, 266–314. New York: The Free Press.

Goodman, Sara. 1995. "'Hand, Heart and Mind'—Technology in the Practice and Tradition of Swedish Midwives." In *Forplantning, Kon og Teknologi*, ed. Bente Rosenbeck and Robin May Schott, 145–63. Copenhagen: Museum Tusculanuns Forlang, Jobenhavns Universitet.

Gordon, Linda. 1988. *Heroes of their Own Lives: The Politics and History of Family Violence*. Madison: University of Wisconsin Press.

———, ed. 1990. *Women, the State and Welfare*. Madison: University of Wisconsin Press.

Gornick, Janet C., Marcia K. Nyers, and Katherine E. Ross. 1997. "Supporting the Employment of Mothers: Policy Variation Across Fourteen Welfare States." *Journal of European Social Policy* 17 (1): 45–70.

Gottfried, Robert S. 1983. *The Black Death: Natural and Human Disaster in Medieval Europe*. New York: The Free Press.

Goudie, Elizabeth. 1983 (1973). *Woman of Labrador*. Agincourt, ON: The Book Society of Canada.

Gould, Jan. 1975. *Women of British Columbia*. Saanichton, BC: Hancock House Publishers.

Gough, Ian. 1979. *The Political Economy of the Welfare State*. London: Macmillan Press.

Gouvernment du Québec. 1997. *New Elements of the Family Policy: Our Children at the Heart of Our Decisions*. Montreal: Bibliotheque nationale du Québec.

Graham, Elizabeth. 1974. "Schoolmarms and Early Teaching in Ontario." In *Women at Work: Ontario, 1850–1930*, ed. Jane Acton, Penny Goldsmith, and Bonnie Shepard, 165–210. Toronto: Canadian Women's Educational Press.

Graham, Hilary. 1983. "Caring: A Labour of Love." In *A Labour of Love: Women, Work and Caring*, ed. Janet Finch and Dulcie Groves, 13–30. London: Routledge and Kegan Paul.

Greenwood, Earnest. 1957. "Attributes of a Profession." *Social Work* 2: 44–55.

Greese, Gillian. 1992. "The Politics of Dependence: Women, Work and Unemployment in the Vancouver Labour Movement Before World War II." In *British Columbia Reconsidered: Essays on Women*, ed. Gillian Greese and Veronica Strong-Boag, 364–90. Vancouver: Press Gang Publishers.

Grimm, James W. 1978. "Women in Female-Dominated Professions." In *Women Working: Theories and Facts in Perspective*, ed. Ann Stolberg and Shirley Harkness, 293–315. Palo Alto, CA: Mayfield.

Haavio-Mannila, Elina and Kaisa Kauppinen. 1992. "Women and the Welfare State in the Nordic Countries." In *Women's Work and Women's Lives: The Continuing Struggle Worldwide*, ed. Hilda Kahne and Janet Giele. Boulder, CO: Westview Press.

Hacker, Jacob S. 1997. *The Road to Nowhere: The Genesis of President Clinton's Plan for Health Security*. Princeton, NJ: Princeton University Press.

Hagan, John and Fiona Kay. 1995. *Gender in Practice: A Study of Lawyers' Lives*. New York: Oxford University Press.

Harrison, Bennett and Barry Bluestone. 1988. *The Great U-Turn: Corporate Restructuring and the Polarising of America*. New York: Basic Books.

Hartmann, Heidi. 1979. "The Unhappy Marriage of Marxism and Feminism: Towards a More Progressive Union." *Capital and Class* 8: 1–33.

Harvey, David. 1989. *The Condition of Postmodernity*. Oxford: Blackwell.

Hatem-Asmar, Marie and Regis Blais. 1997. "Opinions of Certified and Lay Midwives about Midwifery in Quebec: Perspective for the Future of Their Profession." In *The New Midwifery: Reflections on Renaissance and Regulation*, ed. Farah Shroff, 311–30. Toronto: Women's Press.

Hayes, Cheryl, John Palmer, and Martha Zaslow. 1990. *Who Cares for America's Children?* Washington, DC: The Urban Institute Press.

Hearn, Jeff. 1982. "Notes on Patriarchy, Professionalization, and the Semi-Professions." *Sociology* 16 (2): 184–202.

Hedley, R. Alan. 1992. *Making a Living: Technology and Change*. New York: Harper Collins.

Heilbroner, Robert. 1985. *The Act of Work*. Washington, DC: Library of Congress.

Heitlinger, Alena. 1993. *Women's Equality, Demography, and Public Policy: A Comparative Perspective*. London: Macmillan Press.

Helco, Hugh and Henrik Madsen. 1987. *Policy and Politics in Sweden*. Philadelphia: Temple University Press.

Hernes, Helga. 1987. *Welfare State and Woman Power: Essays in State Feminism*. Oslo: Norwegian University Press.

———. 1988. "The Welfare State Citizenship of Scandinavian Women." In *The Political Interests of Gender*, ed. K. Jones and A. Jonasdittir, 187–213. Newbury Park, CA: Sage Publications.

Heron, Craig. 1980. "The Crisis of the Craftsmen: Hamilton's Metal Workers in the Early Twentieth Century." *Labour/Le Travailleur* 6: 7–48.

Hirdman, Yvonne. 1994. "Women—from Possibility to Problem? Gender Conflict in the Welfare State—the Swedish Model." *Research Report, No. 3*. Stockholm: The Swedish Centre for Working Life.

Hirshman, Albert O. 1970. *Exit, Voice, and Loyalty*. Cambridge: Harvard University Press.

Hobsbawm, Eric. 1968. *Industry and Empire*. London: Penguin Books.

Hobson, Barbara. 1993. "Feminist Strategies and Gendered Discourses in Welfare States: Married Women's Right to Work in the United States and Sweden." In *Mothers of the New World: Maternalist Policies and the Origins of Welfare States*, ed. Seth Koven and Sonya Michel, 396–429. London: Routledge.

Hochschild, Arlie. 1983. *The Managed Heart: Commercialization of Human Feeling*. Berkeley: University of California Press.

———. 1989. *The Second Shift*. New York: Avon Books.

Hodson, Randy and Teresa Sullivan. 1995. *The Social Organization of Work*. 2nd ed. Belmont, CA: Wadsworth Publishing.

Hoem, Jan M. 1993. "Public Policy as the Fuel of Fertility: Effects of a Policy Reform on the Pace of Childbearing in Sweden in the 1980s." *Acta Sociologica* 36: 19–31.

Howley, J.P. 1974. *The Beothucks or Red Indians: The Aboriginal Inhabitants of Newfoundland*. Toronto: Coles.

Hughes, Everett Cherrington. 1958. *Men and Their Work*. Glencoe, IL: The Free Press.

———.1971. *The Sociological Eye*. Chicago: Aldine Atherton.

Human Resources Development Canada. 1998. *The New Employment Insurance System*. Ottawa: Human Resources Centre of Canada.

Inter-Parliamentary Union.1997. *Men and Women in Politics: Democracy Still in the Making—A World Comparative Study*. Geneva: IUP.

———.1998. *Women in National Parliaments*. Geneva: IUP.

Jaffe, Abram. J. 1992. *The First Immigrants from Asia: A Population History of the North American Indians*. New York: Plenum Press.

James, Nicki. 1989. "Emotional Labour: Skill and Work in the Social Regulation of Feelings." *Sociological Review* 37: 15–41.

James, Susan. 1997. "Regulation: Changing the Face of Midwifery?" In *The New Midwifery: Reflections on Renaissance and Regulation*, ed. Farah Shroff, 181–200. Toronto: The Women's Press.

Jenson, Jane, Elizabeth Hagan, and Ceallaigh Reddy, eds. 1988. *Feminisation of the Labour Force: Paradoxes and Promises*. London: Polity Press.

Jessop, B. et al. 1987. "Popular Capitalism, Flexible Accumulation and Left Strategy." *New Left Review* 165: 104–23.

Jewson, N.D. 1974. "Medical Knowledge and the Patronage System in 18th-Century England." *Sociology* 8: 369–85.

Johnson, Laura and Janice Dineen. 1981. *The Kin Trade: The Day Care Crisis in Canada*. Toronto: McGraw-Hill Ryerson.

Johnson, Leo. 1974. "The Political Economy of Ontario Women in the Nineteenth Century." In *Women at Work: Ontario, 1850–1930*, ed. Jane Acton, Penny Goldsmith, and Bonnie Shepard, 13–32. Toronto: Canadian Women's Educational Press.

Johnson, Terence. 1972. *Professions and Power*. London: Macmillan.

Jones, Kathleen. 1990. "Citizenship in a Woman-Friendly Polity." *Signs* 15: 781–812.

Jonung, Christina and Inga Persson. 1994. "Combining Market Work and Family." In *Population, Economy, and Welfare in Sweden*, ed. Tommy Bengtsson, 37–64. Berlin: Springer-Verlag.

Kahn, Alfred and Sheila Kamerman, eds. 1988. *Child Support: From Debt Collection to Social Policy*. Newbury Park, CA: Sage Publications.

Kamerman, Sheila and Alfred Kahn. 1991. "Child Care Policies and Programs: An International Overview." *Journal of Social Issues* 47 (2): 179–96.

———. 1981. *Child Care, Family Benefits, and Working Parents: A Study in Comparative Policy*. New York: Columbia University Press.

Karvonen, Lauri and Per Selle, eds. 1995. *Women in Nordic Politics: Closing the Gap*. Aldershot, UK: Dartmouth.

Kaufert, Patricia A. and John O'Neil. 1993. "Analysis of a Dialogue on Risks in Childbirth: Clinicians, Epidemiologists, and Inuit Women." In *Knowledge, Power & Practice*, ed. Shirley Lindenbaum and Margaret Lock, 32–54. Berkeley: University of California Press.

Kealey, Linda. 1991. "Women's Labour Movement Militancy in Canada, 1900–20." Paper presented at the Annual Meeting of the Canadian Historical Association, 3–5 June 1991.

Kiely, Ray. 1998. "Globalization, Post-Fordism and the Contemporary Context of Development." *International Sociology* 13 (1): 95–115.

Klein, Alice and Wayne Roberts. 1974. "Besieged Innocence: The 'Problem' and Problems of Working Women—Toronto, 1896–1914." In *Women at Work: Ontario, 1850–1930*, ed. Jane Acton, Penny Goldsmith, and Bonnie Shepard, 211–60. Toronto: Canadian Women's Educational Press.

Klinge, Matti. 1993. "Finland: From Napoleonic Legacy to Nordic Co-operation." In *The National Question in Europe in Historical Context*, ed. Mikulas Teich and Roy Porter, 317–31. New York: Cambridge University Press.

———. 1997 (1981). *A Brief History of Finland*. Helsinki: Otava Publishing Company.

Korbin, Frances. 1966. "The American Midwife Controversy: A Crisis of Professional-ization." *Bulletin of the History of Medicine* 40: 350-63.

Korpi, Walter. 1985. "Power Resources Approach vs. Action and Conflict: On Casual and Intentional Explanations in the Study of Power." *Sociological Theory* 3: 31–45.

———. 1989. "Power, Politics, and State Autonomy in the Development of Social Citizenship." *American Sociological Review* 54: 309–28.

Kosonen, Pekka. 1994. "European Welfare State Models: Converging Trends." *International Journal of Sociology* 24 (4): 81–109.

Krahn, Harvey and Graham Lowe. 1993. *Work, Industry and Canadian Society*. 2nd ed. Scarborough, ON: ITP Nelson Canada.

———. 1998. *Work, Industry and Canadian Society*. 3rd ed. Scarborough, ON: ITP Nelson Canada.

Krause, Elliott. 1988. "Doctors, Partitocrazia, and the Italian State." *The Milbank Quarterly* 66 (2): 148–66.

Kraut, Alan. 1982. *The Huddled Masses: The Immigrant in American Society, 1880–1921*. Wheeling, IL: Harlan Davidson.

Kuczynski, Jurgen. 1967. *The Rise of the Working Class*. New York: McGraw-Hill.

Laforce, Hélène. 1990. "The Different Stages of the Elimination of the Midwife in Québec." In *Delivering Motherhood: Maternal Ideologies and Practices in the 19th and 20th Centuries*, ed. Katherine Arnup, Andree Levesque, and Ruth Roach Pierson, 36–50. London: Routledge.

Langford, Nanci. 1995. "Childbirth on the Canadian Prairies 1880–1930." *Journal of Historical Sociology* 8 (3): 278–302.

Langley, Winston E. and Vivian C. Fox. 1994. *Women's Rights in the United States: A Documentary History*. Westport, CT: Greenwood Press.

Larkin, Gerald V. 1983. *Occupational Monopoly and Modern Medicine*. London: Tavistock.

Laslett, Peter. 1984. *The World We Have Lost: England Before the Industrial Age*. 3rd ed. New York: Charles Scribner.

Lassey, Marie L., William R. Lassey, and Martin J. Jinks. 1997. *Health Care Systems Around the World*. New Jersey: Prentice Hall.

Laxer, Gordon. 1985. "Foreign Ownership and Myths About Canadian Development." *Canadian Review of Sociology and Anthropology* 22: 311–45.

Laxer, James. 1996. *In Search of a New Left: Canadian Politics After the Neoconservative Assault*. London: Penguin Books.

Leavitt, Gregory. 1977. "The Frequency of Warfare: An Evolutionary Perspective." *Sociological Inquiry* 47 (1): 45–58.

Leavitt, Judith Walzer. 1986. *Brought to Bed: Childbearing in America 1970 to 1950*. New York: Oxford University Press.

Lefkowitz, Mary R. and Maureen B. Fant. 1982. *Women's Life in Greece and Rome: A Source Book in Translation*. London: Duckworth Press.

Leidner, Robin. 1993. *Fast Food, Fast Talk: Service Work and the Routinization of Everyday Life*. Berkeley: University of California Press.

Leira, Arnlaug. 1992. *Welfare States and Working Mothers: The Scandinavian Experience*. New York: University of Cambridge Press.

Lenski, Gerhand, Patrick Nolan, and Jean Lenski. 1995. *Human Societies: An Introduction to Macrosociology*. 7th ed. New York: McGraw-Hill.

Leslie, Genevieve. 1974. "Domestic Service in Canada, 1880–1920." In *Women at Work: Ontario, 1850–1930*, ed. Jane Acton, Penny Goldsmith, and Bonnie Shepard, 71–126. Toronto: Canadian Women's Educational Press.

Lewis, Jane. 1990. "'Motherhood Issues' in the Late Nineteenth and Twentieth Centuries." In *Delivering Motherhood: Maternal Ideologies and Practices in the 19th and 20th Centuries*, ed. Katherine Arnup, Andree Levesque, and Ruth Roach Pierson, 2–19. London: Routledge.

———, ed. 1993. *Women and Social Policies in Europe: Work, Family and the State*. Aldershot, UK: Edward Elgar.

———. 1994. "Choice, Needs and Enabling: The New Community Care." In *The Politics of the Welfare State*, ed. Ann Oakley and A. Susan Williams, 147–80. London: UCL Press.

Linder, Marc. 1997. *The Dilemmas of Laissez-Faire Population Policy in Capitalist Societies*. Westport, CT: Greenwood Press.

Lispet, Seymour Martin. 1986. "Historical Traditions and National Characteristics." *Canadian Journal of Sociology* 11 (2):113–56.

———. 1990. *Continental Divide: The Values and Institutions of the United States and Canada*. New York: Routledge.

Litoff, Judy. 1978. *American Midwives: 1860 to the Present*. Westport, CT: Greenwood.

Livi-Bacci, Massimo. 1991. *Population and Nutrition: Antagonism and Adaptation*. Cambridge: Cambridge University Press.

Lorber, Judith. 1992. "Can Women Physicians ever be True Equals in the American Medical Profession?" *Current Research on Occupations and Professions* 6: 25–37.

———. 1993. "Why Women Physicians Will Never Be True Equals in the American Medical Profession." In *Gender, Work and Medicine: Women and the Medical Division of Labour*, ed. Elianne Riska and Katerina Wegar, 77–94. London: Sage Publications.

———. 1994. *Paradoxes of Gender*. New Haven, CT: Yale University Press.

Lowe, Graham S. 1986. "The Administrative Revolution in the Canadian Office: An Overview." In *Work in the Canadian Context: Continuity Despite Change* (2nd ed.), ed. Katherina L.P. Lundy and Barbara Warine, 100–20. Toronto: Butterworths.

Macionis, John J. 1996. *Society: The Basics*. 3rd ed. Upper Saddle River, NJ: Prentice Hall.

Macionis, John, Cecilia Benoit, and Mikael Jansson. 1999. *Society: The Basics, Canadian Edition*. Scarborough, ON: Prentice Hall Canada.

Maioni, Antonia. 1998. *Parting at the Crossroads: The Emergence of Health Care in the United States and Canada*. Princeton, N.J.: Princeton University Press.

Marie, Gillian. 1980. "Writing Women into British Columbia's History." In *In Her Own Right: Selected Essays on Women's History in BC*, ed. Barbara Latham and Cathy Kess, 1–18. Victoria, BC: Camosun College.

Marland, Hilary and Anne Marie Rafferty, eds. 1997. *Midwives, Society and Childbirth: Debates and Controversies in the Modern Period*. London: Routledge.

Marshall, T.H. 1965. *Class, Citizenship and Social Development*. New York: Anchor Books.

———. 1992. "Social Rights in the Twentieth Century." In *Citizenship and Social Class*, ed. T.H. Marshall and Tom Bottomore, 27–43. London: Pluto Press.

Martin, Leslie E. 1986. "Women Workers in a Masculine Domain: Jobs and Gender in a Yukon Mine." In *Work in the Canadian Context: Continuity Despite Change* (2nd ed.), ed. Katherina L.P. Lundy and Barbara Warme, 248–80. Toronto: Butterworths.

Mason, Mary Ann. 1988. *The Equality Trap.* New York: Simon and Schuster.

McCallum, Margaret. 1986. "Keeping Women in Their Place: The Minimum Wage in Canada 1910–25." *Labour/Le Travail* 17 (Spring): 29-56.

McCormack, Thelma. 1997. "Canadian Feminism: A Tale of Two Eurocentric Cultures and Three Nations." Paper presented at the Annual Meeting of the American Sociological Society (Toronto), Aug. 1997.

McIntoch, Robert. 1996. "Sweated Labour: Female Needleworkers in Industrializing Canada." In *Canadian Women: A Reader*, ed. Wendy Mitchinson et al., 142–71. Toronto: Harcourt Brace and Company.

McIntosh, Mary. 1978. "The State and the Oppression of Women." In *Feminism and Materialism*, ed. Annette Kuhn and Ann Wolpe, 254–89. London: Routledge and Kegan Paul.

McKay, Susan. 1993. "Models of Care: Denmark, Sweden, and the Netherlands." *Journal of Nurse-Midwifery* 38 (20): 114–120.

Merritt, Susane. 1994. *Her Story: Women from Canada's Past*. St. Catharines, ON: Vanwell Publishing.

Millerson, Geoffrey. 1964. *The Qualifying Associations: A Study of Professionalisation*. London: Routledge.

Mishra, Ramesh. 1984. *The Welfare State in Crisis*. Brighton: Wheatsheaf.

———. 1990. *The Welfare State in Capitalist Society*. New York: Harvester Wheatsheaf.

———. 1996. "The Welfare of Nations." In *States Against Markets: The Limits of Globalization*, ed. Robert Boyer and Daniel Drache, 316–33. London: Routledge.

Mitchinson, Wendy et al., eds. 1996. *Canadian Women: A Reader*. Toronto: Harcourt Brace and Company.

Miyoshi, Masao. 1993. "A Borderless World? From Colonialism to Transnationalism and the Decline of the Nation State." *Critical Inquiry* 19 (Summer): 726–51.

Moore Thomas. 1996. *The Disposable Work Force: Worker Displacement and Employment Instability in America*. New York: Aldine de Gruyter.

Morison, S.E. 1971. *The European Discovery of America: The Northern Voyages*. New York: Oxford University Press.

Morton, Suzanne. 1996. "Separate Spheres in a Separate World: African-Nova Scotian Women in Late-19th-Century Halifax County." In *Canadian Women: A Reader*, ed. Wendy Mitchinson et al., 172–93. Toronto: Harcourt Brace and Company.

Myles, John. 1996. "When Markets Fail: Social Welfare in Canada and the United States." In *Welfare States in Transition: National Global Economies*, ed. Gøsta Esping-Andersen, 116–40. London: Sage Publications.

Myrdal, Alva. 1941. *Nation and Family: The Swedish Experiment in Democratic Family and Population Policy*. Stockholm.

National Council on Welfare. 1994. *Poverty Profile 1992*. Ottawa: National Council on Welfare.

Nelson, Barbara. 1984. "Women's Poverty and Women's Citizenship: Some Political Consequences on Economic Marginality." *Signs* 10 (2): 209–31.

Nermo, Magnus. 1996. "Occupational Sex Segregation in Sweden, 1968–1991." *Work and Occupations* 23 (3): 319–32.

Neysmith, Sheila M. and Jane Aronson. 1997. "Working Conditions in Home Care: Negotiating Race and Class Boundaries in Gendered Work." *International Journal of Health Services* 27 (3): 479–99.

Noddings, Nels. 1995. "Caring." In *Justice and Care: Essential Readings in Feminist Ethics*, ed. Virgina Held, 7–30. Boulder, CO: Westview Press.

Noel, Jan. 1996. "'Femmes Fortes' and the Montreal Poor in the Early Nineteenth Century." In *Canadian Women: A Reader*, ed. Wendy Mitchinson et al., 61–86. Toronto: Harcourt Brace and Company.

NORD. 1991. *Yearbook of Nordic Statistics, 1991*. Vol. 29. Stockholm.

———. 1994. *Women and Men in the Nordic Countries: Facts and Figures 1994*. Stockholm.

O'Connor, Julia S. 1993. "Gender, Class, and Citizenship in the Comparative Analysis of Welfare State Regimes: Theoretical and Methodological Issues." *British Journal of Sociology* 44 (3): 501–18.

———. 1996. "From Women in the Welfare State to Gendering Welfare State Regimes." *Current Sociology* 44 (2): 1–125.

Oakley, Ann and A. Susan Williams, eds. 1994. *The Politics of the Welfare State*. London: UCL Press.

———. 1976. *Housewife*. Harmondsworth, UK: Penguin Books.

———. 1984. *The Captured Womb*. London: Basil Blackwell.

———. 1994. "Introduction." In *The Politics of the Welfare State*, ed. Ann Oakley and A. Susan Williams, 1–17. London: UCL Press.

OECD. 1992. *Economic Outlook Historical Statistics*. Paris: OECD.

OECD. 1995. *Labour Force Statistics, 1973–1993*. Paris: OECD.

———. 1998. *Labour Force Statistics, 1997–1997*. Paris: OECD.

———. 1998b. *National Accounts*. Paris: OECD.

———. 1998c. *Employment Outlook, July 1998*. Paris: OECD.

———. 1998d. *OECD Health Data 98*. Paris: OECD.

Offe, Claus. 1984. *Contradictions of the Welfare State*. London: Hutchinson.

Ohlander, Ann-Sofie. 1994. *Women, Children and Work in Sweden 1850–1993*. Report for the International Conference on Population and Development in Cairo. Stockholm: Swedish Government Official Reports: 38.

Ohmae, Kenichi. 1991. *The Borderless World*. London: Fontana.

Olslen, Gregg M. 1994. "Locating the Canadian Welfare State: Family Policy and Health Care in Canada, Sweden, and the United States. *Canadian Journal of Sociology* 19 (3): 303–29.

Olsson, Sven E. 1993. *Social Policy and Welfare State in Sweden*. Lund: Arkiv förlag.

Oppenheimer, Jo. 1983. "Childbirth in Ontario: The Transition from Home to Hospital in the Early Twentieth Century." *Ontario History* 75(1): 36–60.

Orloff, Ann Shola. 1993. "Gender and the Social Rights of Citizenship: The Comparative Analysis of Gender Relations and Welfare States." *American Sociological Review* 58: 303–28.

Palme, Joakim. 1990. *Pension Rights in Welfare Capitalism: The Development of Old-Age Pensions in 18 OECD Countries 1930 to 1985*. Stockholm: Swedish Institute for Social Research Dissertation Series, No. 14.

Parcel, Toby L. 1997. "Introduction to the Special Issue on Work and Family: Research Informing Policy." *Work and Occupations* 23 (4): 349–53.

———. 1999. "Work and Family in the 21st Century: It's About Time." *Work and Occupations* 26(2): 264–74.

Park, Katharine. 1992. "Medicine and Society in Medieval Europe, 500–1500." In *Medicine in Society: Historical Essays*, ed. A. Wear, 59–90. Cambridge: Cambridge University Press.

Parkin, Frank. 1979. *Marxism and Class Theory: A Bourgeois Critique*. London: Tavistock.

Parry, Noel and Jose Parry. 1976. *The Rise of the Medical Profession*. London: Croom Helm.

Parsons, Talcott. 1951. *The Social System*. New York: The Free Press.

———. 1955. "The American Family: Its Relation to Personality and to the Social Structure." In *Family, Socialization and Interaction Process*, ed. Talcott Parsons and R. Bales, 3–21. Glencoe, IL: The Free Press.

———. 1968. "The Professions." In *International Encyclopaedia of the Social Sciences*, 536–47. New York: Macmillan.

Pascall, Gillian. 1986. *Social Policy: A Feminist Analysis*. New York: Tavistock.

Pastore, Ralph T. 1978. *Newfoundland Micmacs: A History of Their Traditional Life*. St. John's: Newfoundland Historical Society Pamphlet No. 5.

Pateman, Carole. 1988a. "The Patriarchal Welfare State." In *Democracy and the State*, ed. A. Gutmann, 231–78. Princeton, NJ: Princeton University Press.

———. 1988b. *The Sexual Contract*. Stanford, CA: Stanford University Press.

———. 1989. *The Disorder of Women: Democracy, Feminism and Political Theory*. Cambridge: Polity Press.

Pennington, Shelley and Belinda Westover. 1989. *A Hidden Workforce: Homeworkers in England, 1850–1985*. London: Macmillan.

Perry, Julia. 1991. *Breadwinners or Childrearers: The Dilemma for Lone Mothers*. OECD Working Party on Social Policy.

Phillips, Paul and Erin Phillips. 1993. *Women and Work*. Rev. ed. Toronto: James Lorimer and Company.

Philp, Margaret. 1997. "Child-care Plan Makes Quebec Distinct." *Globe and Mail* (Toronto), 17 June: A1, A6.

———. 1998. "Public Day Care Pays Off for the Whole Society, Study Says." *Globe and Mail* (Toronto), A5.

Pierson, Ruth Roach. 1986. *"They're Still Women After All": The Second World War and Canadian Womanhood*. Toronto: McClelland and Stewart.

Pleck, Joseph H. 1992. "Work-Family Policies in the United States." In *Women's Work and Women's Lives: The Continuing Struggle Worldwide*, ed. Hilda Kahne and Janet Z. Giele, 248–76. Boulder, CO: Westview Press.

Polakow, Valerie. 1993. *Lives on the Edge: Single Mothers and Their Children in the Other America*. Chicago: The University of Chicago Press.

Polanyi, Karl. 1957. *The Great Transformation*. Boston: Beacon Press.

Pollert, Anna. 1996. "Gender and Class Revisited." *Sociology* 30, No. 4: 639–59.

Porter, Marilyn. 1995. "'She Was Skipper of the Shore Crew': Notes on the History of the Sexual Division of Labour in Newfoundland." In *Their Lives and Times: Women in Newfoundland and Labrador: A Collage*, ed. Carmelita McGrath, Barbara Neis, and Marilyn Porter, 33–47. St. John's, NF: Killick Press.

Prentice, Alison et al., eds. 1996. *Canadian Women: A History*. 2nd ed. Toronto: Harcourt Brace and Company.

Quadagno, Jill. 1994. *The Color of Welfare: How Racism Undermined the War on Poverty*. New York: Oxford University Press.

Queen, Stuart, Robert Habenstein, and Jill Quadagno. 1985. *The Family in Various Cultures*. 5th ed. New York: Harper and Row.

Rainwater, L. and T.M. Smeeding. 1995. *Doing Poorly: The Real Income of American Children in a Comparative Perspective*. Luxembourg Income Study. Working Paper. No. 127.

Ramklawansingh, Ceta. 1974. "Women During the Great War." In *Women at Work: Ontario, 1850–1930*, ed. Jane Acton, Penny Goldsmith, and Bonnie Shepard, 261–308. Toronto: Canadian Women's Educational Press.

Reskin, Barbara and Irene Padavic. 1994. *Women and Men at Work*. Thousand Oaks, CA: Pine Forge Press.

Reich, Robert. 1991. The *Work of Nations: Preparing Ourselves for 21st-Century Capitalism*. New York: Alfred A. Knopf.

———. 1997. "Sky and Ground: What the U.P.S. Strike Delivered." *American Sociological Association Organizations, Occupations, and Work Newsletter* (Fall): 5, 8.

Reiter, Ester. 1996 (1991). *Making Fast Food: From the Frying Pan into the Fryer*. Montreal and Kingston: McGill-Queen's University Press.

Reskin, Barbara and Irene Padavic. 1994. *Women and Men at Work*. Thousand Oaks, CA: Pine Forge Press.

Reverby, Susan. 1987. *Ordered to Care*. Cambridge, MA: Cambridge University Press.

_____. 1989. "A Caring Dilemma: Womanhood and Nursing in Historical Perspective." In *Perspectives in Medical Sociology*, ed. Phil Brown, 470–85. Belmont, CA: Wadsworth.

Rich, Adrienne. 1975. "The Theft of Childbirth." *The New York Review of Books* 22: 25–30.

_____. 1978. *Dream of a Common Language*. London: Norton and Company.

Rifkin, Jeremy. 1995. *The End of Work*. New York: G.P. Putnam's Sons.

Rinehart, James. *The Tyranny of Work: Alienation and the Labour Process*. 3rd ed. Toronto: Harcourt Brace Canada.

Riska, Elianne and Katarina Wegar. 1993. *Gender, Work and Medicine: Women and the Medical Division of Labour*. London: Sage Publications.

Ritchie, Laurell et al. 1997. "Pension Policy." In *The National Action Committee on the Status of Women's Voters' Guide: A Woman's Agenda for Social Justice*, ed. Nandita Sharma, 124–32. Toronto: James Lorimer and Company.

Ritzer, George. 1993. *The McDonaldization of Society: An Investigation Into the Changing Character of Contemporary Social Life*. Thousand Oaks, CA: Pine Forge Press.

Romlid, Christina. 1997. "Swedish Midwives and Their Instruments in the Eighteenth and Nineteenth Centuries." In *Midwives, Society and Childbirth: Debates and Controversies in the Modern Period*, ed. Hilary Marland and Anne Marie Rafferty, 38–60. London: Routledge.

Rooks, Judith. 1997. *Midwifery and Childbirth in America*. Philadelphia: Temple University Press.

Ross, Catherine and John Mirowsky. 1988. "Child Care and Emotional Adjustment to Wives' Employment." *Journal of Health and Social Behaviour* 29: 127–38.

Rotenberg, Lori. 1974. "The Wayward Worker: Toronto's Prostitutes at the Turn of the Century." In *Women at Work: Ontario, 1850–1930*, ed. Jane Acton, Penny Goldsmith, and Bonnie Shepard, 33–70. Toronto: Canadian Women's Educational Press.

Rubery, Jill, C. Fagan, and M. Smith. 1995. *Changing Patterns of Work and Working-Time in the European Union and the Impact of Gender Divisions*. Report for the Equal Opportunities Unit. Manchester: DGV, EU Commission.

Rubio, Mary and Elizabeth Waterson, eds. 1986. *Selected Journals of L.M. Montgomery, Volume 1 (1889–1910)*. Toronto: Oxford University Press.

Ruggie, Mary. 1984. *The State and Working Women*. Princeton, NJ: Princeton University Press.

Russell, Bob. 1990. *Back to Work? Labour, State, and Industrial Relations in Canada*. Scarborough, ON: ITP Nelson.

Sainsbury, Diane. 1993. "The Swedish Social Democrats and the Legacy of Continuous Reform: Asset or Dilemma?" *West European Politics* 16 (1): 39–61.

————. 1996. *Gender, Equality and Welfare States*. Cambridge, MA: Cambridge University Press.

Saks, Mike. 1998. "Professionalism and Health Care." In *Sociological Perspectives on Health, Illness and Health Care*, ed. David Field and Steve Taylor, 175–91. London: Blackwell.

Samuel, Raphael, ed. 1981. *People's History and Socialist Theory*. London: Routledge and Kegan Paul.

Sandall, Jane. 1995. "Choice, Continuity and Control: Changing Midwifery, Towards a Sociological Perspective." *Midwifery* 11: 201–09.

Sarvasy, Wendy. 1992. "Beyond the Difference versus Equality Policy Debate: Postsuffrage Feminism, Citizenship, and the Quest for a Feminist Social Citizenship." *Signs* 17 (2): 329–62.

Schor, Juliet B. 1991. *The Overworked American: The Unexpected Decline of Leisure*. New York: Basic Books.

Schwartz, Felice N. 1989. "Management, Women, and the New Facts of Life." *Harvard Business Review* 89 (1): 65–76.

Sharma, Nandita, ed. 1997. *The National Action Committee on the Status of Women's Voters' Guide: A Women's Agenda for Social Justice.* Toronto: James Lorimer and Company.

Shaver, Sheila. 1998. "Patterns of Change: Gender and Welfare State Restructuring in Australia and Sweden." Paper presented at the Annual Meeting for the American Sociological Association (San Francisco), 21–25 Aug. 1998.

Shorter, Edward. 1982. *A History of Women's Bodies.* New York: Basic Books.

Shostak, Marjorie. 1981. *Nisa: The Life and Words of a Kung Woman.* Cambridge, MA: Harvard University Press.

Shroff, Farah, ed. 1997. *The New Midwifery: Reflections on Renaissance and Regulation.* Toronto: The Women's Press.

Sidel, Ruth. 1986. *Women and Children Last: The Plight of Poor Women in Affluent America.* New York: Viking.

Simpson, Richard and Ida Harper Simpson. 1969. "Women and Bureaucracy in the Semi-Professions." In *The Semi-Professions and Their Organization*, ed. Amitai Etzioni, 196–265. New York: The Free Press.

Skocpol, Theda. 1988. "The Limits of the New Deal and the Roots of Contemporary Welfare Dilemmas." In *The Politics of Social Policy in the United States*, ed. Margaret Weir, Ann Shola Orloff, and Theda Skocpol, 293–312. Princeton, NJ: Princeton University Press.

———. 1992. *Protecting Soldiers and Mothers: The Political Origins of Social Policy in the United States.* Cambridge: The Belknap Press of Harvard University Press.

Skolnick, Arlene. 1991. *Embattled Paradise: The American Family in an Age of Uncertainty.* New York: Basic Books.

Smith, Adam. 1937 (1776). *An Inquiry into the Nature and Causes of the Wealth of Nations.* New York: The Modern Library.

Smith, Joan. 1984. "The Paradox of Women's Poverty: Wage-earning Women and Economic Transformation." *Signs* 10 (2): 291–310.

Snedden, David. 1919. "Probable Economic Future of American Women." *American Journal of Sociology* 24: 528–65.

Sorel, Ruth Caldwell. 1984. *Ever Since Eve: Personal Reflections on Childbirth.* New York: Oxford University Press.

Stacey, Margaret. 1981. "The Division of Labour Revisited, or Overcoming the Two Adams." In *Practice and Progress: British Sociology 1950–1980*, ed. P. Abrams et al. London: Allen and Unwin.

Stainsby, Jill. 1994. "It's the Smell of Money: Women Shoreworkers of British Columbia." *BC Studies* 103 (Autumn): 59–82.

Starr, Paul. 1982. *The Social Transformation of American Medicine.* New York: Basic Books.

Statistics Canada. 1995. *Women in Canada: Third Edition.* Ottawa: Ministry of Industry. Catalogue No. 89-503E.

———. 1997. *Education in Canada, 1996.* Ottawa: Ministry of Industry.

———. 1998. "Work Arrangements in the 1990s." Ottawa: Ministry of Industry. Catalogue No. 71-535-MPB, no. 8.

———. 1998b. *Labour Force Update: Canada-US Labour Market Comparison.* Autumn 1998. Ottawa: Minister of Industry. Catalogue No. 71-005-XPB.

———. 1998c. *The Daily* (12 May).

Statistics Sweden. 1999. *Labour Force Survey.* Stockholm: Central Bureau of Statistics.

Stein, Leonard I. 1967. "The Doctor-Nurse Game." *Archives of General Psychiatry* 16: 699–703.

Stephens, John D. 1996. "The Scandinavian Welfare States: Achievements, Crisis, and Prospects." In *Welfare States in Transition: National Global Economies*, ed. Gøsta Esping-Andersen, 32–65. London: Sage Publications.

Stone, Lawrence. 1977. *The Family, Sex and Marriage in England 1500–1800.* Abridged ed. New York: Harper Torchbooks.

Stone, Leroy O. 1994. *Dimensions of Job-Family Tension.* Statistics Canada Catalogue No. 89-540E. Ottawa: Ministry of Industry, Science and Technology.

Sullivan, Deborah A. and Rose Weitz. 1988. *Labor Pains: Modern Midwives and Home Birth.* New Haven: CT: Yale University Press.

Sundström-Feigenberg, Kajsa. 1983. "Reproductive Health and Reproductive Freedom: Maternity Health Care and Family Planning in the Swedish Health Care System." *Women and Health*: 35–55.

Sundström, Marianne. 1993. "The Growth in Full-Time Work Among Swedish Women in the 1980s." *Acta Sociologica* 36: 139–50.

The Swedish Institute. 1992. "The History of Sweden." *Fact Sheets on Sweden*. Stockholm.

———. 1994a. "Equality Between Men and Women in Sweden." *Fact Sheets on Sweden*. Stockholm.

———. 1994b. "Immigrants in Sweden." *Fact Sheets on Sweden*. Stockholm.

———. 1995. "Swedish Labour Market Policy." *Fact Sheets on Sweden*. Stockholm.

———. 1997. "Equality Between Men and Women." *Fact Sheets on Sweden*. Stockholm.

Tausky, Curt. 1996. *Work and Society: An Introduction to Industrial Sociology*. Itasca, IL: F.E. Peacock Publishers.

Taylor, Frederick W. 1911. *The Principles of Scientific Management*. New York: Harper and Row.

Thompson, E.P. 1978. *The Poverty of Theory and Other Essays*. London: Merlin Press.

Thompson, Paul. 1989. *The Nature of Work*. 2nd ed. London: Macmillan.

Thorne, Barrie. 1983. "Feminist Rethinking of the Family: An Overview." In *Rethinking the Family*, ed. Barrie Thorne and Marilyn Yalom. New York: Longman.

Tilly, Chris. 1991. "Reasons for the Continuing Growth of Part-time Employment." *Monthly Labor Review* 114: 10–18.

Tilly, Chris and Charles Tilly. 1997. Capitalist Work and Labour Markets." In *The Sociology of Labour Markets: Efficiency, Equity, Security*, ed. Axel Van Den Berg and Joseph Smucker, 89–118. Scarborough, ON: Prentice Hall Canada.

Tilly, Louise A. and Joan W. Scott. 1978. *Women, Work and Family*. New York: Holt, Rinehart and Winston.

Titmuss, Richard. 1974. *Social Policy: An Introduction*. London: George Allen and Unwin.

Tooker, Elisabeth. 1984. "Women in Iroquois Society." In *Extending Rafters: Interdisciplinary Approaches to Iroquoian Studies*, ed. Michael K. Foster, 109-23. Albany: State University of New York Press.

———. 1996. "Women in Iroquois Society." In *Canadian Women: A Reader*, ed. Wendy Mitchinson et al., 19–32. Toronto: Harcourt Brace and Co.

Towler, Jean and Joan Bramall. 1986. *Midwives in History and Society*. London: Croom Helm.

Twaddle, Andrew. 1996. "Health System Reforms—Toward a Framework for International Comparison." *Social Science and Medicine* 43 (5): 637–53.

Twaddle, Andrew and R. Hessler. 1987. *A Sociology of Health*. 2nd ed. New York: Macmillan.

Tyyskä, Vappu. 1998. "Insiders and Outsiders: Women's Movements and Organizational Effectiveness." *Canadian Review of Sociology and Anthropology* 35 (3): 391–410.

Udy, Stanley H. 1967 (1959). *Organization of Work: A Comparative Analysis of Production Among Nonindustrial Peoples*. New Haven: Hraf Press.

United Nations Development Programme. 1995. *Human Development Report 1990*. New York: Oxford University Press.

Upton, L.F.S. 1978. "The Beothucks: Questions and Answers." *Acadiensis* 8 (2): 150–55.

Ursel, Jane. 1988. "The State and the Maintenance of Patriarchy: A Case Study of Family, Labour, and Welfare Legislation in Canada." In *Gender and Society: Creating A Canadian Women's Sociology*, ed. Arlene Tigar McLaren, 108–45. Toronto: Copp Clark Pitman.

US Bureau of Census. 1996. *Statistical Abstract of the United States: 1996*. 116th ed. Washington, DC: US Government Printing Office.

US Bureau of Labor Statistics. 1997. "Union Members in 1997." Washington, DC. http//stats.bls.gov/news.release/union2.txt.

Vallgarda, Signild. 1996. "Hospitalization of Deliveries: the Change of Place of Birth in Denmark and Sweden from the Late Nineteenth Century to 1970." *Medical History* 40: 173–96.

Valpy, Michael. 1998. "Welfare-to-Work: The Workaday World of Allison Wilson." *Globe and Mail* (Toronto), D1, D3.

Van den Berg, Axel and Joseph Smucker, eds. 1997. *The Sociology of Labour Markets: Efficiency, Equity, Security*. Scarborough, ON: Prentice Hall Canada.

Van Kirk, Sylvia. 1980. *Many Tender Ties: Women in the Fur Trade Society, 1670–1870*. Winnipeg: Watson and Dwyer.

Veblen, Thorstein. 1943 (1899). *The Theory of the Leisure Class: An Economic Study of Institutions*. Modern Library Edition. New York: Random House.

Walby, Sylvia. 1986. *Patriarchy at Work: Patriarchal and Capitalist Relations in Employment*. Cambridge: Polity Press.

———. 1990. *Theorizing Patriarchy*. Oxford: Blackwell.

Waldram, James B., D. Ann Herring, and T. Kue Young. 1997. *Aboriginal Health in Canada: Historical, Cultural, and Epidemiological Perspectives*. Toronto: University of Toronto Press.

Wallerstein, Immanuel. 1974. *The Modern World-System: Capitalist Agriculture and the Origins of the European World-Economy in the Sixteenth Century*. New York: Academic Press.

Walsh, Mary Roth. 1977. *Doctors Wanted: No Women Need Apply: Sexual Barriers in the Medical Profession, 1835–1975*. New Haven, CT: Yale University Press.

Watson, Tony J. 1987. *Sociology, Work and Industry*. 2nd ed. London: Routledge and Kegan Paul.

Weir, Margaret, Ann Shola Orloff, and Theda Skocpol. 1988. *The Politics of Social Policy in the United States*. Princeton, NJ: Princeton University Press.

Weitz, Rose. 1996. *The Sociology of Health, Illness, and Health Care*. Boulder, CO: Wadsworth.

Wertz, Richard and Dorothy Wertz. 1977. *Lying-In. A History of Childbirth in America*. New York: Schocken Books.

Williams, Christine. 1992. "The Glass Elevator: Hidden Advantages for Men in the 'Female' Professions." *Social Problems* 39: 253–67.

Wilson, Dorothy. 1979. *The Welfare State in Sweden: A Study in Comparative Social Administration*. London: Heinemann.

Wilson, Susan. 1991. *Women, Families and Work*. 3rd ed. Toronto: McGraw-Hill Ryerson.

Witz, Anne. 1990. "Patriarchy and Professions: The Gendered Politics of Occupational Closure." *Sociology* 24 (1): 675–90.

Wilson, William. 1886. *Newfoundland and its Missionaries*. Cambridge, Mass.: Dakin and Metcalfe.

———. 1992. *Professions and Patriarchy*. London: Routledge.

The World Bank. 1997. *World Development Indicators*. New York: The World Bank.

Credits

Table: © Judith Lorber, *The Paradoxes of Gender*. 1994. Yale University Press. Reprinted with permission of Yale University Press.

Extract from poem, "*Song for the Dead*," from *Daughters of Copper Woman* by Anne Cameron, Press Gang Publishers, 1981.

Excerpt from Elizabeth Tooker, "Women in Iroquois Society," in Michael K. Foster, ed., *Extending the Rafters: Interdisciplinary Approaches to Iroquoian Studies*. Albany: State University of New York, 1984.

Excerpt from Elizabeth Jane Errington, *Wives and Mothers and Scullery Maids*. McGill-Queen's University Press.

Excerpt from *Women in Canada*, 1995, p. 72; Table from *Statistics Canada, Work Arrangements in the 1990s*, p. 77; and Excerpt from *Daily*, Friday, January 22, 1999: Statistics Canada.

Statistics Canada information is used with the permission of the Minister of Industry, as Minister responsible for Statistics Canada. Information on the availability of the wide range of data from Statistics Canada can be obtained from Statistics Canada's Regional Offices, its World Wide Web site at http://www.statcan.ca, and its toll-free access number 1-800-263-1136.

Excerpt entitled "Status of Women Canada," from *Economic Gender Indicators*, 1997, p. 41. Reprinted with the permission of the Minister of Public Works and Government Services Canada, 1999.

Table: Reprinted by permission of Sage Publications Ltd. from Janet Gornick et al., "Supporting the Employment of Mothers." *Journal of European Social Policy* Vol. 7(1): 45-70. © Sage Limited, 1999.

Table from *The Progress of Nations*, P. Adamson, ed.: Reprinted with permission. *The Progress of Nations*, 1996, UNICEF, New York, p. 44.

Table from "Women in National Parliaments as of 5 December 1998, Selected Countries": *Women in National Parliaments*, IPU Web Site: http://www.ipu.org, Inter-Parliamentary Union.

Index